Learn to Program in Arduino™ C:

18 Lessons, from setup() to robots

William P. Osborne holds a BSEE and an MIT (master's degree in teaching) from Seattle University and an MBA and an MS from Stanford University. His career has included consulting to technology manufacturers, running a small software company, and ten years at the Microsoft Corporation, primarily in the Windows operating system division. He teaches computer science and engineering at a public high school.

Earlier versions of this book were shared on the author's website, LearnCSE.com.

Printed in the United States of America

Published by Armadillo Books
Printed by CreateSpace

ISBN: 978-0-9981287-1-9

Edited by Margo Paddock
Book design by Margo Paddock
Cover design by Abby Osborne
Photographs by Abby Osborne and Caroline Osborne

Contents

HOW-TOs

Introduction

The Arduino™ is an extremely popular single-board computer that can be used to make a vast variety of intelligent devices. With this book you will learn how to work with the Arduino™ itself, to identify and control common electronic components used with an Arduino™, and, most important of all, to write programs for the Arduino™.

This book is for you if you want to understand, program, and use the Arduino™ to make things that work. It is also for you if you want to teach Arduino™ programming. We believe this mastery is valuable for three reasons:

1. Industry demands and career opportunity: The key component of the Arduino™ is a microcontroller from the Atmel Corporation. Learning to program and apply an Arduino™ is also learning to program and apply a microcontroller, a skill that is in heavy demand in industry.

2. As a basis for learning other programming languages: The Arduino™ is programmed in a version of the C programming language. Consequently, knowledge of the syntax of Arduino™ C transfers to learning higher-level languages, including C++, C#, Java, and Python, which are all currently used in industry.

3. Satisfaction and fun: The Arduino™ can be used as the computing component for many different kinds of devices. Students who have completed the lessons in this book have gone on to design, build, and program robots that walk, sensors that record and report data, musical instruments, and quadcopters that fly, among other things.

You will guide and pace your own learning. Each lesson builds upon and extends the content of the preceding lessons. And each lesson is constructed as it would be presented in a classroom, beginning first with key concepts and ending with exercises in applying that knowledge:

Big Idea: The major concept or skill the lesson conveys. Everything else in the lesson supports this idea.

Background: The underlying theory, and, when appropriate, the science behind the content of the lesson. Understanding the background of new material enhances your ability to apply that knowledge.

Vocabulary: New terms are highlighted in yellow when they introduced in text. Those terms and their definitions are also conveniently arranged in a table (with a yellow banner heading) for reference.

Description: Further detail of the concepts covered in the lesson and other information that will put the lesson's procedure and exercises into the context of the Big Idea.

Goals: The specific set of concepts you will learn and skills you will develop while completing the lesson.

Materials: A list of the electronic materials and tools used in the lesson. Each item on the list has a number linking it to a Parts Catalog (available at LearnCSE.com), which provides information about where the part can be purchased.

Procedure: A set of ordered steps for conducting the experiment or building the project that illustrates the content of the lesson.

Exercise(s): A set of one or more additional experiments or projects you can do in order to apply and reinforce what you have learned in the lesson.

Support in the form of sample programs (referred to as "sketches") for the Arduino™, FAQs, the Parts Catalog, new topics and projects, and a blog can be found at www.LearnCSE.com.

The lessons in this book have been classroom tested. Students have created projects of their own designs based on what they've learned with earlier versions of these lessons. They have made model helicopters and airplanes, elaborate rolling robots, musical instruments, light panels, keyboards to drive synthesizers, "laser" tag games, hover boards, Segway-like vehicles, and more.

Whether you are exploring this book for yourself or to teach others, I hope you find the content engaging and useful. I invite you to share your thoughts, suggestions, and cool projects of your own. Visit us anytime at www.LearnCSE.com.

Lesson 1 Microcontrollers and SBCs 1

The Big Idea:

This book is about computer science.

It is not about the Arduino,™ the C programming language, electronic components, or the mathematics of electricity—even though we refer to them extensively in the lessons in this book.

The Arduino,™ the C programming language, electronic components, and the mathematics of electricity are the *tools* this book uses to teach computer science.

These tools allow readers to learn by doing, to learn with their hands. Every lesson is either an experiment or a project. Some projects, lighting LEDs, for example, are simple. Others are complex. Laser tag is an excellent example. But simple or complex, none of the projects does anything unless some computer science has been applied to bring them to life.

Background: What, precisely, is computer science?

For the purposes of this text, computer science is the application of numbers and logic to make devices, algorithms, and languages that, together, can model just about anything. This book uses the tools listed in Table 1-1.

Table 1-1. Tools this book uses

Tool	Description
devices	The Arduino™ family of Single-Board Computers (SBCs).
algorithms	The collection of programming techniques, tools, and libraries we use to build our models.
language	The C programming language.

The key word is *model*. Consider Table 1-2, examples of the uses of models in computing.

Table 1-2. Examples of models in computing

Example	What is modeled	How model connects to world
League of Legends	A fantasy world where characters possess magical and physical powers.	Players (humans) participate by controlling the actions of some of the characters. High quality graphics and game play allow the user to suspend disbelief and pretend the world is real and that the player is actually the character being controlled.
Digital medical imaging via Magnetic Resonance	The detailed densities of the portions of the body being scanned.	By collecting data about minute movement of molecules in response to a changing magnetic field, a model of the scanned object is created. This model is presented to the user as startlingly detailed 2D and 3D images of what would be found if the subject were opened surgically.
Microsoft Word	The appearance of formatted text as if it were typed directly onto a piece of paper.	The user can add to and modify both the content and appearance of this text and can cause a copy of the model to be printed on paper.
Aircraft Autopilot	The stable flight of an aircraft.	The computer collects data (speed, direction, physical orientation of the aircraft, altitude) and uses the model to control wing surfaces and engine speed.

Notice that in each case the computer creates and maintains a model. That model might be something that exists in reality or something entirely fictional. And the *output* from the model may be information that appears on a screen, instructions that control physical devices, or a physical product, such as text or graphics printed on paper or plastic.

The important takeaway is this: ***all computer programs are models***.

The lessons in this book contain experiments and projects that explore concepts and build models that control lights, make sounds, run robots, turn motors, detect and compose messages, and more. Some of these models will collect and respond to data from their environments. Some will provide text as their output, and others will control physical devices. But every experiment and project is controlled by an Arduino™ running a model of what is being built. And, that model will be written with the *C programming language*.

1

Table 1-3. Vocabulary

Term	Definition
algorithm	A means of or steps to performing a specific task. For a computer, an algorithm is usually expressed in a set of computer program instructions.
Arduino™	A single-board computer and an open-source electronics platform based on easy-to-use hardware and software. It's intended for anyone making interactive projects.
C programming language	The programming language used to write sketches for the Arduino™ SBC. The syntax is similar to several other commonly used programming languages, including C++, C#, and Java.
Integrated Development Environment (IDE)	A collection of computer programs used to create other computer programs.
microcontroller	A complete self-contained computer in a chip, including the memory for a program and its data. This small microprocessor also contains the necessary electronics to communicate with external devices.
microprocessor	A complex electronic integrated circuit that performs the processing tasks of a computer, including input, output, and computation.
output	Information of any sort that comes out of a computer.
single-board computer (SBC)	An entire microcomputer on a single printed circuit board. Abbreviated SBC. Examples include the Arduino™ and the Raspberry Pi.
sketch	A computer program written for the Arduino™.

Description:

Arduino™ is a name given to a family of *single-board computers (SBCs)*. The particular family member used in lessons in this book is the Arduino™ Uno. All Arduinos™ contain an integrated circuit called a *microcontroller*. A microcontroller is a small but complete microprocessor capable of input, output, and computation. In addition, a microcontroller includes storage memory for a computer program and its data.

Figure 1-1. The Arduino™ Uno

Surrounding this microcontroller are the electronic components, connectors, and rows of sockets necessary to bring power to the microcontroller, allow it to receive information from the outside world, and to transmit information.

The term *single-board* means that the entire computer fits on a single circuit board. Different members of the Arduino™ family have different features. Some are small and light enough to be sewn into clothing, while others are sufficiently powerful to perform complex tasks very quickly. But they are a family in that they are all programmed with the same language. The syntax of this language is so very close to C that it is referred to as the C language. Mastery of this language serves as an excellent base for other commonly used programming languages, including C++, C#, and Java.

The upcoming lessons explore most of the features of the Arduino™ Uno. This first lesson begins with installation and testing of the set of computer programs used to write and install Arduino™ sketches. This collection of computer programs is called the *Arduino™ Integrated Development Environment (IDE)*. A program written for the Arduino™ is called a *sketch*.

Goals:

1

By the end of this lesson you will:

1. Know the purpose of an Integrated Development Environment (IDE).
2. Know how to locate, download, and install the Arduino™ IDE.
3. Be able to modify, save, upload, and run simple sketches for the Arduino™.
4. Know that sketch refers to a computer program written for the Arduino™.

Materials:

Quantity	Part	Image	Notes	Catalog Number
1	Arduino™ Uno		Single-board computer. This board is delicate and should be handled with care. When you are not using it, keep it in a box or plastic bag.	3102
1	USB Cable		This is the standard USB adapter cable with the flat connector on one end and the square connector on the other.	2301
1	Computer with at least one USB port and access to the Arduino™ website, http://www.Arduino.cc.	---	The operating system of this computer must be Windows, Macintosh OS/X, or Linux.	---

Procedure:

Important	These instructions are for Windows and will work in most situations. For Macintosh and Linux, refer to the instructions on the Arduino™ website: http://www.Arduino.cc

Part I: Download, install, and test the Integrated Development Environment

1. Open Internet Explorer or another Internet browser and navigate to the Arduino™ website http://www.Arduino.cc.

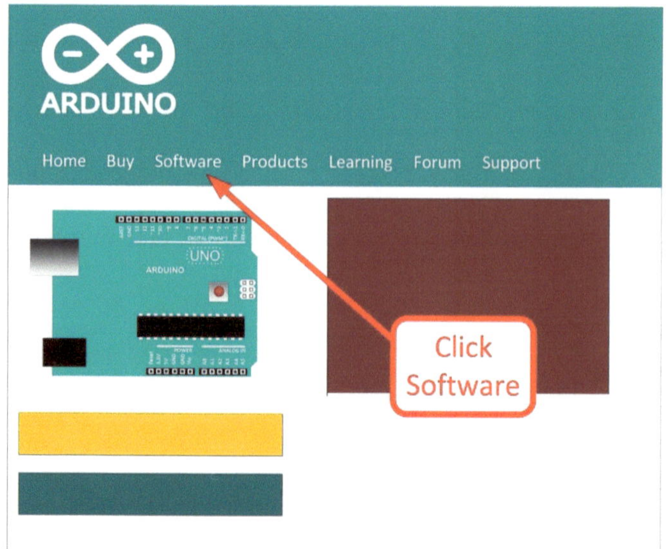

2. Locate the "Download" section of the page and select [Windows]. This will begin the download of the package that will install the IDE.

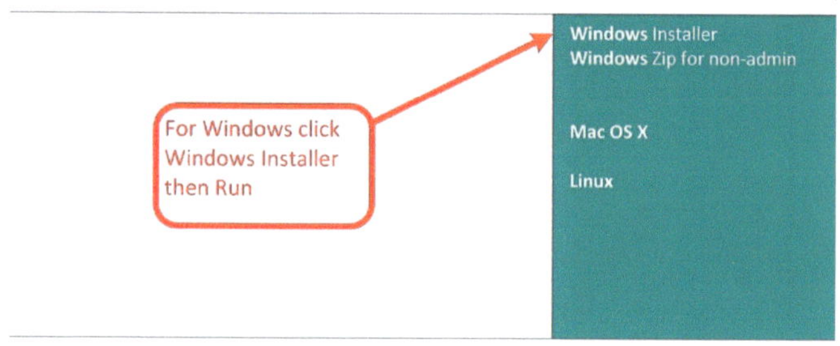

3. Double-click the Arduino™ icon.

   A warning message may appear. If it does, click the [Run] button.

4. The IDE work space should then appear.

Part II: Connect and test the Arduino™ Uno

1. Connect the Arduino™ Uno to the computer using the USB cable. A small green light should appear on the Arduino,™ indicating it has power.

   A small message may appear in the lower-right tray of Windows indicating to which COM port the Arduino™ is assigned. If it does, remember it because it may be needed later.

2. Click the [Tools] menu at the top of the IDE. From the dropdown menu select [Board], and from that menu select [Arduino™ Uno].

3. Select [File]. From the dropdown menu, select [Examples], then [Basics], then [Blink]. An Arduino™ program, called a sketch, will appear in the IDE. Notice that the name of the sketch, `Blink`, is in the tab.

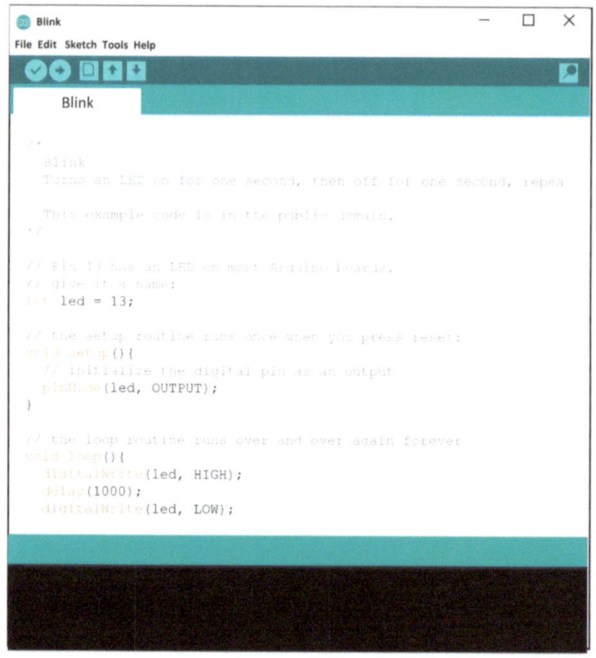

4. Verify the IDE is communicating with the Arduino™ by clicking the [Upload] button on the IDE toolbar.

   If communication is successfully established, the message "Uploading to I/O board" will appear at the bottom of the IDE. It will be followed by the message "Done uploading." A small light should now be blinking: on for one second, then off for one second.

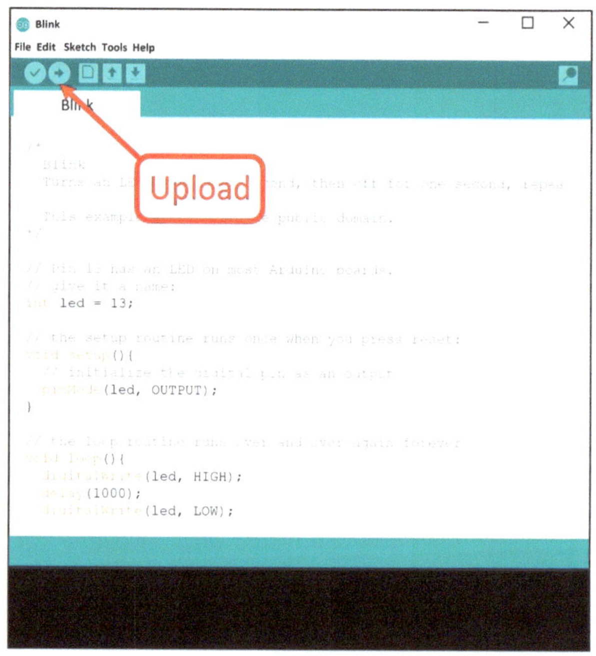

Exercises:

1

Exercise 1-1. Verify success of `Blink` sketch

1. Under the File menu is a submenu called Preferences. Open [Preferences] to verify that the Sketchbook location is the Arduino™ folder in Documents.

   Then click [OK] at the bottom of the screen.

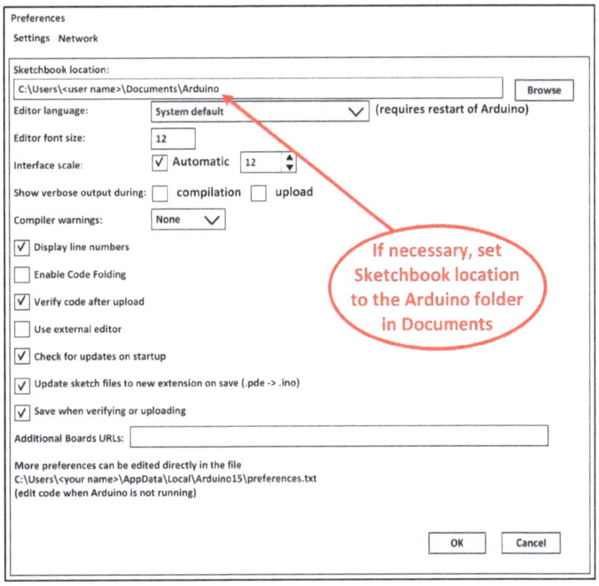

2. Save the `Blink` sketch as `MyBlink` by selecting the [File] menu, then [Save as], then naming the file [MyBlink]. Click the [Save] button.

   Notice that the tab in the IDE should now say [MyBlink].

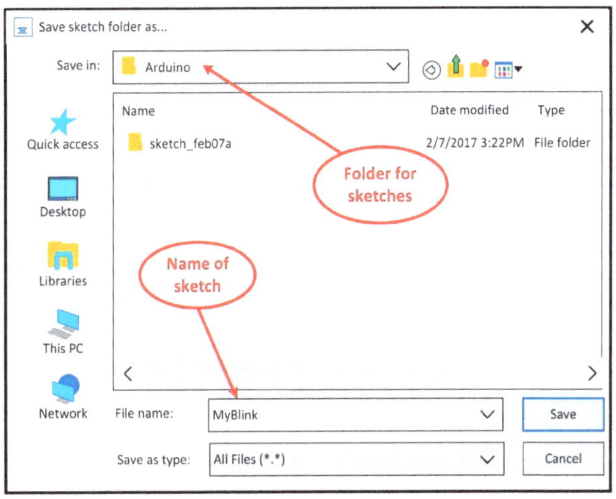

3. Modify the `MyBlink` sketch to make the light blink on and off at half-second intervals by changing the number `1000` to `500` in the two `delay` statements. Don't be concerned about understanding the sketch at this time. The intent of this step is simply to verify the proper operation of the Arduino™ Uno and the IDE.

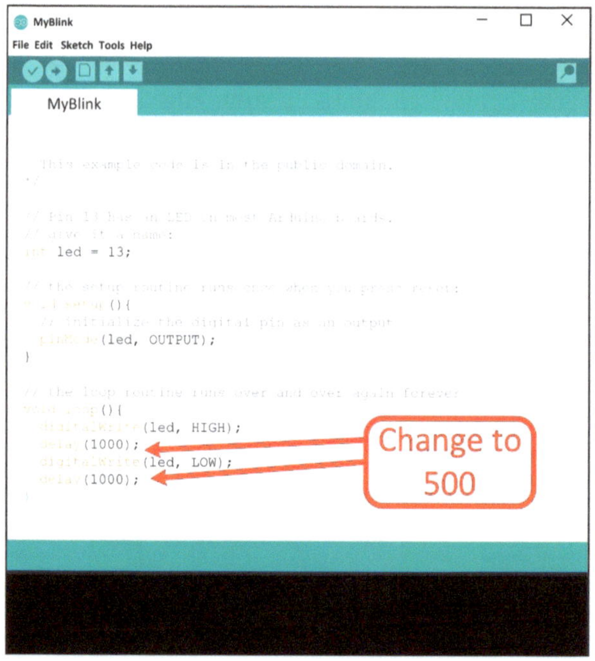

4. Save the modified sketch by selecting [File] then [Save].

5. Upload the sketch to the Arduino™. If you're successful, the light should blink twice as fast as before.

Exercise 1-2. Verify sketch runs on Arduino™ and experiment with time delays

1. Verify that the modified sketch is, in fact, running on the Arduino™ and not on the computer to which the Arduino™ is connected. This can be done by unplugging the Arduino™ from its USB cable and providing power to the Arduino™ by means of a wall-plug power supply (3101 in Parts Catalog) or a battery pack. Note: The light should blink even though the Arduino™ is now independent of the computer.

2. The number used in the delay statement, `delay(500);`, is a measure of time in milliseconds. The number "500" is 500 milliseconds, or one half second. This is a common technique used to save power. For example, roadside flashers turn their lights on for short periods of time while leaving them off for a longer period. Experiment with the values of `MyBlink` to find the shortest blink time that still appears to be long enough to be noticed by a casual observer.

1

3. Experiment with at least six values of `delay` for time on.

   Set the `delay` for the light off to be one second. That is 1000 milliseconds. Complete Exercise Table 1-1.

Exercise Table 1-1. Time delay experiment table

Condition	Time On, in Milliseconds
Light on longer than necessary:	________
Light not on long enough to be noticed reliably:	________
Optimal time on:	________

Lesson 2 | Communicating with the Arduino™

2

The Big Idea:

An Arduino™ can be programmed to send messages to and receive messages from the computer being used to write and upload sketches. A feature called the *serial port* makes this communication possible. This lesson shows how to use the serial port to send messages from an Arduino™ sketch and to use a feature of the Arduino™ IDE called the *Serial Monitor* to view those messages.

Background:

Any computer must have, at a minimum, the features listed in Table 2-1.

Table 2-1. Computer features, purposes, and examples

Feature	Purpose	Examples
input	To receive information from the outside world.	Keyboard, mouse, network connection, touch screen, voltage sensor
output	To display information or to control devices.	Monitor, lights, printer, motor, network connection
processor	To manipulate information.	Intel Core i5, Atmel ATmega 328
storage	To contain programs to be run and data to be accessed.	Memory, hard disk, cloud storage

Serial Port

The Arduino™ is a complete computer possessing each of the features listed in Table 2-1. In this lesson, you will have the opportunity to write your first Arduino™ sketches. The sketches take advantage of the output ability of the Arduino™ to send text messages to the Arduino™ Integrated Development Environment (IDE) via a built-in serial port. This port is composed of some electronic components specifically designed to send data to and receive data from another device, in this case a computer via USB, some special hardware designed to communicate text. The port can also send data out pin 1 of the Arduino™ and receive it via pin 0. These pins are marked TX for transmit and RX for receive.

Figure 2-1. USB connector and pins controlled by the serial port

The ability of the port to transmit and receive data is very handy. It is especially useful for discovering why sketches don't always operate as expected. The process of fixing things that are wrong with a sketch is called *debugging*. A common technique for debugging is building into a sketch the sending of text messages to the IDE.

The Arduino™ Sketch

To make use of the serial port, or any other feature of the Arduino,™ a *sketch* is required. A sketch is a collection of instructions for your Arduino.™ A specific instruction within a sketch is called a *programming statement*. An example of a statement is shown in Example 2-1.

Example 2-1. Programming statement

```
Serial.print("Hello");
```

Note	Programming statements end with a semicolon.

The programming statement in Example 2-1 instructs the Arduino™ to send the word `"Hello"` out the serial port.

Statements that, taken together, perform a specific task may be grouped and named. Such a group is called a *method*. A method is a collection of programming statements that, when executed in order, perform some subtask essential to the overall purpose of the sketch. If the sketch operates a robot, for example, one subtask is to detect surrounding obstacles. Another subtask controls motors. Yet another detects and decodes messages from a remote control. Each of these subtasks appears in the sketch as a method. Each method has a name, parameters, a return type, and some programming statements.

2

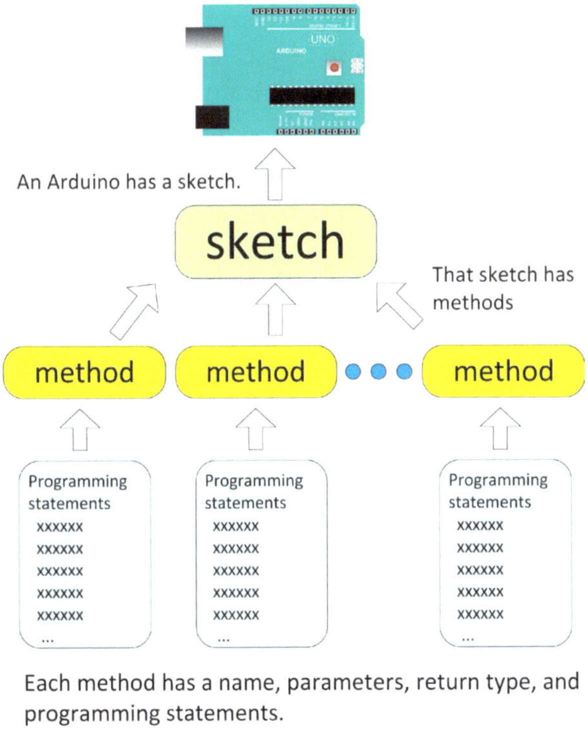

Figure 2-2. Hierarchical diagram of Arduino™ sketch, methods, and programming statements

Example 2-2 is an Arduino™ method that might be found within a sketch. This particular method has parameters: the length and width of a rectangle. It has a return type of `int`, meaning integer, because the method "returns" the calculated area. (The use of return values is included in a later lesson.)

Example 2-2. Arduino™ method

return type — name of method — parameters

```
int calcAreaOfRect(int length, int width){
  int area;
  area = length * width;
  return area;
}
```

programming statements

Curly braces enclosing statements

Important	The programming statements necessary to calculate area and then return that value are contained within a pair of curly braces.

All methods comply with this format. If a method does not have parameters, then empty parentheses are used in the name. (A parameter is a special kind of *variable* used by a method to refer to data provided as input.) If no values are to be returned, then the return type is `void`. Example 2-3 is an Arduino™ method that has no parameters and no values returned. This method merely plays some sounds.

Example 2-3. Example of Arduino™ method with no parameters

```
void playSounds(){
   tone( 5, NOTE_A4, 50);
   delay( 600);
   tone( 5, NOTE_E4, 50);
   delay( 300);
   tone( 5, NOTE_C4, 80);
   delay( 400);
}
```

Every Arduino™ sketch must use, at a minimum, the two methods listed in Table 2-2.

Table 2-2. Methods required in every Arduino™ sketch

Method	What the statement does	Return Type
`setup()`	Initializes the Arduino™ and its components	`void`
`loop()`	Performs a task	`void`

Both `setup()` and `loop()` have `void` as the return type (or type of data that the method yields) because neither ever has any values to return. Neither method has any parameters, which is why their names are followed by empty parentheses. To help other people understand what you, the programmer, have done and when and to aid you when you revisit a sketch, you can embed notes within a sketch. These notes have nothing to do with how the sketch works; they are for information only.

One way of entering a note is to begin with a pair of slashes. When the Arduino™ is executing programming statements, it ignores anything following a pair of slashes. The following programming statement has a note:

```
Serial.println("Greetings.");  // First line the user sees
```

Another method of entering a note is to use slash-asterisk bookends: /* and */. The content between them becomes a comment, and the Arduino™ ignores the comment when it is carrying out programming statements.

Example 2-4.

```
/* MyFirstArduino™Sketch
   <author>
 <date>
 */
```

Finally, some words have special meaning to the C language as it is used with the Arduino.™ These are called *keywords*. A keyword cannot be used for any other purpose. The programming statement `delay()` uses the keyword `delay`.

Other commonly used keywords are: `double int switch void while long return short signed if goto for else do const char case break false true`

In this lesson you will create the sketch shown in Sketch 2-1. Note the comments, methods, and programming statements.

Sketch 2-1. First Arduino™ sketch

```
/* MyFirstArduino™Sketch.ino
   W. P. Osborne
   6/30/15
*/

void setup(){
    Serial.begin(9600);
}

void loop(){
    // print message at one second intervals
    Serial.println("Hello, world!");
    delay(1000);
}
```

Note	Throughout this book, sketches and snippets that the reader will type on her or his keyboard appear in a gray box, as seen in Sketch 2-1.

In the sketch shown in Sketch 2-1, the first three lines are comments. The first line is the name of the sketch; the second line names the author; the third notes the date the sketch was created.

The sketch also has two methods: `setup()` and `loop()`. The `setup()` method contains only one programming statement while the `loop()` method contains two. The `loop()` method also includes a comment.

Table 2-3. Vocabulary

Term	Definition
baud	A unit of measure of the speed of data going into and out of a serial port.
comment	Text inside a sketch that is present to provide the human reader of the sketch insight into some aspect of the sketch's operation but that is ignored by the Arduino™ as it obeys programming statements.
debugging	Finding and fixing improper behaviors in an Arduino™ sketch (and in other computer programs).
escape sequence	An escape sequence is a pair of characters embedded in text where the first character is a backslash (\). The second character is a command to do something special when that text is printed on a computer screen via the `Serial.print()` and `Serial.println()` programming statements. The second characters are: the double quote ("), used to print the quotation mark as text, the lower-case letter t, which advances printing to the next tab, the lower-case letter n, which moves printing to a new line, and the backslash character itself (\), which prints the backslash as text.
keyword	A word that has a specific and predefined meaning in the C programming language.
`loop()` **method**	One of the two essential methods in each Arduino™ sketch. The C-language statements in this method run over and over.
method	A collection of C-language statements that perform a specific task. A method always has a name. Some methods can receive and return data.
programming statement	A computer language instruction. A set of pre-written C-language instructions that are used to send and receive data via a serial port.
serial library	A set of pre-written C-language instructions that are used to send and receive data via a serial port.
serial port	A service built into each Arduino™ specifically to send to and receive data from outside devices, including another computer.
Serial Monitor	A feature of the Arduino™ IDE that allows sending text to and getting text from the sketch running on the Arduino.™
`setup()` **method**	One of the two essential methods in each Arduino™ sketch. The C-language statements in this method run only once, when the sketch first starts. These statements initialize the Arduino™, any attached devices, and the sketch itself prior to running.
sketch	A collection of instructions for your Arduino.™

Goals:

1. Know that the Arduino™ pins 0 and 1 are used to receive and transmit data.
2. Know that the serial port is configured in the setup method and that the rate of data exchange is set at this time. Understand that the Arduino™ IDE includes a tool called the Serial Monitor for exchanging text with the Arduino.™
3. Know how to find and open the Serial Monitor.
4. Know how to invoke the text transmission from the Arduino™ to the Serial Monitor using the C-language statements `Serial.print()` and `Serial.println()`.
5. Be able to write, save, upload, and run simple programs for the Arduino.™
6. Understand and know how to use escape sequences to format text.

Materials:

Quantity	Part	Image	Notes	Catalog Number
1	Arduino™ Uno		Single-board computer. This board is delicate and should be handled with care. When you are not using it, keep it in a box or plastic bag.	3102
1	USB Cable		This is the standard USB adapter cable with the flat connector on one end and the square connector on the other.	2301
1	Computer with at least one USB port and access to the Arduino™ website, http://www.arduino.cc.	---	The operating system of this computer must be Windows, Macintosh OS/X, or Linux.	---

Procedure:

Set up, upload, and run the first Arduino™ sketch

1. Connect the Arduino™ Uno to the serial cable and that cable to the computer.
2. Start the Arduino™ IDE (Integrated Development Environment) by clicking the Arduino™ icon.
3. The Arduino™ IDE will appear. The white space is where you will type the program code.

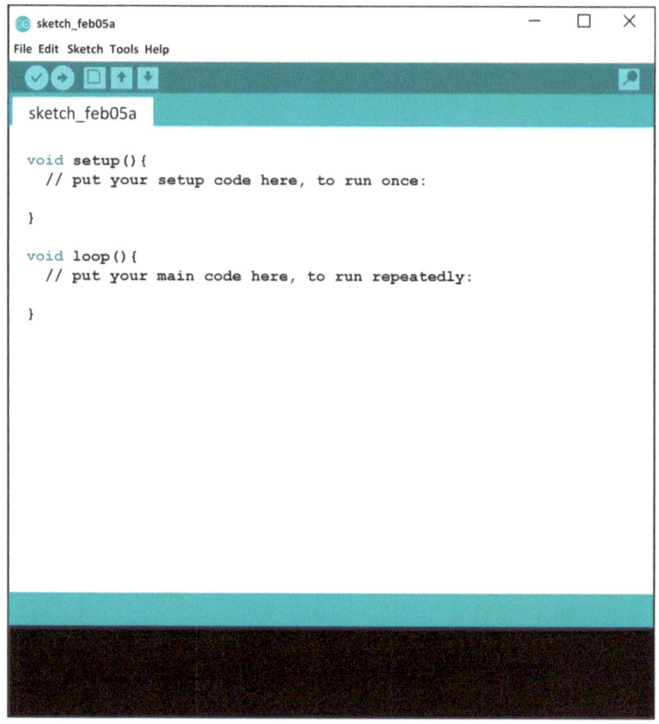

2

4. Enter the header comments. These comments identify the sketch, the author, and the date the sketch was created.

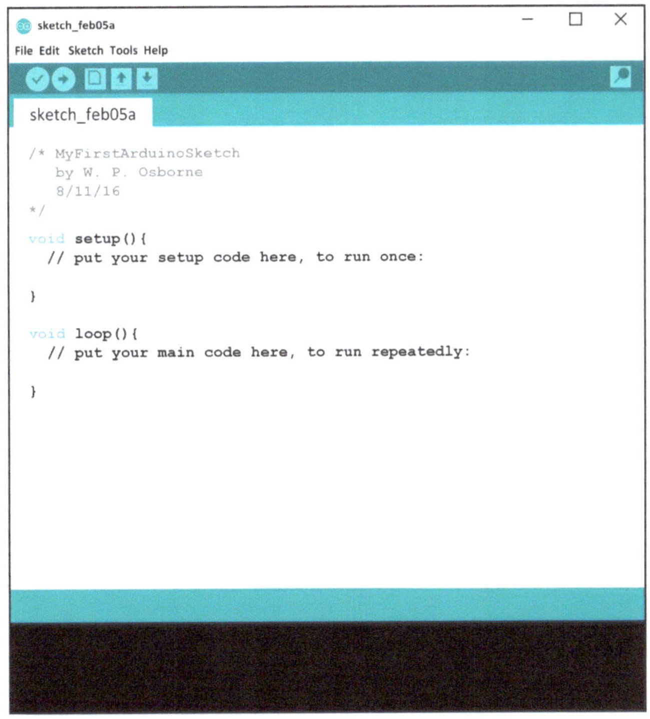

5. Enter the programming statements for the `setup()` method as shown in Sketch 2-1 (shown again below for reference).

   This method runs when the Arduino™ is first started.

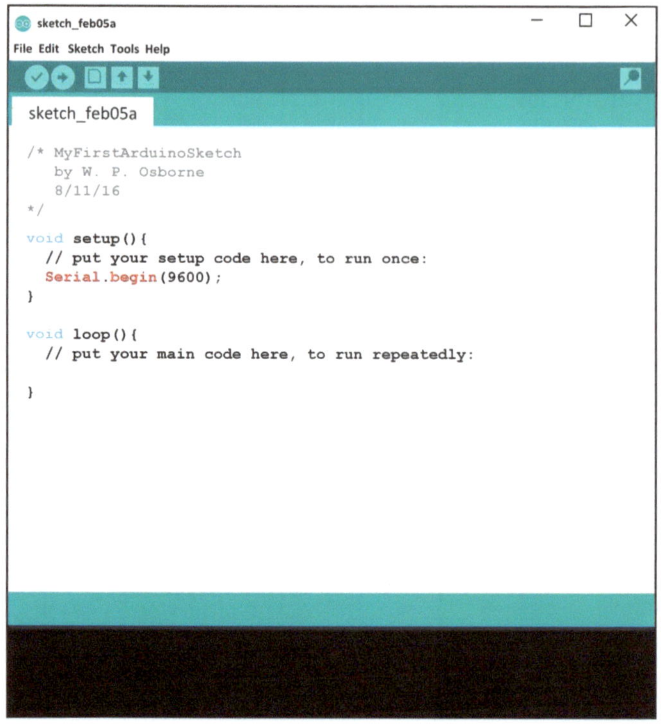

Complete listing 2-1. First Arduino™ sketch

```
/* MyFirstArduino™Sketch.ino
   <author>
   <date>
*/

void setup(){
   Serial.begin(9600);
}

void loop(){
   // send text to the Serial Monitor
   Serial.println("Hello, world!");
   // pause for one-half second
   delay(500);
}
```

6. Next add the `loop()` method. This method runs over and over and over and over — continuously repeating the programming statements.

   In this case the `loop()` method is sending the message

   `Hello, world!`

   repeatedly to the Serial Monitor.

   The programming statement

   `delay(500)` pauses the Arduino™ for 500 milliseconds (one-half a second).

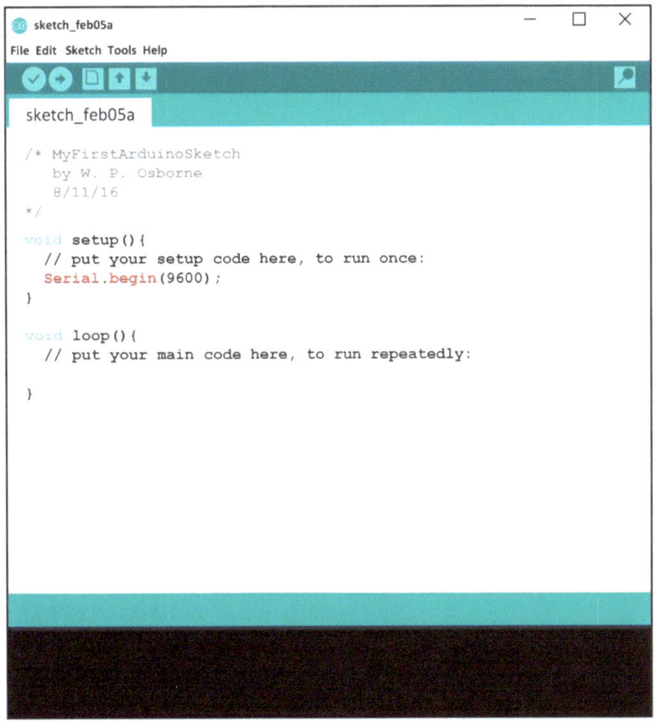

7. Under the File, click [Save As], change the file name to `MyFirstArduino™Sketch` and make sure that the folder file name appearing in the [Save in:] box is the Arduino™ folder in Documents.

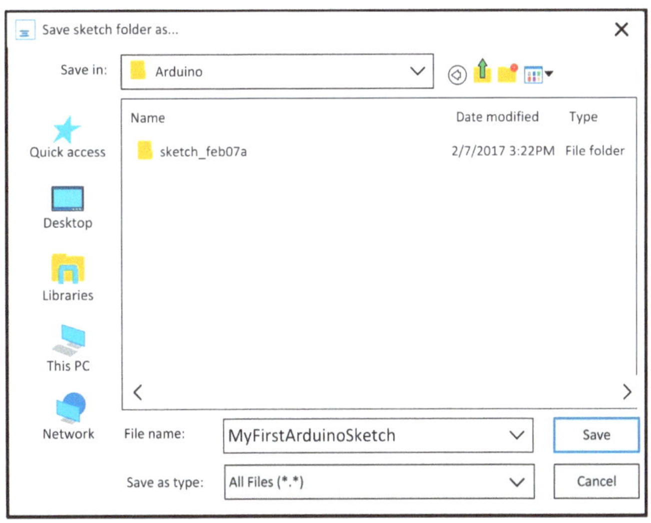

8. Connect the Arduino™ to your computer, then click the [Upload] button. Wait for the program to be uploaded to the Arduino.™

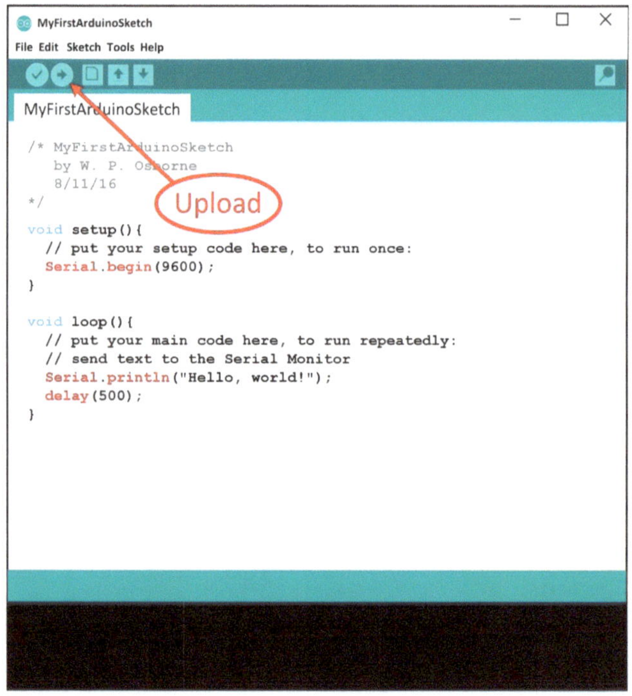

9. Open the Serial Monitor by clicking Serial Monitor under the Tools menu.

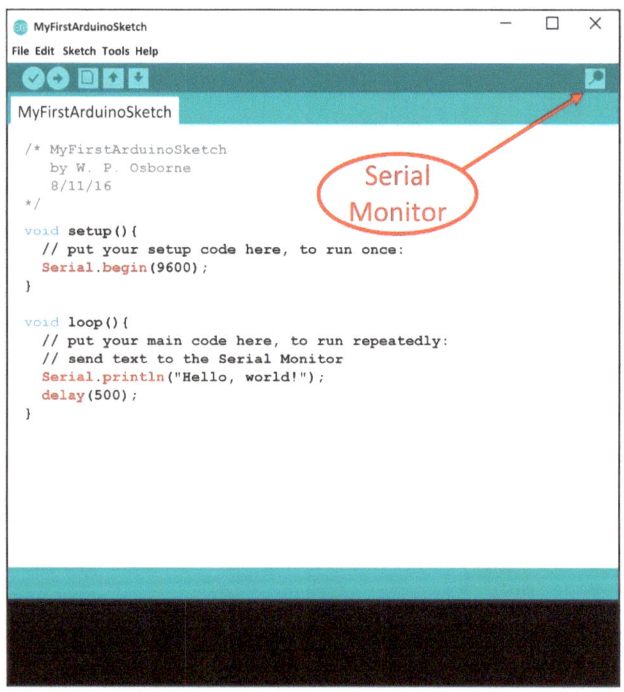

10. The words "Hello, world!" should be scrolling through the text window in the Serial Monitor. If they are not, make certain the box marked Autoscroll is checked.

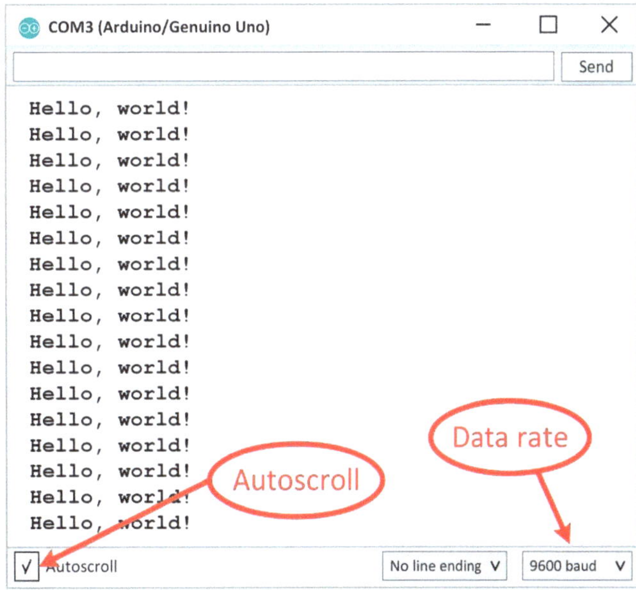

Check the baud rate that appears in the Combo Box at the lower right. It should be set to 9600, the rate used in the

```
Serial.begin(9600)
```

statement in the `setup` method.

Baud is a measure of data transfer speed.

2

Exercises:

Exercise 2-1. Experiment with formatting text

Perform the tasks listed in Table 2-4 and record your observations in its right-hand column.

Table 2-4. Observation table

Task	Observations
1. Replace the `Serial.println` command with:`Serial.println("test");`	
2. Replace the word `println` with `print`.	
3. Add a second double quote. `Serial.print("test \"");` Note: The \ (backslash) character followed by the quotation mark is called an *escape sequence*. It allows for the quotation mark to be printed rather than interpreted as the end of the text.	
4. Replace the second quote with a second backslash. `Serial.print("test \\");`	
5. Replace the second backslash with the letter n followed by another word. `Serial.print("test \n hello");`	
6. Use what you have learned to cause the words "Snoopy is a dog." to be printed, including the quotation marks. Write the new statement in the box to the right.	

Important	In Exercise 2-1, the use of the backslash before the double quote, a second backslash, and the letter n are called escape sequences. There are others, but these are the primary ones. More information about programming the serial port can be found at http://arduino.cc/en/Reference/Serial.

Exercise 2-2. Create a rocket

Save and close `MyFirstArduino™Sketch`. Then, using "new" under the File menu, create a new Arduino™ sketch. Name this sketch `Rocket`.

Add the `setup()` method to this sketch. Have it initialize the serial port to `9600` baud, just as you did in `MyFirstArduino™Sketch`.

Add the `loop()` method. Place it in the programming statements necessary to draw the rocket, as shown in Example 2-3, in the Serial Monitor. Don't forget that some of the characters require escape sequences.

Insert a half-second delay between the drawing of each line. The statement `delay(500)` will accomplish this.

Example 2-4. Rocket, as it appears in Serial Monitor

```
  /\
 /  \
/    \
+----+
+    +
+    +
+----+
+    +
+----+
+    +
+    +
+----+
  /\
 /  \
/    \
```

Lesson 3 | Variables and Strings

The Big Idea:

This lesson extends what we know about working with text in an Arduino™ sketch by adding the ability to change it as the sketch is running.

Background:

In Lesson 2, an Arduino™ sketch used the serial port to send text to a computer screen, where it appeared in the Serial Monitor. The programming statement that sent the text was:

```
Serial.println("Hello, world!");
```

The text was contained inside double quotation marks. Such information is pre-set. It cannot be changed as the sketch runs. It is used literally. Such information that is programmed exactly as it is to be used is called a *literal*.

Further, a collection of characters, such as the `Hello, world!` message, is called a *String*.

A String (note that this word always begins with a capital letter) is a kind of data. Kinds of data are referred to as *types*. Putting these together, then, the String in the programming statement is a *String literal*. Another way of saying this is that the message `Hello, world!` is a literal of type `String`.

Most Arduino™ sketches, including nearly all the lessons in this book, need a way to store values so the values can change over time and so that multiple parts of the sketch can access the values. This is accomplished by employing a *variable*. You may be familiar with variables from algebra. Here the variable X is set equal to the number 42.

```
X = 42
```

The variable name is X. The value is the integer 42.

Computer programming languages, including C, provide ways to create and name variables. Along with each variable name C also sets aside spaces in computer memory to store the values being represented. Once created, a variable may be assigned a value. That value may be retrieved or replaced with another whenever the sketch requires.

What use would a sketch have for a variable? Making cool sketches possible. Table 3-1 provides some examples.

Table 3-1. Uses of variables in sketches

Kind of sketch	Possibly use for a variable
Laser Tag	A variable to store energy level is set when the game is started. The sketch refers to the variable when tagging or receiving a tag.
Quad Copter	A variable to store the desired throttle setting to detemine if the copter is climbing, hovering or descending. Its value is set by the user's manipulation of a control and is compared to the copter's actual throttle setting.
Digital Musical Keyboard	Lots of variables are used to hold the frequencies of different notes and to provide the correct note output when the corresponding key is pressed.

Just as in algebra, variables have names. Unlike with algebra, however, programmers can give variables meaningful names, which aid in making the programming instructions in an Arduino™ sketch understandable. Suppose, for example, a sketch that programs the Arduino™ to play a game. A variable to keep track of a player's name might be `playerName`.

Notice this name is really two words: player and name. How they are combined into one is by means of a naming convention called *camel notation*. Under this convention the first letter of the first word of the variable is always lowercase, and there are no spaces between words. The first letters of all subsequent words in the variable are capitalized.

The process of setting aside memory space for a variable and assigning that variable's name to that space is called *declaration*. Before it can be used, a variable must be declared. The programmer has the option of assigning an initial value to the variable at that time.

Table 3-2. Vocabulary

Term	Definition
assignment operator	The symbol used in a programming statement to store a value to a variable. The symbol is the equals sign, =.
camel notation	A convention for naming variables where words are joined together to form a meaningful phrase to describe what is being assigned. Example of a possible variable in camel notation: `playerHighScore`
concatenation	The process of appending the value of one `String` variable to the value of another `String` variable.
declaration	A programming statement that sets aside memory for a particular type of data and assigns the variable name that will refer to that type.
delimiter	The character used to identify the beginning and end of the values for some types of data. For data of the type `String` the delimiter is the quotation mark: "

Term	Definition
initialization	The initial value assigned to a newly declared variable.
literal	A notation for representing a fixed value in source code. Its value cannot be changed as a sketch runs. Literals are often used to initialize variables.
scope	The portions of an Arduino™ sketch where a variable can be accessed. Scope comes in two kinds: • global: the variable is declared at the beginning of the sketch and may be accessed anywhere. • local: the variable is declared within a set of curly braces and may be accessed only within those curly braces. This will be discussed in a later lesson.
String	A sequence of characters treated as one object. Example: "Hello, World!".
type	The kind of data to be assigned to a variable. The type used in this lesson is `String`. Other types, which will be introduced in future lessons, are: `boolean`, `int`, `double`, and `char`.
variable	A name given to a location in memory where a value can be stored. A variable is for a specific type. The name must follow some naming rules. Putting a value into memory is referred to as assigning that value to the variable.

3

Description:

The rules for using variables in C are:

1. Declare a variable before assigning a value to it.
2. Assign a value to a variable before using it for some other purpose, such as printing or having its value assigned to another variable.
3. Give variables valid names, meaning the names follow some simple rules.
4. Give variables meaningful names in accordance with good practices. Do not access a variable outside of its scope. Local variables may be accessed only from within their set of curly braces, while global variables may be accessed from anywhere within a sketch. The limitation on access is referred to as scope.

Declaring variables

In order for an Arduino™ sketch to use a variable, the sketch must first know two things about the variable: its name and its type.

Naming variables

A variable can be given any name, subject to the following rules:

1. A variable name may not begin with a number but can begin with an underbar (_) or a dollar sign ($).

2. A variable name may not contain spaces.

3. A variable name may not contain mathematical operators: `+ - / * % =`

4. A variable name may not contain the symbols for logical operators: `> < !`

5. A variable name may not contain a comma.

Table 3-3. Examples of names of variables

Example	Comment
`volumeOfCube`	valid and descriptive.
`correct_answer`	valid.
`3ForAChange`	invalid; cannot begin with a number.
`answerForQuestion5`	valid; number is allowed, just not the first character.
`location of Wumpus`	invalid; contains a space.
`tax%rate`	invalid; contains mathematical operator.
`age1,age2`	invalid as one name. C will interpret this as two variables, one named age1 and the other named age2.
`FrodoLives`	valid but not good practice since the name is not likely to be meaningful in the context of the sketch.

Declaration

A *declaration* is the C-language programming statement that makes a variable available to a sketch.

For these first few lessons, all variables will be given global scope, meaning they are declared near the top of the sketch, before the `setup()` method.

The declaration statement consists of two required parts and one optional part. The type and the name are required. As part of declaring a variable, the programmer has the option of giving the variable an initial value. The format of the variable declaration is simple, consisting of three parts: the type, followed by the name and, optionally, an initial value for the variable.

Example 3-1. `String` variable declarations in the C language

```
String nameOfAccountHolder;
String playerName = "Deputy Dog";
String capital;
```

Notice the following about each of the declarations in Table 3-4:

1. Each declaration begins with the type of variable. In this case each variable is of type `String`.
2. The type of variable is followed by the variable name.
3. These names follow the naming rules, convey meaning, and comply with the camel notation naming convention. 3
4. The variable `playerName` is assigned an initial value.

Assigning and using values

Once declared, a variable can be assigned a value by using the equals sign. In C, the equals sign is referred to as the *assignment operator*. That value may be replaced by the assignment of a new value. For example, the statement:

```
nameOfAccountHolder = "Flintstone";
```

stores the `String literal` `Flintstone` to the variable `nameOfAccountHolder`.

This statement:

```
Serial.println(nameOfAccountHolder);
```

will cause the `String Flintstone` to appear on the Arduino™ IDE's Serial Monitor.

This statement changes the value stored to the variable `nameOfAccountHolder:`

```
nameOfAccountHolder = "Rubble";
```

Now the statement:

```
Serial.println(nameOfAccountHolder);
```

will cause the `String Rubble` to appear on the Serial Monitor.

Concatenation

Finally, the plus sign (+) may be used to append one String to another. This is called *concatenation.* For example, consider the following two declarations:

```
String actorFirstName = "Yogi";
String actorFamilyName = "Bear";
```

Suppose the programmer needs to have the full name stored to another variable, called `actorFullName`. Further, a space is required between the two names. One way to do this is with concatenation, where the first name, a space `String literal`, and the last name are combined. See Example 3-2.

Example 3-2.

```
String fullName;
fullName = actorFirstName + " " + actorLastName;
```

The statement

```
Serial.println(fullName);
```

results in the following to appear on the Serial Monitor:

```
Yogi Bear
```

Goals:

By the end of this lesson readers will:

1. Know that a variable is a name that can be assigned a value.
2. Be able to follow naming rules and conventions.
3. Know that before a variable can be used it must be declared.
4. Be able to declare variables.
5. Be able to declare variables and assign initial values as part of the declaration.
6. Know how to work with the `String` data type, including use of the concatenation operator +.

Materials:

Quantity	Part	Image	Notes	Catalog Number
1	Arduino™ Uno		Single-board computer. This board is delicate and should be handled with care. When you are not using it, keep it in a box or plastic bag.	3102
1	USB Cable		This is the standard USB adapter cable with the flat connector on one end and the square connector on the other.	2301

Quan-tity	Part	Image	Notes	Catalog Number
1	Computer with at least one USB port and access to the Arduino™ website, http://www.arduino.cc.	---	The operating system of this computer must be Windows, Macintosh OS/X, or Linux.	---

3

Procedure:

Part I: Set up, upload, and run the first sketch.

1. Connect the Arduino™ to the computer then start the Arduino™ Integrated Development Environment (IDE).

Arduino™ IDE as it appears when first opened. Notice the type of Arduino™ and the COM port being used appear in the lower-right corner.

COM refers to the communications port. This is assigned by the computer's operating system and may change from time to time.

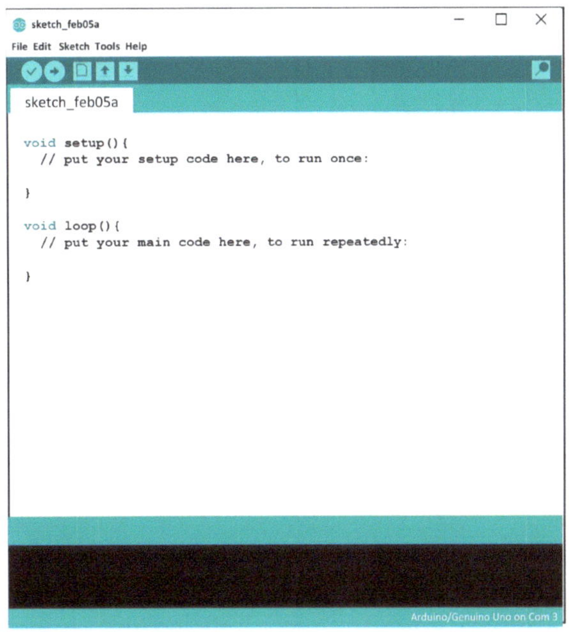

2. Enter the header comments as shown in Snippet 3-1.

Snippet 3-1.

```
/* Lesson3LearnStringVariables
   <author>
   <date>
*/
```

3. Declare three `String` variables just below the header comments as shown in Snippet 3-2. By declaring them here, outside of any methods, the variables are global and can be accessed anywhere in the sketch.

Snippet 3-2.

```
...
String str1 = "Hello,";
String str2 = "world!";
String str3;
```

4. Add the `setup()` method to your sketch as shown in Snippet 3-3. Use it to send the initial values to the Serial Monitor:

Snippet 3-3.

```
...
void setup(){
    Serial.begin(9600);

    Serial.print("str1 is: ");
    Serial.println(str1);
    Serial.print("str2 is: ");
    Serial.println(str2);
}
```

5. Add the `loop()` method, as shown in Snippet 3-4, but place no programming statements within it.

Snippet 3-4.

```
...
void loop(){

}
```

6. Save the sketch as `Lesson3LearnStringVariables`.

7. Upload the sketch, then open the Serial Monitor. The following should appear:

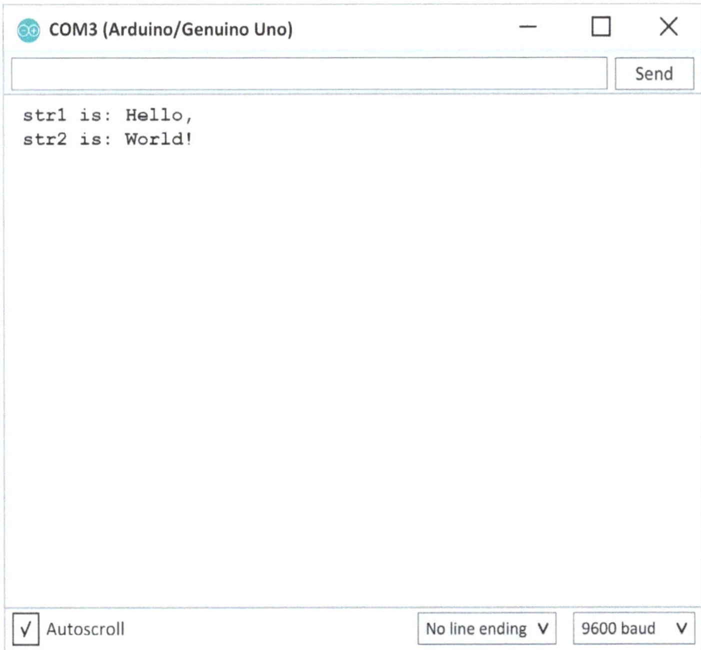

Notice the text does not repeat. This is because the print statements are inside the `setup()` method. Since the `setup()` method is run only once, these statements are run only once.

Part II: Experiment with concatenation.

As in Part I, these steps will place programming statements in the `setup()` method. Keep in mind that they could easily be put in the `loop()` method instead. But statements in the `loop()` method are executed over and over. This means the text will be sent to the Serial Monitor over and over.

8. Add the programming statements to the bottom of the `setup()` method (existing statements are in gray, new statements in black), as shown in Snippet 3-5.

Snippet 3-5.

```
...
void setup(){
   Serial.begin(9600);

   Serial.print("str1 is: ");
   Serial.println(str1);
   Serial.print("str2 is: ");
   Serial.println(str2);

// Concatenate str1 with a space
// and str2 to produce the message
// hello world!
// Assign result to str3 then
// print it.
   str3 = str1 + " " + str2;
   Serial.println(str3);
}
...
```

9. `str3` now contains the concatenation of `str1` with a space, followed by `str2`. The next line sends the contents of `str3` to the Serial Monitor.

10. Save the sketch, then upload to the Arduino.™ Open the Serial Monitor. The Serial Monitor should look like this:

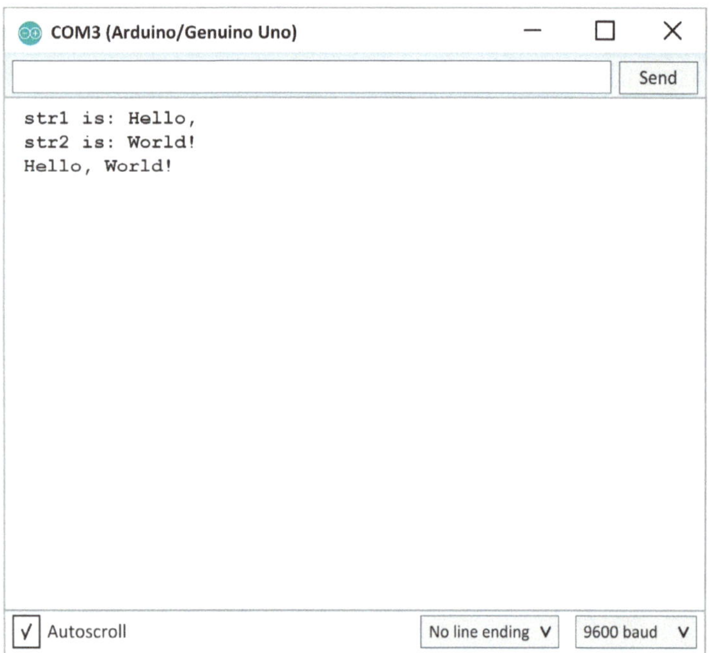

Exercise:

Exercise 3-1. "There was an old lady"

Create a new sketch called `SpiderLady.ino`. Pattern this sketch after `Lesson3LearnStringVariables.ino` Initialize variables `str1` and `str2` as follows:

3

```
String str1 = "There was an old lady who swallowed a ";

String str2 = "I don't know why she swallowed a ";

String sentence;
```

Then, after initializing the Serial port in `setup()` add the programming statements necessary to print a truncated version of the children's poem. The first few statements will look like this:

```
sentence = str1 + "fly";

Serial.println(sentence);

sentence = str2 + "fly";

Serial.println(sentence);

sentence = str1 + "spider";

Serial.println(sentence);
```

… and so on through the critter of bird.

Note	The Arduino™ does not have sufficient data storage for this sketch to print the entire poem.

Lesson 4 | Digital Pins and Constants

The Big Idea:

4

This lesson is the first step toward learning to connect the Arduino™ to its surrounding world. You will connect lights to your Arduino™ and then write sketches to turn them on and off in any desired pattern. In the process you will learn how to configure the digital pins of the Arduino™ in order to control devices and to turn those devices on and off. You will also learn how to use a solderless bread-board to connect electronic devices together and to the Arduino.™ Later lessons expand this connection ability to control motors, make sounds, detect light, and receive and transmit messages.

Background:

In Lesson 3, sketches used the serial port to send text from the Arduino™ Uno to the computer running the Arduino™ IDE. In Lesson 4, you will learn to make things happen by taking advantage of Arduino™ pins.

A *pin* is a connection with which the Arduino™ can be wired to external devices — everything from motors and switches to display panels.

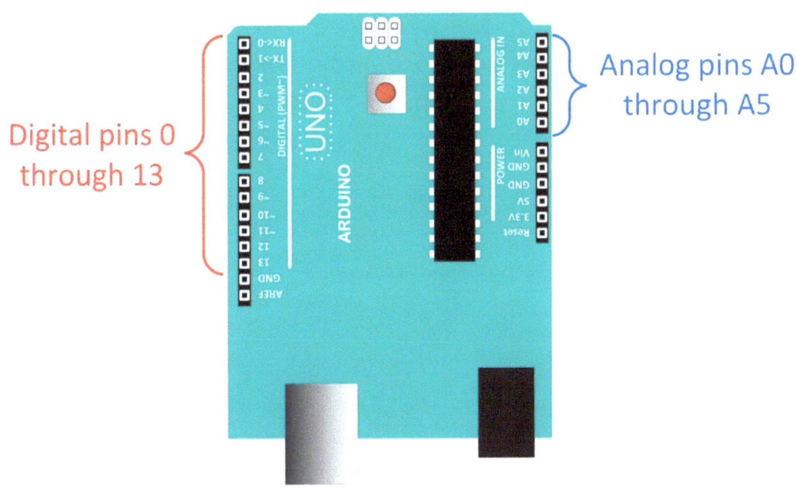

Figure 4-1. Arduino™ Uno with digital and analog pins called out

The Arduino™ Uno has two kinds of pins for receiving and sending information: analog and digital. The six analog pins, pictured on the upper right side of the Arduino™ in Figure 4-1, are the subject of a future lesson. This lesson is about digital pins, of which the Arduino™ has 14. These are numbered from 0 through 13 and are found along one side of the board.

A digital pin has only two states; on or off. The names for these states are `HIGH` and `LOW`. A `HIGH` state means that a volt meter connected to that pin would measure +5 volts. `LOW`, by contrast, means a measurement of zero volts.

Suppose a pin is HIGH. Where do the +5 volts come from? This depends on the mode of that pin. A digital pin can be set to detect the presence or absence of +5 volts coming from outside the Arduino.™ This voltage can come from a battery or some sort of sensing device. A digital pin that is set to detect the presence or absence of +5 volts from an outside source is said to be in the INPUT mode. Such a pin can detect signals from the outside world.

But an Arduino™ sketch itself can set a pin to HIGH or LOW. A pin that can have its voltage set from within a sketch is said to be in the OUTPUT mode. Pins in OUTPUT mode are used to turn devices on and off, to send signals, to control motors, and to generate sounds.

Table 4-1. Summary of modes and states of pins

Pin Mode	Pin Status	Meaning*
OUTPUT	HIGH (on)	The Arduino™ raises the voltage of the pin to +5 volts, meaning that devices connected to this pin have access to electricity. A light, for example, could come on, or a motor could start to turn.
	LOW (off)	The Arduino™ sets the voltage of the pin to zero volts. A light connected to this pin would go dark; a motor would stop.
INPUT	HIGH (on)	The presence of +5 volts is detected on this pin. This voltage is coming from outside the Arduino™ and can be from a switch or a sensor. Some sensors are +5 volts when nothing is detected.
	LOW (off)	The voltage of the pin is determined to be zero. This may reflect a button being pushed or a sensor detecting a signal.

*The meanings in this table are merely possibilities that reflect what commonly happens. What actually happens depends on the device and how it is wired to the Arduino.™ For example, in these lessons push buttons are usually connected in such a way as to produce +5 volts on a pin in INPUT mode when the button is not being pushed. The voltage drops to zero when the button is pushed.

This lesson will confine itself to digital pins in the OUTPUT mode. It also introduces some new electronic components and the schematic diagram.

Table 4-2. Vocabulary

Term	Definition
breadboard	As a verb, to construct an electronic circuit for purposes of testing. The components and wires of such circuits are plugged onto a special device designed for this purpose called a **bread-board**.
constant	A predefined value that is used in Arduino™ sketches to describe the state of a pin and the mode of a pin.
current	The number of electrons moving per unit of time. The unit of measure is the ampere.
`HIGH`	A constant meaning the voltage of a digital pin is +5.
`INPUT`	A constant meaning the mode of a pin is set to sense the voltage being applied from an outside source.
jumper wires	The wires that connect components to each other and to the Arduino™ on the bread-board.
light-emitting diode (LED)	An electronic device that lights up when it is properly connected to an Arduino™ pin set to the `OUTPUT` mode and `HIGH`.
`LOW`	A constant meaning the voltage of a digital pin is zero.
Ohm's Law	An equation that defines the mathematical relationship of voltage, current, and resistance.
`OUTPUT`	A constant meaning the mode of a pin is being set by the Arduino™ sketch. This voltage may be used by an outside device connected to this pin.
parameter	A parameter is a special kind of variable used by a method to refer to data provided as input. A value placed inside parentheses for some C-language commands or method.
pictorial	A picture or drawing; for purposes of this book, it is specifically a picture or drawing of the components wired and connected to digital pins on the Arduino.™
pin	A pin is a connection with which the Arduino™ can be wired to external devices — everything from motors and switches to display panels.
resistance	The tendency of materials to resist the movement of electrons. Metal has low resistance; glass has very high resistance.
resistor	A component that attempts to inhibit the flow of electrons, among other uses. In this lesson, a resistor is used to limit the electrical current that goes through an LED.
schematic	A drawing shorthand used by engineers to show how components are wired together.
voltage	The force of electricity, sometimes referred to as the determination of electrons to move. Lightning, for example, has very high voltage—several hundred million volts. A double-A battery, by contrast, has merely +1.5 volts.

Description:

This lesson introduces electronic components for the first time—in particular, the light-emitting diode (LED) and the resistor. It also includes some drawings of how these components are to be wired and connected to digital pins on the Arduino.™ A picture or drawing of this connection is called a *pictorial*.

The nice thing about a pictorial wiring diagram is that it is easy to duplicate. Just connect the wires as shown. The trouble with the pictorial, however, is that showing even modestly complex circuits becomes very difficult. Engineers use a kind of drawing shorthand, called the *schematic*, for showing how components are wired together. A schematic is concise; it does an excellent job of showing how electricity is expected to move through a circuit. Complex circuits are much easier to diagram. More to the point, it is far easier for a programmer or engineer to understand complex circuitry by reading a schematic rather than a pictorial.

But schematics are also abstract. They reflect how the electricity flows, not how the parts and wires are physically arranged. Reading a schematic is a learned skill. As components are introduced, their images are accompanied by their schematic symbol. For the next few lessons, wiring diagrams will be presented in both pictorial and schematic form. Later lessons present wiring diagrams in schematic form only.

Components

This lesson introduces the light-emitting diode (LED) and the resistor. These are added to the big component that's been in use since Lesson 1, the Arduino™ itself. Each has a pictorial and a corresponding schematic symbol.

Light-emitting diodes

An *LED* is a semiconductor device that lights up when properly connected to a source of electrical current. A proper connection means that the anode is positive relative to the cathode. For an Arduino™ this usually means the cathode is connected to ground (GND).

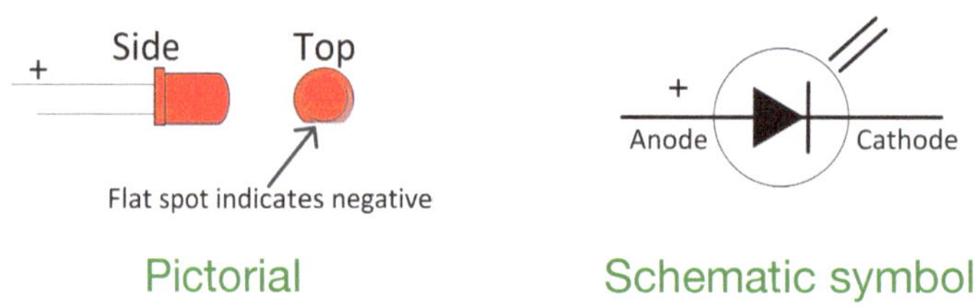

Figure 4-2. LED shown in pictorial and schematic forms

Resistors

A *resistor* is a component that attempts to inhibit the flow of electrons. A resistor has many uses, but in this case it is used to limit the electrical current that goes through an LED. Most resistors are made from some carbon compound. They come is a wide variety of values; color stripes indicate the value of an individual resistor.

Pictorial Schematic symbol

Figure 4-3. Resistor shown in pictorial and schematic forms

4

Arduino™

Important	Notice that, as with the other components, each connector on the physical Arduino™ Uno board has its counterpart on the schematic diagram.

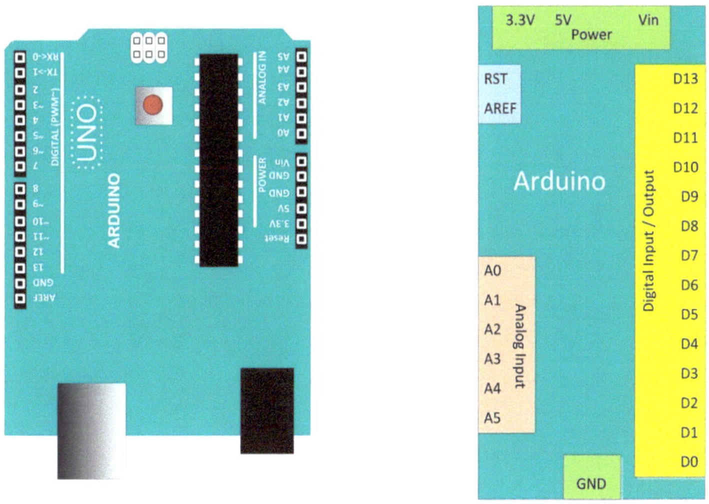

Pictorial diagram Schematic diagram

Figure 4-4. Arduino™ Uno shown in pictorial and schematic forms

Tools

Bread-board

A bread-board is a prototyping tool used to temporarily connect electronic components to each other to prototype circuits. It is not a true electronic component, and, thus, it does not appear in schematics or have a schematic symbol.

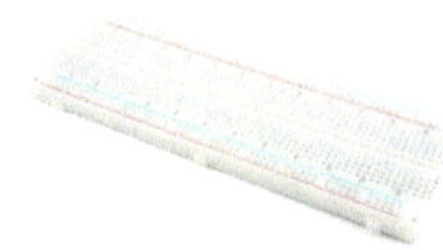

Figure 4-5. Bread-board

Jumper wires

For purposes of this book, jumper wires connect components to each other and to the Arduino™ on the bread-board. Jumper wires come in a variety of sizes and colors, which vary to distinguish the objects to which they are connected. Male-to-male jumper wires are used to make the electrical connections between components. Female-to-female jumper wires simply extend male jumpers too small for a job.

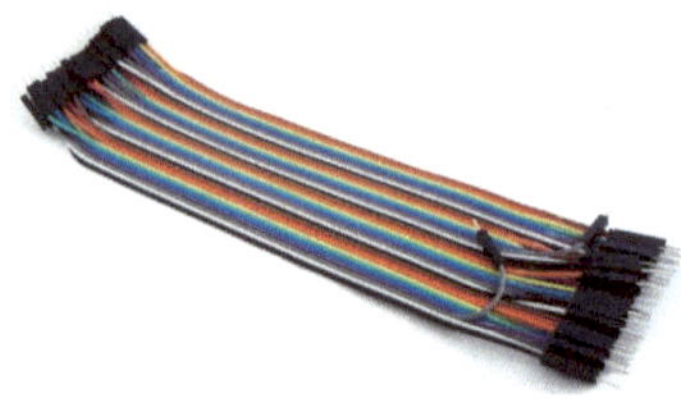

Figure 4-6. Jumper wires

Programming a Digital Pin

In this lesson digital pins are used to light LEDs. This requires setting each pin to the status of `OUTPUT`.

Two new C-language statements are required, `pinMode()` and `digitalWrite()`. Both of these statements require parameters. These are the pin number and desired mode for `pinMode()` and pin number and status for `digitalWrite()`.

`pinMode()` and `digitalWrite()`

`pinMode( pinNumber, mode)`

`pinNumber:` integer that specifies which pin is to be accessed.

`mode:` constant specifying the pin's direction.

`OUTPUT`: program can set the pin's voltage to +5V or 0v.

`INPUT`: program can detect a voltage applied to the pin.

```
example: pinMode( 2, OUTPUT); // sets pin 2 to output
```

`digitalWrite( pinNumber, status)`

`pinNumber:`	integer that specifies which pin is to be accessed.
`status:`	constant specifying whether that pin is to be set to +5v or 0 volts. `HIGH`: sets pin to +5 volts. `LOW`: sets pin to 0 volts.
`example:`	`digitalWrite( 3, HIGH); // sets pin 3 to 5v.`

4

Electronics and Ohm's Law

Underlying everything the Arduino™ does are *voltage*, *current*, and *resistance*. These will appear again and again, so taking some time now to understand them will make future challenges easier. Electricity is all about electrons — how many there are, how badly they want to get from one place to another, and how difficult it is for them to move.

Table 4-3. Components of Ohm's Law

Voltage:	The difference in electric potential between two points in space, measured in volts. How badly some electrons want to get from one place to another.
Current:	A flow of electric charge, measured in amperes (amps). How many electrons want to move.
Resistance:	The degree of opposition an electrical current will encounter when passing through an electrical conductor, measured in ohms. How much trouble electrons will encounter in attempting the move.

The relationship of these is described by Ohm's Law:

Ohm's Law: $V = IR$

where:
V is voltage, in volts
I is current, in amps
R is resistance, in ohms

The LED is a device made from semiconducting material, usually silicon. This silicon in an LED is modified to conduct electrical current easily but only in only one direction. A problem occurs when the LED is connected to power because the LED has a low resistance. A quick look at Ohm's law shows that if the resistance (R) is low, the current (I) will be high.

For that reason, an LED is always connected to power in series with a resistor, usually 220 ohms for a source of +5 volts. This is the value of the resistor used in these lessons.

Goals:

By the end of this lesson the reader will:

1. Know how to identify the pins by number on the Arduino™ Uno.
2. Know how to configure any particular pin as `INPUT` or `OUTPUT`.
3. Know the meaning of and how to use the constants `INPUT` and `OUTPUT`.
4. Know how to set the output of a digital pin to `HIGH` or `LOW`.
5. Know the meaning of and how to use the constants `HIGH` and `LOW`.
6. Be able to identify an LED, including which lead is the anode (+) and which is the cathode (-).
7. Be able to identify a 220-ohm resistor and know that it is used in this case as a way of limiting how much current passes through the LED.
8. Be able to connect an LED to an Arduino™ pin and control that LED with an Arduino™ sketch.

Materials:

Quantity	Part	Image	Notes	Catalog Number
1	Arduino™ Uno		Single-board computer. This board is delicate and should be handled with care. When you are not using it, keep it in a box or plastic bag.	3102
1	USB Cable		This is the standard USB adapter cable with the flat connector on one end and the square connector on the other.	2301
1	Computer with at least one USB port and access to the Arduino™ website, http://www.arduino.cc	---	The operating system of this computer must be Windows, Macintosh OS/X, or Linux.	---
6	Light-emitting diodes (LEDs)		Single color, about 0.02 amps rated current, diffused.	1301
6	220 ohm resistors		¼ watt, 5% tolerance. Color code is red–red–brown-gold.	0102
1	Bread-board	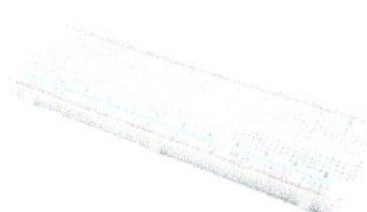	Used for prototyping.	3104
As-req'd.	Jumper wires		Used with bread-boards for wiring the components.	3105

Procedure:

Part I: Set up and test a set of six LEDs connected to pins 2 through 7 of the Arduino.™

1. Connect the Arduino™ to a set of six LEDs and resistors as shown in Figure 4-7.

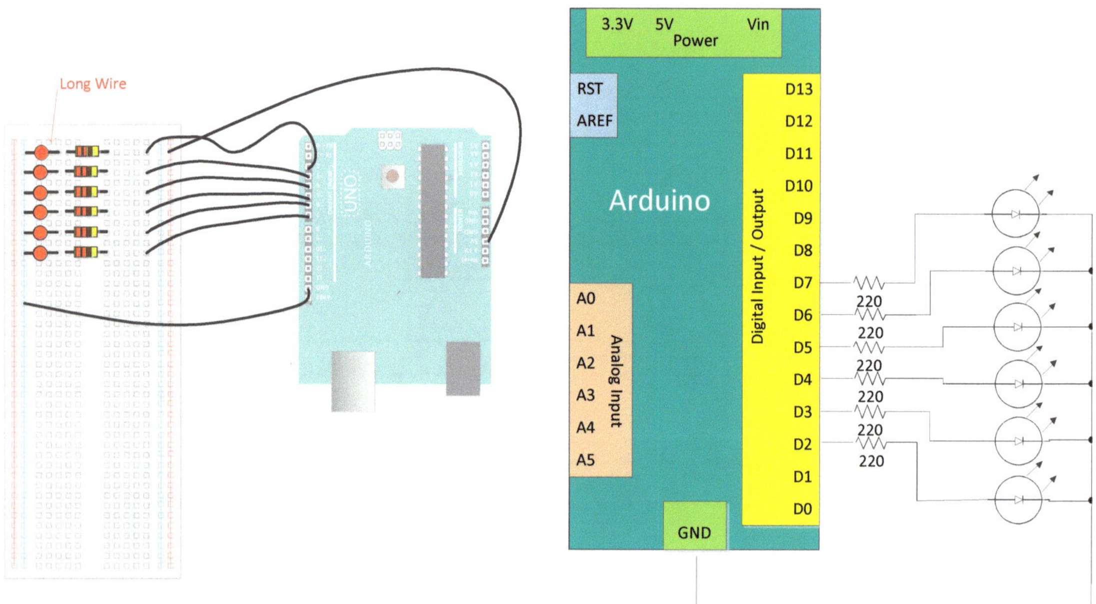

Pictorial diagram | Schematic diagram

Figure 4-7. Pictorial and schematic diagrams of LED connections to the Arduino™

Important	Notice the difference between the Pictorial diagram and the Schematic diagram. The Pictorial diagram shows exactly where parts are placed on the bread-board and how wires are connected. The Schematic diagram, by contrast, shows components in abstract form. The electrical connections are clear, but the images don't match the real thing.

Schematic diagrams are the common way of illustrating how something is wired. Later lessons and projects in this book will provide only the schematic diagram, leaving the details of the wiring up to the programmer.

2. Connect the Arduino™ to the computer. Then start the Arduino™ Integrated Development Environment (IDE).

3. Enter the header comments for this lesson's sketch as shown in Snippet 4-1. Enter the programmer's (author's) name in place of W. P. Osborne. Enter the date on the next line.

Snippet 4-1.

```
/* Lesson4DigitalPins
  by W. P. Osborne
  <date>
*/
```

4

4. Add the `setup()` method as shown in Snippet 4-2. Within it, initialize pins 2 and 3 for `OUTPUT`. Notice that the other pins wired in step 1 are not being used yet.

Snippet 4-2.

```
...
void setup(){
     pinMode(2, OUTPUT);
     pinMode(3, OUTPUT);
}
```

5. Add the `loop()` method to cause the LEDs connected to pins 2 and 3 to blink alternately.

Snippet 4-3.

```
...
void loop(){
    digitalWrite(2, HIGH);
    digitalWrite(3, LOW);
    delay(500); // wait

    digitalWrite(2, LOW);
    digitalWrite(3, HIGH);
    delay(500);
}
```

6. Save the sketch as `Lesson4DigitalPins`. Upload to the Arduino™ and observe.

Exercises:

Exercise 4-1. LED thermometer

Make a sketch called `Thermometer` that makes all six LEDs light up, going from pin 2 through pin 7, and then go dark from pin 7 through pin 2, with 1/10th second between each change, thermometer style.

The sketch must:

- Begin with all LEDs off.
- Light the LED connected to pin 2, then wait 1/10th second.
- Leaving the LED connected to pin 2 on, light the LED connected to pin 3. Wait 1/10th second.
- Leaving the first two LEDs (pins 2 and 3) on, light the LED connected to pin 4. Wait 1/10th second, and continue until the LEDs on pins 2 through 7 are on.
- After leaving all LEDs on for 1/10th second, extinguish the LED connected to pin 7 and wait 1/10th second.
- Leaving the LED connected to pin 7 extinguished, turn off the LED connected to pin 6 and wait 1/10th second, and continue until all LEDs are off. Wait 1/10 second. By placing the code that does this in the `loop()` method, the pattern should repeat over and over.

Exercise 4-2. Pattern sketch

Create a new Arduino™ sketch that creates some sort of pattern and does something different than what has already been done in this lesson.

Lesson 5 | Integers and Math

5

The Big Idea:

In algebra we all learned to deal with numbers in the abstract by using letters to represent numbers. The equation for a straight line, for example, is y = mx + c. In this equation we know that y is a value that is found by evaluating the expression mx + c. But all the letters—y, m, x, and c—are simply names for placeholders of actual values. The equation expresses how they relate to each other.

These names are called *variables*. Variables to store text (called `Strings`) were first introduced in Lesson 2. The C language also uses variables to store numbers. In this unit you will learn to work with variables and to be aware of some of the subtle differences between how they are used in C and in algebra.

Background:

Lesson 3 introduced variables, in particular variables of the type `String`. `String` variables are useful when the programming task is collecting, manipulating, and displaying text. But Arduino™ sketches also need the ability work with numbers. A sketch used to control a quad copter, for example, must sense the angle of the craft relative to the earth and use that information to adjust the speed of the motors. This cannot be done without mathematics, and mathematics requires numbers.

In addition to the `String` type for text, the C language provides several variable types to use with numbers, as shown in Table 5-1.

Table 5-1. Variables used in lessons in this book

Type	Description	Examples
`String`	A collection of characters; a type of data	Hello, world!
`int`	signed integer with no decimal point. Range is from -32767 to 32767	5, 18, -2776, 0, 83, -21822
`double`	Precise number with a decimal, useful for most mathematic purposes	98.6, 0.7, -236.99, 0.0, -5280.1
`float`	Number with a decimal, not as precise as a double but with a large range—from -3.4028235E+38 to 3.4028235E+38	6.02E+23, 3.7E+8, 7.0, -89.2234E18

The Arduino™ website reference for float numbers cautions that the lack of precision of float numbers may make for some strange behaviors when compared with other numbers.

Important	This lesson works only with integers. For most applications of the Arduino,™ integer math is all that is required.

Mathematics in the C language for the Arduino™ is similar, but not identical, to the math commonly seen in algebra.

Table 5-2. Differences between algebraic math and math in C

	Algebra	**C Programming language**

Equals sign (=)	Indicates equality. That is, the expression on the left of the equals sign evaluates to the same result as the expression on the right.
	
	Examples:
	5 + 2 = 7
	
	4 + 8 = 7 + 5
	
	AB + AC = A(B + C)
		Does not indicate equality. The symbol is called the assignment operator. The left side must be the name of a variable. The right is an arithmetic expression. The results of the evaluation of that expression are "assigned to" the variable. That is, the result is stored to the variable.
		
		Example: The following declares a variable named `myInt` then assigns the result of an arithmetic expression to that variable.
		
		`int myInt;`
		`myInt = 7 + 12;`
		
		The variable, `myInt`, has been assigned the value of 19.
		
		The following programming statement modifies this value.
		
		`myInt = myInt + 3;`
		
		The expression on the right retrieves the value assigned to `myInt`, adds 3 to it, then stores the result to `myInt`. The value of `myInt` is now 22.

	Algebra	C Programming language

Division (/)	One integer divided by another may yield a quotient that contains a decimal. For example:
	15 / 4 = 3.75
		No decimals are allowed. Instead, the integer portion of the quotient is the only result, and it is not rounded.
		
		`int myInt;`
		`myInt = 15 / 4;`
		
		The value assigned to `myInt` is 3.

Modulus (%)	Frequently called the modulo operator, the modulus has several uses in mathematics.	Determines the remainder of integer division.
		
		`int myInt;`
		`myInt = 13 % 4;`
		
		The value assigned to `myInt` is 1.

5

Table 5-3. Vocabulary

Term	Definition
arithmetic operator	A symbol representing a mathematical operation. C has six operators: + - * / % =
assignment operator	The arithmetic operator with the symbol =. The expression to the right of the operator is evaluated. The results are stored to the variable to the left. The act of storing a value to a variable is called assignment.
`double`	A precision number with a decimal.
`float`	A number with a decimal with a very large range but less precision than a `double`.
`int`	A numeric data type for integers. A variable of type `int` may have any value from -32767 through +32767.
library	A library is a set of prewritten Arduino™ sketches, each of which perform a particular service.
Math library	A set of mathematical operations prewritten for the C language.
variable	A name given to a location in memory where a value can be stored. A variable must be named according to certain rules, and a data type must be assigned to the variable.

Description:

Declaring number variables

Example 5-1. Form for declaring number variables

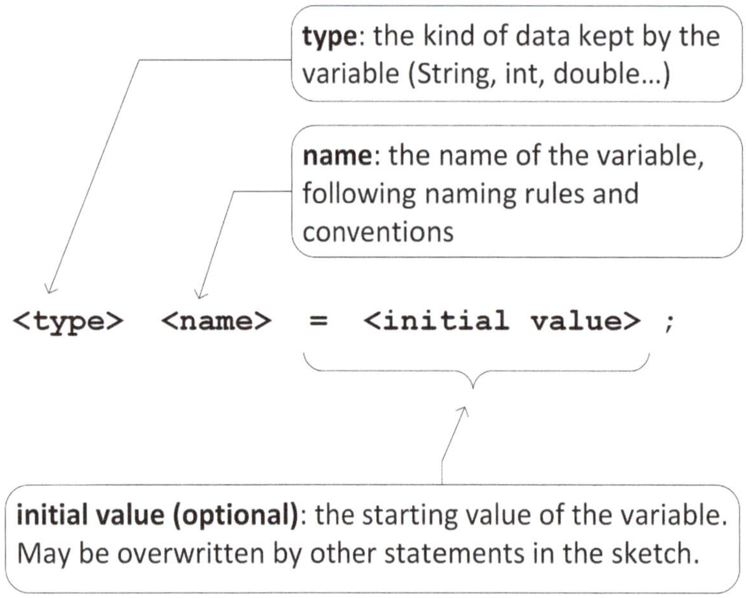

Just as with `String` variables discussed in Lesson 3, number variables must be declared; their names must follow the same naming rules and conventions; and a variable may be assigned an initial value.

Example 5-2. Number variables

```
int ageOfParticipant = 17;  // initialized variable

int highScore;
```

Mathematical operators and equations

Arithmetic Operators:

Just as with algebra, mathematics in C involves addition, subtraction, multiplication, and division. In addition, C also has assignment and modulus. These are called arithmetic operators. Each has a symbol that is used to indicate the operation in a programming statement.

In Table 5-4, assume the letters A, B, and C are declared numeric variables of some type.

Table 5-4. Arithmetic operators used in C programming

Operator	Symbol	Description	Exam-ple
Addition	+	Adds two values.	A + B
Subtraction	-	Subtracts the second value from the first.	A - B
Multiplication	*	Multiplies two values.	A * B

Operator	Symbol	Description	Exam-ple
Division	/	Divides the first value by the second.	A / B
Assignment	=	Stores the value of the right side of the operator to the variable on the left.	C = A + B
Modulus (only works with integers and variables of type `int`)	%	Finds the remainder when the first integer is divided by the second integer.	A % B

5

Equations:

Mathematical expressions in C are similar to those in algebra, except the equals sign serves a different purpose. Called the *assignment operator*, it causes the expression to the right of the operator to be resolved and the numeric results placed in the variable to the left. The code segment in Snippet 5-1 is an illustration. Additional examples appear in the practice sketch in Exercises 5-1 and 5-2.

The equation in Snippet 5-1 is:

```
areaOfRectangle = width * height;
```

Notice how a `String` variable is used to print the results in the Serial Monitor. Concatenation can be used to append integer values to a `String` variable.

Snippet 5-1. Illustration of use of assignment operator

```
...
int areaOfRectangle;
int width;
int height;

// assign width and height values
width = 3;
height = 7;

...
// calculate area and store value to areaOfRectangle
areaOfRectangle = width * height;

// use String, Serial, and concatenation
// to show results in the Serial Monitor
String results = "Area of the rectangle is: ";
results += areaOfRectangle;
Serial.println(results);
...
```

The Serial Monitor will display:

```
Area of the rectangle is: 21
```

The Math library

The Arduino™ IDE includes many prewritten services that can be accessed via libraries. A *library* is a set of pre-written Arduino™ sketches, each of which perform a particular service. Later lessons will make use of many libraries. For now you only need to know the following:

1. The *Math library* offers many services such as square root, raising one number to the power of another, determining absolute value, and trigonometric functions. The last service is very useful for writing sketches that perform navigation, such as is used with quad copters.

2. The services of the Math library can be accessed by name simply by placing the statement #include <math.h> at the top of an Arduino™ sketch, just under header comments.

Note	The statement in Snippet 5-2 is not followed by a semicolon.

3. Snippet 5-2 illustrates the use of the Math library to calculate the square root of an integer. A description of the complete services of the Arduino™ Math library can be found at http://www.arduino.cc/en/Math/H.

Snippet 5-2. Use of the Math library

```
...
#include <math.h>

int myNumber;

...
myNumber = 67;

int squareRootOfMyNumber;
squareRootOfMyNumber = sqrt(myNumber);

String results = "The square root of ";
results += myNumber;
results += " is: ";
results += squareRootOfMyNumber;
Serial.println(results);
...
```

The Serial Monitor will display something like:

```
The square root of 67 is: 8
```

Notice that the square root is an integer. When working with integers, C returns only integers. Further, as with integer division, integer square roots are not rounded. Thus, the square root of 9 and the square root of 15 are both 3.

Goals:

By the end of this lesson readers will:

1. Know how to declare and use number variables of type `int`.
2. Know how to use all six arithmetic operators used in C.
3. Understand that the structure of an equation in C is an expression, the results of which are assigned to a variable.
4. Know that integer division in C yields only the integer quotient and does not round.
5. Know how to use the modulus operator to retrieve the remainder of integer division.
6. Know how to use the Arduino™ Math library.
7. Be able to apply `String` concatenation to prepare `String` values that contain integers.
8. Be able to write Arduino™ sketches that perform mathematical operations.

Materials:

Quan-tity	Part	Image	Notes	Catalog Number
1	Arduino™ Uno		Single-board computer. This board is delicate and should be handled with care. When you are not using it, keep it in a box or plastic bag.	3102
1	USB Cable		This is the standard USB adapter cable with the flat connector on one end and the square connector on the other.	2301
1	Computer with at least one USB port and access to the Arduino™ website, http://www.arduino.cc.	---	The operating system of this computer must be Windows, Macintosh OS/X, or Linux.	---

Procedure:

1. Begin by connecting your Arduino™ to the computer. Then start the Arduino™ Integrated Development Environment (IDE).

2. In the Arduino™ IDE, enter the multi-line header comments as shown in Snippet 5-3.

Snippet 5-3.

```
/* Lesson5IntegersAndMath
   by <your name here>
   <date goes here>
*/
```

Substitute the programmer's name and the actual date where indicated by the angle brackets.

3. Underneath the heading comments, import the Math library as shown in Snippet 5-4.

Snippet 5-4.

```
...
#include <math.h>
```

4. Declare three variables of type `int` as shown in Snippet 5-5. Notice how multiple variables can be created in a single programming statement if the names are separated by commas.

Snippet 5-5.

```
...
int integerA, integerB, integerC;
```

5. Add the `setup()` method as shown in Snippet 5-6. This sketch allows time for the serial port to initialize. Next, a ready message is sent to the Serial Monitor.

Snippet 5-6.

```
...
void setup(){
    Serial.begin(9600);
    Serial.println("Ready for numbers.");
}
```

6. Add the `loop()` method as shown in Snippet 5-7. Do not put any programming statements into it yet.

Snippet 5-7.

```
...
void loop(){

}
```

7. Save the sketch as `Lesson5IntegersAndMath`.

8. Upload the sketch to the Arduino™ and open the Serial Monitor. If successful the Serial Monitor should display the following: 5

```
Ready for numbers.
```

9. Add programming statements to the `loop()` method of the sketch, as shown in Snippet 5-8. These statements initialize the first two integers and show them to the user. Also add the `while(true)` statement at the very end of the `loop()` method. This prevents the `loop()` method from running more than once. This statement should remain the last one in the `loop()` method for this sketch.

Snippet 5-8.

```
...
void loop(){

    // exploring integers
    integerA = 37;
    integerB = 12;

    String message;
    message = "Exploring integers. For the following:";
    message += "\n  integerA = ";
    message += integerA;
    message += "\n  integerB = ";
    message += integerB;
    Serial.println(message);  // show values of integers

    while(true);  // keep this the last line of the loop
    // method
}
```

Upload the sketch and open the Serial Monitor. The following should appear:

```
Ready for numbers.
```

```
Exploring integers. For the following:
  integerA = 37
  integerB = 12
```

10. Above the `while(true)` programming statement, add the programming statements shown in Snippet 5-9 to demonstrate the addition of integers:

Snippet 5-9.

```
...
    // perform integer calculations
    message = "integerA plus integerB is: ";
    integerC = integerA + integerB;
    message += integerC;
    Serial.println(message);

    while(true);
}
```

The Serial Monitor should now display:

```
Ready for numbers.
Exploring integers. For the following:
  integerA = 37
  integerB = 12
integerA plus integerB is: 49
```

11. Adding statements similar to those in Snippet 5-9 that illustrate subtraction and multiplication are left as an exercise (Exercise 5-1). Next, as shown in Snippet 5-10, add statements that demonstrate integer division.

Snippet 5-10.

```
...
    //   subtraction exercise goes here
    //   multiplication exercise goes here
    //   division
    message = "integerA divided by integerB is: ";
    integerC = integerA / integerB;
    message += integerC;
    Serial.println(message);

    while(true);
}
```

The Serial Monitor should now display:

```
Ready for numbers.
Exploring integers. For the following:
  integerA = 37
  integerB = 12
integerA plus integerB is: 49
integerA divided by integerB is: 3
```

5

12. The division operation is not complete without determining and displaying the remainder. This is the function of the modulus operator. Add the programming statements shown in Snippet 5-11 to the `loop()` method just before the `while(true)` statement.

Snippet 5-11.

```
...
    //   remainder
    message = "the remainder of integerA / integerB is: ";
    integerC = integerA % integerB;
    message += integerC;
    Serial.println(message);

    while(true);
}
```

The Serial Monitor will display:

```
Ready for numbers.
Exploring integers. For the following:
  integerA = 37
  integerB = 12
integerA plus integerB is: 49
integerA divided by integerB is: 3
the remainder of integerA divided by integerB is: 1
```

13. Finally, use the Math library function to find the square root of an integer by adding the programming statements shown in Snippet 5-12 to the `loop()` method just above the `while(true)` statement:

Snippet 5-12.

```
...
    // library function, square root
    integerA = 143;
    integerC = sqrt(integerA);
    message = "the square root of ";
    message += integerA;
    message += " is ";
    message += integerC;
    Serial.println(message);

    while(true);
}
```

The Serial Monitor should display:

```
Ready for numbers.
Exploring integers. For the following:
  integerA = 37
  integerB = 12
integerA plus integerB is: 49
integerA divided by integerB is: 3
the remainder of integerA divided by integerB is: 1
the square root of 143 is 11
```

14. Save the sketch to preserve your work.

Exercises:

Exercise 5-1. Create subtraction and multiplication examples

Add the subtraction and multiplication examples to the `Lesson5IntegersAndMath` sketch.

Exercise 5-2. Calculate area and perimeter

Write a new sketch called `AreaAndPerimeter` that calculates and displays the area and perimeter of a rectangle. Set the width to 27 and the height to 40.

Lesson 6 | Serial Input

6

The Big Idea:

Information coming into an Arduino™ sketch is called *input*. This lesson focuses on text in the form of characters that come from the user via the Serial Monitor. The Serial Monitor can also be used to send text back to the Arduino.™

Background:

To read the incoming text, the programmer needs to be able to detect that a character is ready to be read and have a way to retrieve the waiting character. To do so, three new programming statements are introduced. These are:

1. `Serial.available()` returns the number of characters waiting to be read from the serial port.
2. `Serial.read()` retrieves a character from the serial port and assigns it to a character variable.
3. `if(<condition>)` is a means of performing some programming statements if the condition evaluates to true.

Later lessons focus on methods used to transmit information to a sketch running on the Arduino,™ including push buttons, switches, sensors of all sorts, even gravity and movement. The Arduino™ has many ways of responding to that information, including movement, lights, sounds, and text on liquid crystal panels.

About Serial

`Serial.print` and `Serial.println` have been used without examining what *serial* means. Think for a moment about Samuel Morse, who is frequently credited with developing the first practical electrical telegraph in the United States in the 1830s. That telegraph consisted of wire that allowed operators to send and receive messages one character at a time. For example, to transmit the word "hello" first the letter "h" was sent, then the "e," then the "l" (twice), and finally the "o." Each character was identified by a series of pulses, some long and some short. Each pulse was sent one at a time.

Table 6-1. Serial communication via Morse Code

Letter	Pulses (in order)
h	short short short short
e	short
l	short long short short
l	short long short short
o	long long long

This is called *serial communication* because each letter, in fact each pulse for each letter, is sent one at a time, in order, first to last.

If, however, the word "hello" were simply written on a card and that card handed to the recipient, all letters would be sent and received at the same time. This is called *parallel communication*.

Serial has the advantage over parallel that only a few wires are needed to send as much information as could be wanted.

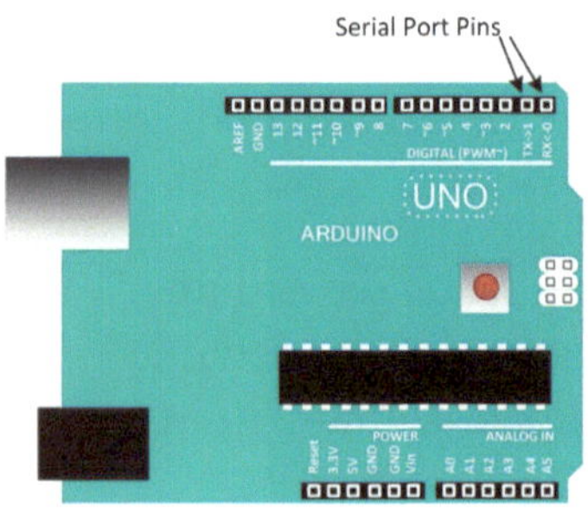

Figure 6-1. Arduino™ Uno with serial port called out

The Arduino™ Uno has one serial port. When it is not being used to communicate with the IDE's Serial Monitor, it can transmit data via pin 1 and receive it via pin 0. A close look at these ports will reveal they are identified as TX and RX. (Other Arduino™ single-board computer models may have more than one. The Arduino™ Mega, for example, has four serial ports.)

About characters

So far the Arduino™ has sent messages to the Serial Monitor using letters, such as in "Hello, world!" But computers don't really know anything about letters. Rather, to a computer everything is a number. In order for a letter to appear, two things must happen. First, the computer must be given, or select, the number to be sent representing a letter and then be given the instructions necessary to read or display that number as a letter.

Table 6-2. Data types

Data Type	Description	Examples
`char`	character, a single letter or number to be interpreted as text	`char my Char;` `myChar` can be set to ‘a,’ ‘3,’ ‘!,’ ‘B,’ and any other character.
`int`	an integer	`int myInt;` `int` can be set to 3, 19, -212, and any other integer.
`String`	a collection of characters	`String myStr;` `myStr` can be set to "The answer is 42," "Heck no, I won't go," or any other collection of characters.

6

This lesson examines the relationship of characters to the integers used to represent them inside the Arduino.™ The capital letter *A*, for example, is stored in the Arduino™ as the integer 65. Whether the Arduino™ chooses to display it as 65 or the character *A* is determined by how the variable to contain it is declared. Either way, what is communicated is the number 65. In binary format this number is 01000001. The serial port sends each bit, in order, one at a time. This serial communication of the bits of the number 65, which, in turn, translate to the letter *A* is, for the Arduino,™ the equivalent of Samuel Morse's short and long pulses of the telegraph.

About `if` testing

The sketch in this lesson uses a statement, `Serial.available()`, that returns an integer greater than or equal to 0. This integer is the number of characters waiting to be read from the serial port after the [Send] button is clicked.

The keyword `if` is a test. The result of that test must be true or false. In this lesson the number returned from `Serial.available` is tested to see if it is greater than zero. If it is, then the statements between the curly braces are executed. Otherwise, these statements are skipped.

Lesson 8 covers `if` in more detail.

Table 6-3. Vocabulary

Term	Definition
`BIN`	BIN is binary, the number base used by computers.
`DEC`	DEC is decimal, which is in common use by people. Its base is 10 symbols, 0 through 9.
`HEX`	HEX is hexadecimal, the numbering scheme used by computer science to economically represent binary values. It has 16 symbols, 0 through 9 plus A, B, C, D, E, and F.

Term	Definition
input	Information going into an Arduino™ sketch from the Serial Monitor.
parallel communication	Communication method in which multiple bits of data are conveyed simultaneously.
serial communication	Comunication method in which data is conveyed one bit at a time.
Unicode	The parent container of computer characters. It includes the commonly used ASCII characters plus characters from most of the world's major languages.

Description:

Sending text to the Arduino from the Serial Monitor is pretty simple. The desired text is entered into the Text Input Box. The contents of this box are sent to the Arduino one character at a time when the [Send] button is clicked.

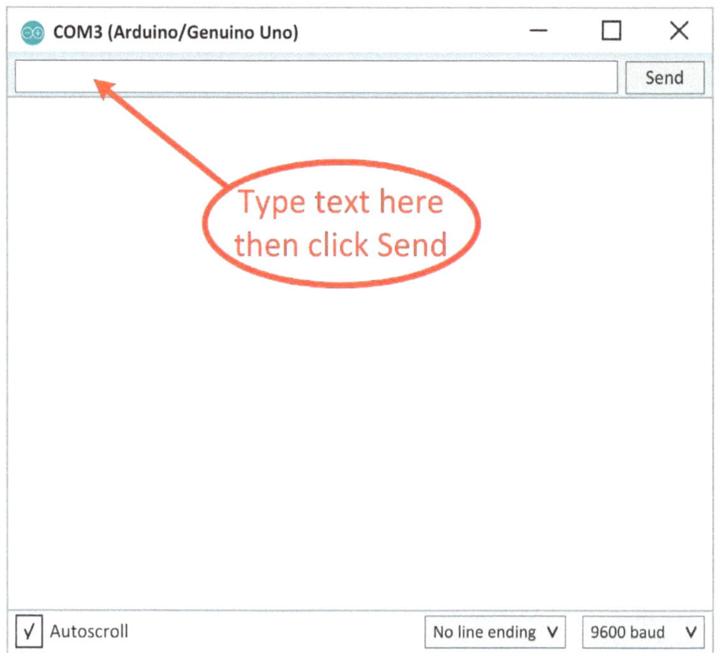

The new programming statements shown in Table 6-4 are used to read characters from the serial port.

Table 6-4. Programming statements used to read characters from the serial port

Programming Statement	Description
`Serial.available()`	Returns the number of characters waiting to be read
`Serial.read()`	Retrieves the character

Example 6-1 illustrates the use of `Serial.available()` and `Serial.read()` plus the character data type to first determine if a character is ready to be read and, if it is, retrieve it and store it to a character variable.

Example 6-1. Use of `Serial.available()` *and* `Serial.read()`

```
char myChar;  // declare variable to contain a character
if(Serial.available() > 0) {  // test, is character waiting?
    myChar = Serial.read();  // yes, retrieve and
                             // assign value to myChar
```

Notice the character is not retrieved and assigned to `myChar` unless the serial port indicates at least one is available. This is what the `if(<condition>)` does. The condition, in this case, is that `Serial.available()` is greater than zero.

6

Goals:

By the end of this lesson readers will:

1. Know how to accept text from the user and store it to a variable.
2. Know how to design and program an interactive program, one that responds to input from the user.
3. Know how to capture and display an entry as a character and as an integer.

Materials:

Quantity	Part	Image	Notes	Catalog Number
1	Arduino™ Uno		Single-board computer. This board is delicate and should be handled with care. When you are not using it, keep it in a box or plastic bag.	3102
1	USB Cable		This is the standard USB adapter cable with the flat connector on one end and the square connector on the other.	2301

Quantity	Part	Image	Notes	Catalog Number
1	Computer with at least one USB port and access to the Arduino™ website, http://www.arduino.cc.	---	The operating system of this computer must be Windows, Macintosh OS/X, or Linux.	---

Procedure:

Part I: Set up, upload, and run the first program.

1. Connect the Arduino™ to the host computer and open the Arduino™ IDE.
2. Type in the heading comments, then declare the variables to be used.

Snippet 6-1.

```
/* Lesson6SerialRead
   <author>
   <date>
*/

int incomingInteger;
char incomingCharacter;
```

3. Add the `setup()` method. It need only initialize the serial port so that communications can be established with the Serial Monitor.

Snippet 6-2.

```
...
void setup(){
    Serial.begin(9600);
}
```

4. Add the `loop()` method with the test for an incoming character and the ability to read and print that character.

Snippet 6-3.

```
...
void loop(){
    // are characters waiting to be read?
    if(Serial.available() > 0){
        // Yes, so read next one as a character
    incomingCharacter = Serial.read();

    Serial.print("The Arduino™ received the character: ");
    Serial.println(incomingCharacter);
    }
}
```


5. Save the sketch, upload it to the Arduino™ and open the Serial Monitor.
6. Type the word `hello` into the text input box, then click [Send]. The Serial Monitor should look like this:

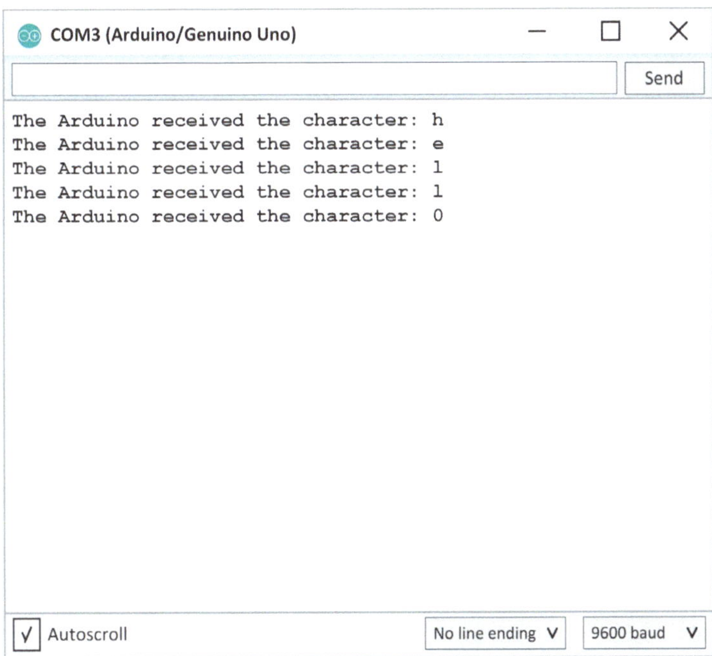

7. Add some programming statements to display the numbers that are sent to the Arduino™ to be interpreted as characters. This is done by first assigning the value of the read character to an integer variable, then printing that value. Remember, the Arduino™ knows nothing of characters, really. It simply knows to print a character if the variable that contains it is of type `char`. But if the variable is of type `int` the actual number will be printed.

Snippet 6-4.

```
...
void loop(){
    // are characters waiting to be read?
    if(Serial.available() > 0){
        // Yes, so read next one as a character
    incomingCharacter = Serial.read();

    Serial.print("The Arduino™ received the character: ");
    Serial.println(incomingCharacter);

    // assign the character to an int variable
    // then print it.
    incomingInteger = incomingCharacter;
    Serial.print("The actual integer sent was: ");
    Serial.println(incomingInteger);
    }
```

8. Save the sketch, upload it to the Arduino™, and open the Serial Monitor. Type the word `hello` into the input text box and click [Send]. The Serial Monitor should look like this:

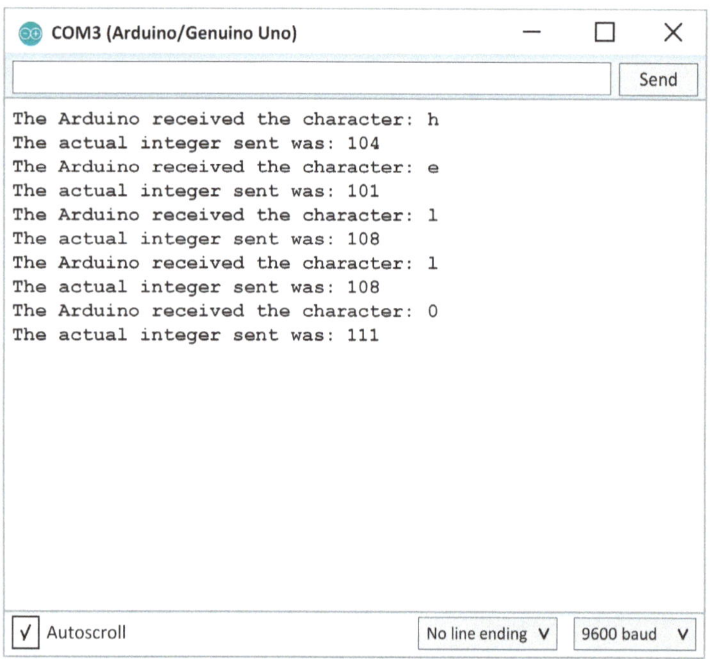

Exercises:

Exercise 6-1. Show characters and integer

Modify the sketch `Lesson6SerialRead.ino` to print the character and its corresponding integer on one line, in the following format:

```
The character h has the integer value 104
The character e has the integer value 101
...
```

Use this table to prepare a set of characters, numbers, and punctuation. Then compare this with the ASCII Table found at http://www.asciitable.com.

6

Exercise 6-2. Show `String` of characters

Write an original sketch, called `Lesson6Exercise2.ino`, that reproduces the characters exactly as entered. The sentence Hello, World! typed into the input text box appears as `Hello, World!` when the [Send] button is clicked.

Exercise 6-3. Show character values and hexadecimal values

The programming statement `Serial.print` can be forced to use a specific format for displaying a character. This is done by adding a comma and a formatting instruction as follows:

```
char myChar = 'A';  // character literals are
                    //delimited by single quotes
Serial.println(myChar);  // prints the letter A
Serial.println(myChar, DEC); // prints 65
Serial.println(myChar, HEX); // prints 41
Serial.println(myChar, BIN); // prints 1000001
```

DEC, HEX, and BIN indicate a number base. DEC is decimal, which is in common use by people. Its base is 10 symbols, 0 through 9.

HEX is hexadecimal, the numbering scheme used by computer science to economically represent binary values. It has 16 symbols, 0 through 9 plus A, B, C, D, E, and F.

BIN is binary, the number base used by computers.

Write a short sketch called `Lesson6Exercise3.ino` that accepts characters from the Serial Monitor and displays both their character values and hexadecimal values. Then verify these values are correct by looking up the characters on the Unicode Character Set found at http://unicode-table.com/en/#control-character.

Unicode is the parent container of computer characters. It includes the commonly used ASCII characters plus characters from most of the world's major languages.

Complete listing 6-1. Lesson6SerialInput

```
/* Lesson6SerialInput
   by W. P. Osborne
   6/30/15
*/

int incomingInteger;
char incomingCharacter;

void setup(){
  Serial.begin(9600);
}

void loop(){
  // are characters waiting to be read?
  if(Serial.available() > 0){
    // Yes, so read next one as a character

    incomingCharacter = Serial.read();

   Serial.print("The Arduino™ received the character: ");
   Serial.println(incomingCharacter);

   // assign the character to an int variable
   // then print it.
   incomingInteger = incomingCharacter;
   Serial.print("The actual integer sent was: ");
   Serial.println(incomingInteger);
  }
}
```

Lesson 7 For Loops

The Big Idea:

This lesson simplifies the control of digital pins by assigning the pin numbers to an integer variable and by calling the `digitalWrite` command multiple times by means of a `for` loop.

Background:

Lesson 4 introduced digital pins. The sketches written turned light-emitting diodes on and off. The program code in those sketches has two characteristics that, while appropriate for an early lesson, are considered inefficient. These are:

1. The same programming statement appears multiple times, as shown in Example 7-1.

Example 7-1. `digitalWrite`

```
digitalWrite( 2, HIGH);
digitalWrite( 3, HIGH);
digitalWrite( 4, HIGH);
digitalWrite( 5, HIGH);
digitalWrite( 6, HIGH);
digitalWrite( 7, HIGH);
```

2. The pin number parameter (2, 3, 4, 5, 6, and 7 in Example 7-1) is an integer `literal`. Good practice is to replace it with an integer `variable`.

A `for` loop is a way of performing a set of tasks a fixed number of times. Consider the host of a child's birthday party. At the end of the party each child is thanked for his or her gift, given a gift bag to take home, thanked for coming, sent out the door to be met by a parent. This is a kind of `for` loop that can be written as a set of instructions as follows:

For each child:

- Thank for the gift.
- Hand a gift bag.
- Thank for coming.
- Escort through door to parent.

When writing sketches for the Arduino,™ the programmer often needs to perform a set of programming statements a fixed number of times. In the example of the LEDs shown here, there is only one statement, the one that turns the LED on by setting the output `HIGH`. The process is:

For each digital pin:

- Set the output `HIGH`

For that matter, in the `setup()` method a `for` loop can be used to set the digital pins to output mode:

For each digital pin:

- Set each pin to `OUTPUT`

Table 7-1. Vocabulary

Term	Definition

comparison operator	Also called logical operators, these are used in logical tests. The C language has six:
	`>` `greater than`
	`<` `less than`
	`>=` `greater than or equal to`
	`<=` `less than or equal to`
	`==` `equal to`
	`!=` `not equal to`

curly brace { }	A symbol that indicates the beginning and ending of a group of C-language statements. The beginning of the group is indicated by the **{** symbol, the ending by the **}**. These are referred to as the *opening* curly brace and the *closing* curly brace.
`for` **loop**	A type of loop in which the number of times the statements in a loop run is numerically defined.
increment	The addition of the value 1 to some integer variable. For example, if `myNumber` is the name of an integer variable and the current value is 6, the increment of `myNumber` results in replacing that value with 7.
logical test	A logical expression that evaluates to either true or false. Both terms are C-language keywords. For example, if `myNumber` is an integer variable to which a value has been assigned, a logical statement that must evaluate to true or false is: `myNumber > 6` This statement is either true or false.
loop	A group of C-language programming statements enclosed in a set of curly braces. This group is intended to be run multiple times.

Description:

The `for` loop concept

The `for` *loop* is used to execute a set of programming statements multiple times. It consists of two parts. These are the set of programming statements to be run and the `for` loop programming statement that sets the criteria for allowing them to be run and determining when execution should stop.

As illustrated in Figure 7-1, the programming statements to be executed are contained within a set of *curly braces* {} immediately following the `for` loop statement.

The `for` loop statement itself has three parts. Each places a role in setting up and running a logical test that determines how many times the statements are executed. These are the initial condition, the test, and the increment. Each contains one or more Java programming statements.

Eventually the programming statements in increment will create a situation where the test no longer evaluates to true. When this happens, the programming statements within the curly braces are no longer executed, and the program will move to what comes after the `for` loop.

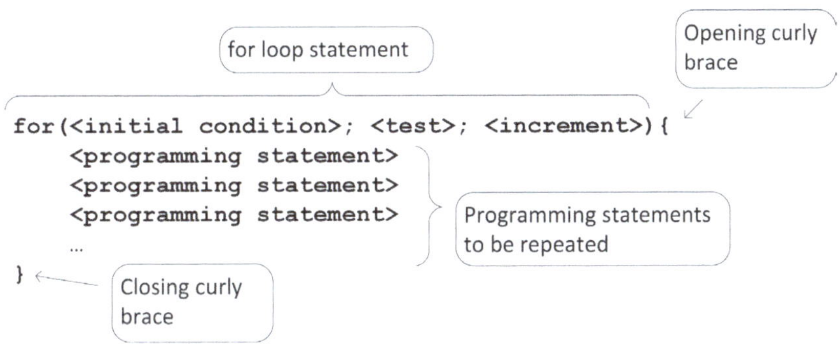

Figure 7-1. Parts of the `for` loop statement

The `for` loop statement itself has three parts. The underlying idea is that an integer counter is created to keep track of the number of times the programming statements are run. Each time they run is called a *loop*. After each loop, the counter changes somehow. This is the *increment*. After the increment, the counter is tested to see if the loop should run again.

Suppose, for example, someone you know has enrolled in a public speaking course. As part of this course, she is to perform the following set of tasks five times:

- Locate a complete stranger.
- Introduce herself.
- Learn something about this stranger.
- Record the stranger's name and what was learned.

This set of tasks to be completed for each stranger is the real world equivalent of the programming statements to be repeated. Suppose, further, that this person wants perform her tasks in an organized manner. She might then take the following approach:

Step 1: Before beginning, write the number 1 on a piece of paper. This is a counter and reflects which attempt she is about to undertake. This is the initial condition. Her first attempt is attempt number 1. So the counter is set to 1.

Step 2: Examine the counter on the piece of paper. Is it less than or equal to 5? If yes, she isn't done and must make one more attempt. But if it is greater than 5, then she has completed five attempts and will stop.

Step 3: Perform the four tasks: locate, introduce, learn, and record.

Step 4: Increment the counter by adding 1 to it and recording the new value.

Step 5: Go to Step 2.

The `for` loop in C

Referring back to Lesson 3, suppose the `setup()` method is to initialize pins 2 through 7 to the `OUTPUT` mode so that the attached LEDs can be turned on and off in the `loop()` method. Instead of having six separate and nearly identical `pinMode` statements, a `for` loop can be used to simplify the initialization as shown in Example 7-2:

Example 7-2. Simplifying code using a `for` loop

```
for(int pinNum = 2; pinNum <= 7; pinNum = pinNum + 1){
    pinMode(pinNum, OUTPUT);
}
```

These statements instruct the Arduino™ to do the following:

Step 1: Create an integer variable to represent the pin being addressed. This is the counter. Initialize it to the number of the first pin to be set to `OUTPUT`.

Step 2: Have all the pins through pin 7 been configured? If yes, quit.

Step 3: Initialize the pin represented by the current value of `pinNum` to the `OUTPUT` mode.

Step 4: Increment `pinNum` by adding 1 to it.

Step 5: Go to Step 2.

Comparison operators

The portion of the `for` loop that tests to see if the loop should be run again is shown in Example 7-3.

Example 7-3.

```
pinNum <= 7;
```

This is a comparison of the value of the variable `pinNum` with the integer literal 7. The result of this comparison is either true or false. The symbols <= combination is called a *comparison operator.* This particular one is read as, "less than or equal to" and is one of six comparison operators in the C language. The set of six comparison operators appears in Table 7-2.

Table 7-2. Comparison operators

Operator	Symbol	Example	Meaning
Greater than	>	a>b	True if the value of a is greater than the value of b. Otherwise false.v
Greaterv than or equal to	>=	a>=b	True if the value of a is greater than the value of b or if a is equal to b. Otherwise false.
Less than	<	a<b	True if the value of a is less than the value of b. Otherwise false.
Less than or equal to	<=	a<=b	True if the value of a is less than the value of b or if a is equal to b. Otherwise false.
Equal to	==	a==b	True if the value of a is equal to the value of b. Otherwise false.
Not equal to	!=	a!=b	True if the value of a is not the same as the value of b. Otherwise false.

Materials:

Quan-tity	Part	Image	Notes	Catalog Number
1	Arduino™ Uno		Single-board computer. This board is delicate and should be handled with care. When you are not using it, keep it in a box or plastic bag.	3102
1	USB Cable		This is a standard USB adapter cable with a flat connector on one end and a square connector on the other.	2301
1	Computer with at least one USB port and access to the Arduino™ website, http://www.arduino.cc	---	The operating system of this computer must be Windows, Macintosh OS/X, or Linux.	---

Quantity	Part	Image	Notes	Catalog Number
6	Light-emitting diodes (LEDs)		Single color, about 0.02 amps rated current, diffused.	1301
6	220 ohm resistors		¼ watt, 5% tolerance. Color code: red-red-brown-gold.	0102
1	Bread-board	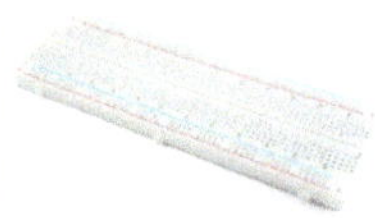	Used for prototyping.	3104
As req'd	Jumper wires		Used with bread-boards for wiring the components.	3105

Procedure:

Part 1: Explore `for` loops

1. Open the Arduino™ IDE. Create a new Arduino™ sketch and name it `Lesson7ForLoopsText`.

2. Add the header and the `setup()` method.

Snippet 7-1.

```
/* Lesson7ForLoopText
   <author>
   <date>
*/

void setup(){
    Serial.begin(9600);
}
```

3. Insert the simple `for` loop into the `loop()` method as shown in Snippet 7-2.

Snippet 7-2.

```
...
void loop(){
    Serial.println(); // insert a blank line

    Serial.println("Beginning loop");
    for(int counter = 1; counter <= 6; counter++){
        Serial.println("Hello, world!");
    }


    Serial.println("Finished loop");
    while(true); // stop here
}
```

7

Open the Serial Monitor. It should show the String `Hello, world!` six times. Above and below should be the messages indicating the loop is about to start and that it has finished.

```
Beginning loop
Hello, world!
Hello, world!
Hello, world!
Hello, world!
Hello, world!
Hello, world!
Finished loop
```

4. For step 3, the programming statement inside the `for` loop is printed the first time when counter = 1, the second time when counter = 2, the third time when counter = 3, and so on until the counter is equal to 6. When the counter is next incremented, it equals 7, and the test for the counter <= 6 fails. The loop stops, and the program execution jumps to the next statement after the `for` loop's curly braces.

Remember that counter is an `integer` variable. Its value can be printed from inside the loop. Verify this by replacing the programming statement inside the `for` loop curly brace as shown in Snippet 7-3.

Snippet 7-3.

```
...
void loop(){
    Serial.println(); // insert a blank line

    Serial.println("Beginning loop");
    for(int counter = 1; counter <= 6; counter++){
        Serial.print("The counter is: ");
        Serial.println(counter);
    }

    Serial.println("Finished loop");
    while(true); // stop here
}
```

The Serial Monitor will now show:

```
Beginning loop
The counter is: 1
The counter is: 2
The counter is: 3
The counter is: 4
The counter is: 5
The counter is: 6
Finished loop
```

5. The counter does not have to begin at 1. Nor does it have to count up. Nor does the increment value have to be 1. Modifying the `for` loop to read as shown in Snippet 7-4 has the counter counting down from 20 by 3's.

Snippet 7-4.

```
...
void loop(){
    Serial.println(); // insert a blank line

    Serial.println("Beginning loop");
    for(int counter = 20; counter >= 0; counter -= 3){
        Serial.print("The counter is: ");
        Serial.println(counter);
    }
```

```
    Serial.println("Finished loop");
    while(true); // stop here
}
```

The Serial Monitor will display:

```
Beginning loop
The counter is: 20
The counter is: 17
The counter is: 14
The counter is: 11
The counter is: 8
The counter is: 5
The counter is: 2
Finished loop
```


6. Save and close the Arduino™ sketch.

Part 2: Controlling digital pins with `for` loops

The following steps require the same bread-board configuration used for Lesson 4.

1. Connect the LEDs to their current limiting resistors and these, in turn, to the Arduino.™

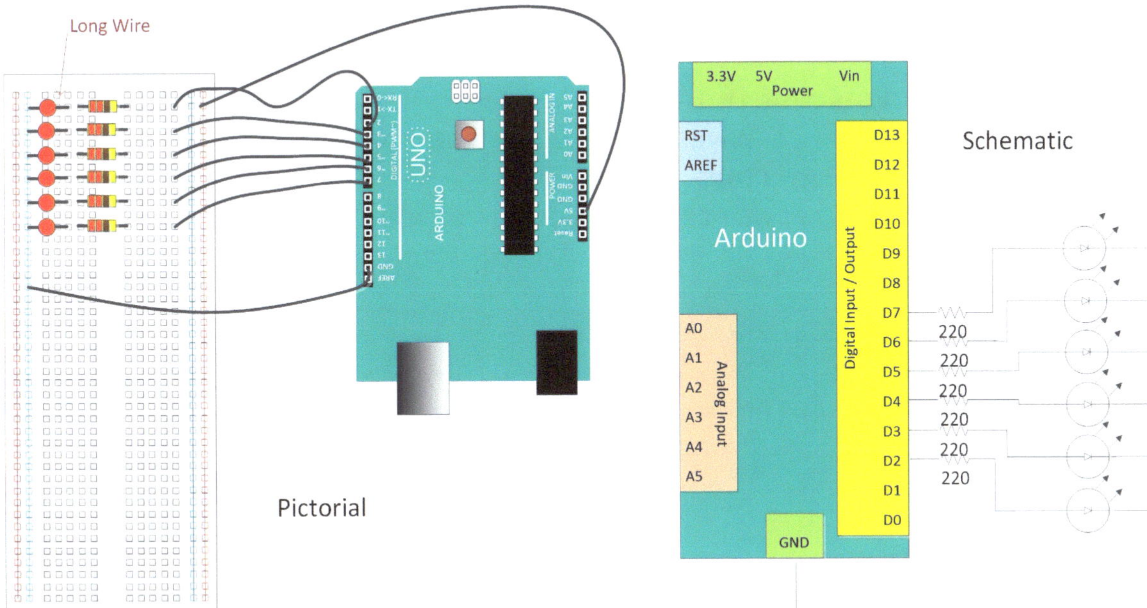

Figure 7-2. Pictorial and schematic diagrams of connection of LEDs to Arduino™

2. Create a new Arduino™ sketch. Name this one `Lesson7ForLoopsLED`. The header should be similar to that for the previous sketch but with the new sketch name and date.

3. Below the header comments, add the `setup()` method. It will take advantage of a `for` loop to simplify initializing the modes of the digital pins. Notice the counter begins at 2 because this is the first digital pin wired to an LED. It ends by initializing pin 7 because that is the last digital pin connected to an LED.

Snippet 7-5.

```
/* Lesson7ForLoopsLEDv
   <author>
   <date>
*/

void setup(){
    for(int pinNum = 2; pinNum <= 7; pinNum++){
        pinMode(pinNum, OUTPUT);
    }
}
```

4. Now add a `loop()` method that will light each of the LEDs in pin number order and then extinguish them in reverse order. It should look something like Snippet 7-6.

Snippet 7-6.

```
...
void loop(){
    // turn on in ascending order
    for(int pinNum = 2; pinNum <= 7; pinNum++){
        digitalWrite(pinNum, HIGH);
        delay(500); // wait 1/2 second
    }

    // turn off in descending order
    for(int pinNum = 7; pinNum >= 2; pinNum--){
        digitalWrite(pinNum, LOW);
        delay(500);
    }
}
```

Upload the sketch to the Arduino.™ The LEDs should now be lighting and going out much like a thermometer going up and down. Take time to understand how the `for` loops are being used to accomplish this.

5. Comment out the `delay(500)` programming statement inside the turn off `for` loop. Then upload the sketch. The lights should still come on in order but appear to all go off at once. In fact, they are going off in turn, just as before, but so quickly the actions appear to be simultaneous.

6. Save the sketch.

Exercises:

Exercise 7-1. Light LEDs one at a time

Write an Arduino™ sketch (name it `Lesson7Exercise1`) that uses a `for` loop to light each LED in turn, beginning with the one wired to pin 2 and ending with the LED wired to pin 7. But only one LED is lit at a time. The result should look like a light moving from LED to LED, from pin 2 through pin 7. Set the delay between each LED to 1/10 second. 7

Exercise 7-2. Odds and evens

Write an Arduino™ sketch (name it `Lesson7Exercise2`) that uses `for` loops to alternately flash the LEDs attached to even-numbered pins (2, 4, 6) and LEDs attached to odd-numbered pins (3, 5, 7). The interval should be 1/10 second.

Exercise 7-3. LEDs move in pairs

Write an Arduino™ sketch (name it `Lesson7Exercise3`) that has a pair of LEDs light up so that they appear to move as a pair from pin 2 through pin 7. The interval should be 1/10 second. The lighting pattern is:

pin 2 `HIGH`
pins 2 and 3 `HIGH`
pins 3 and 4 `HIGH`
pins 4 and 5 `HIGH`
pins 5 and 6 `HIGH`
pins 6 and 7 `HIGH`
pin 7 `HIGH`
all off
pattern repeats

Lesson 8 — Digital Input, If Else

The Big Idea:

This lesson adds the ability of an Arduino™ sketch to respond to its environment, taking different actions for different situations. If some condition is true, then execute one set of programming statements. If it is not, then execute a different set.

Background:

With the sole exception of reading text from and sending it back to the Serial Monitor, all of the Arduino™ sketches so far have been passive. No information has been sensed from the world outside the Arduino.™ Nor has any sketch made any decisions based on outside information.

8

But the ability to receive and send information is essential for any useful robotic-type application of the Arduino.™ A robot that can navigate a maze, which is an upcoming, must be able to sense the walls. A quad copter must sense pitch, roll, yaw, altitude, and direction. A musical instrument needs to know which keys are being pressed and be able to send the information needed to generate the appropriate sounds.

This ability to send and receive information is referred to as Input / Output, or IO for short. The mechanics, electronics, and programming of IO is often specified in published industry standards, in order for devices and software from different companies to work together. The Arduino™ Uno offers several of these, including implementations of the industry standards TWI, also known as the Inter Integrated Circuit Standard (I2C) and Serial Peripheral Interface (SPI).

This lesson focuses on the simplest of inputs, the detection of a voltage at a digital pin. If about +5 volts is applied to a digital pin, and if that pin's mode has been set to `INPUT`, then an attempt to read that pin will return a status of `HIGH`. If that pin has no voltage applied, then that same read attempt will return a status of `LOW`. Program commands exist in the C language to set this mode, to read the pins, and to test the results.

These commands will be used to detect the status of a push button. It is either being pushed or it is not. The results of this reading will be used to turn an LED on when the button is pushed and off when it is not.

But program commands are not sufficient. Some new electronics are required to connect the push button, and some new C-language commands need to be applied to act on the results of the reading of the pin. These commands are `if` and `else`.

In this lesson a digital pin will have its mode set to `INPUT`, meaning its state may be read with the programming statement `digitalRead()`. If left unconnected to anything, such a pin will have a state that is unpredictable. Sometimes `digitalRead()` will return `HIGH` and sometimes `LOW`.

To avoid such ambiguity, a digital pin for input is usually preset to a default state. This lesson uses a resistor, called a *pull-up resistor*, to place +5 volts on an input pin. The default state for that pin, then, is `HIGH`.

A push button or other device can be connected directly between that pin and ground. When pushed, the state of the digital pin immediately drops to `LOW`.

Table 8-1. Vocabulary

Term	Definition
closed circuit	A circuit with a path for electrical current to travel from +5 volts to ground.
ground	The zero-voltage counterpart to +5 volts. Electrical current will flow between +5 volts and ground. On an Arduino™, the three ground pins are marked GND. These pins are electrically identical and their use interchanged.
open circuit	An electrical circuit that does not provide current a complete path from +5 volts to ground. Often, a switch is part of a circuit in such a way that when it is set off the circuit is open.
pull-up resistor	A high-value resistor, usually 10,000 ohms, connected between a digital pin and +5 volts to set that pin HIGH by default.

Description:

Before a sketch can be written to test a digital pin and turn an LED on or off, based on the results, a circuit must be wired that includes a push button, some resistors, an LED, and some connections to the Arduino.™

For now, assume the digital pin 12 is to be connected to the push button and the LED to be lit or extinguished is connected to digital pin 5.

The electronics

The wiring on an LED and its current-limiting resistor were covered in Lesson 4. The push button, access to voltage on the Arduino™, and the pull-up resistor are new.

The push button

The push buttons used in these lessons have four legs and, when used on a breadboard, are inserted straddling the channel that runs lengthwise down the center. The legs, or pins, are electrically connected when the button is pushed but not connected when it is not pushed.

On is referred to as *closed circuit* and off as *open circuit*.

Figure 8-1. Push button

The schematic symbol for the push button is simply two pins that are electrically connected when the button is pushed. The push button illustrated by the schematic in Figure 8-2 is not pushed. Its circuit is open.

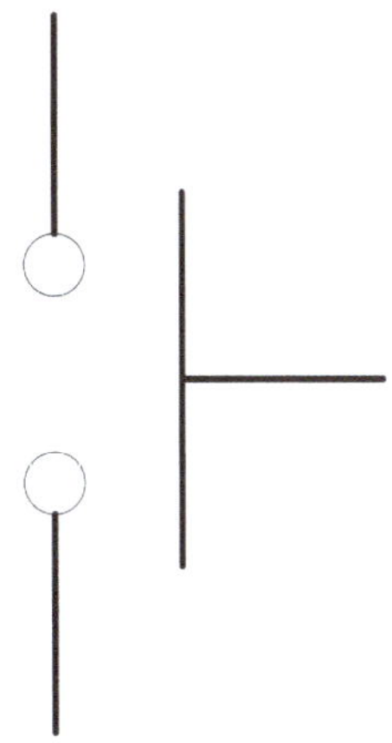

Figure 8-2. Schematic of push button with circuit open

8

Arduino™ +5v and GND

The convention used in these lessons for a push button connected to a digital pin is that when open, the pin should be at +5 volts, and when closed, that is, when the button is pushed, the pin should be at zero volts.

The Arduino™ provides pins for both of these. +5 volts may be found at the pin marked +5v and zero at the pin marked GND. GND is an abbreviation for *ground*, meaning zero volts. The Arduino™ Uno has three such pins for wiring convenience. Any one of the GND pins may be used for this lesson.

Figure 8-3. Arduino™ GND and +5 volt pins

The pull-up resistor

One side of the push button is wired to ground, the other to an Arduino™ digital pin configured for the `INPUT` mode. When the button is pushed, then the voltage at that pin will be zero. But the voltage is to be +5 volts when the button is not pushed. To bring the pin voltage to +5 when the button is open, a high-value resistor is used. A typical value is 10,000 ohms. This resistor looks just like the current-limiting resistor used for the LED except that the color stripes are brown, black, orange.

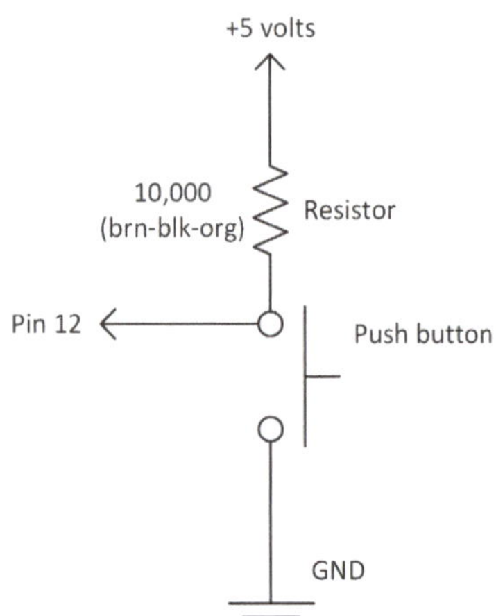

Complete push button schematic. Notice the push button connects the Arduino™ pin 12 to ground when pushed. But when not pushed +5 volts is at pin 12 via the 10,000 ohm pull-up resistor. The resistor is "pulling the pin voltage up to +5."

Figure 8-4. Schematic diagram of Arduino™ push button circuit

Programming statements

Reading from a digital port

To read from a digital port, the port must first be configured for input mode. This is accomplished with the `pinMode` command.

```
pinMode(pin, mode);
```

`pin`: the number of the pin to be read from or written to

`mode`: either `INPUT` if the pin is to be read from or `OUTPUT` if written to

The actual reading is accomplished with the `digitalRead` command. This command returns a status of either `HIGH`, reflecting +5 volts is present, or `LOW`, indicating the voltage at the pin is zero.

```
int status = digitalRead(pin);
```

`status:` `HIGH` if +5 volts is present, else `LOW`

`pin`: the number of the pin to be read

The code segment shown in Example 8-1 sets pin 12 to the `INPUT` mode, reads its status, and stores that status to a status variable.

Example 8-1. Setting a pin to `INPUT` and reading and storing its status

```
int pinNum = 12;
int statusOfPin12;
pinMode(pinNum, INPUT);  // set pin to be read
statusOfPin12 = digitalRead(pinNum);
```

`if-else`

Lesson 7 introduced the logical operators and their application in logical statements that resolve to either true or false. These same operators may be used to direct the flow of an Arduino™ sketch. If such-and-such condition is true, then do these things. Else, do those different things.

`if` and `else` are C-language keywords.

The `if` statement:

The general form of an `if` statement is:

```
if(<logical expression>){
  <programming statement>
  <programming statement>
  <programming statement>
  ...
}
```

Programming statements to be executed if the logical expression resolves to true

Figure 8-5. General form of an `if` statement

For example, suppose `energyLevel` is an integer with a value assigned, and the programmer wants the Arduino™ sketch to print this if the value is above 15. The program code would look something like that shown in Example 8-2.

Example 8-2. The `if` statement

```
if( energyLevel > 15){
    Serial.print("Energy level is: ");
    Serial.println( energyLevel);
}
```

Notice that nothing is printed if the energy level is equal to or less than 15. But what if the programmer wishes the message, "Energy level is CRITICAL!" to be printed in this situation? This is accomplished by the `if-else` combination.

The `if-else` combination:

The general form for the `if-else` combination is:

```
if(<logical expression>){
    <programming statement>
    <programming statement>
    <programming statement>
    ...
} else {
    <programming statement>
    <programming statement>
    <programming statement>
    ...
}
```

Programming statements to be executed if the logical expression resolves to true

Programming statements to be executed if the logical expression resolves to false

Figure 8-6. General form of `if-else` statement

Example 8-3. The `if-else` statement

```
if( energyLevel > 15){
    Serial.print("Energy level is: ");
    Serial.println( energyLevel);
} else {
    Serial.println("Energy level is CRITICAL!");
}
```

Goals:

By the end of this lesson the reader will:

1. Know how to configure an Arduino™ pin for digital input.
2. Know that by "digital input" is meant that the port can be tested by a sketch to see if it has a voltage.
3. Know how to wire a push button such that a voltage is applied or removed from an Arduino™ pin if that button is pushed or released.
4. Understand that this is the first of several "input" capabilities of the Arduino™ Uno.
5. Be able to use `if` and `if-else` statements in the C programming language.

Materials:

Quan-tity	Part	Image	Notes	Catalog Number
1	Arduino™ Uno		Single-board computer. This board is delicate and should be handled with care. When you are not using it, keep it in a box or plastic bag.	3102
1	USB Cable		This is a standard USB adapter cable with a flat connector on one end and a square connector on the other.	2301
1	Computer with at least one USB port and access to the Arduino™ website, http://www.arduino.cc.	---	The operating system of this computer must be Windows, Macintosh OS/X, or Linux.	---
2	Light-emitting diodes (LEDs)		Single color, about 0.02 amps rated current, diffused.	1301
2	220 ohm resistors		1/4 watt, 5% tolerance. Color code: red-red-brown.	0102
1	10,000 ohm resistor		1/4 watt, 5% tolerance. Color code: brown-black-orange.	0104
1	Push button		Bread-board and PCB friendly.	3106
1	Bread-board		Used for prototyping.	3104
As req'd	Jumper wires		Used with bread-boards for wiring the components.	3105

Procedure:

1. Using the bread-board, construct a push button circuit and an LED circuit. Connect them to the Arduino.™

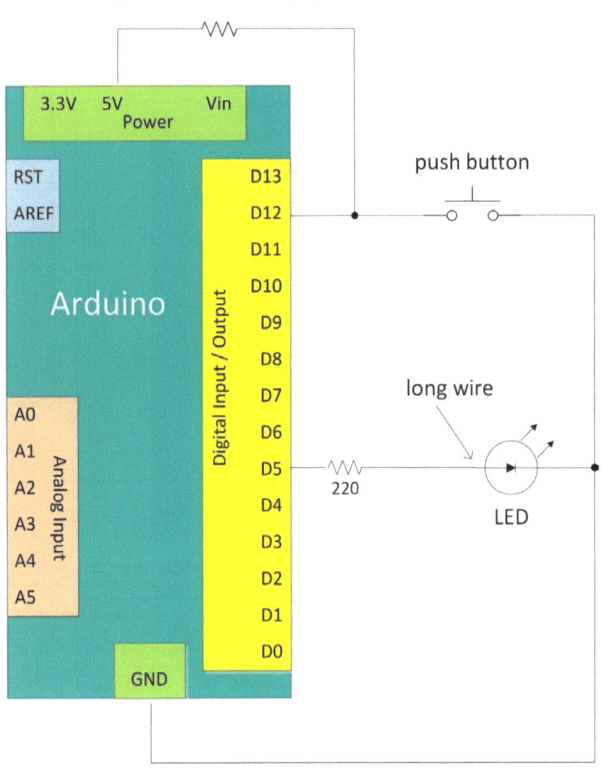

Figure 8-7. Schematic wiring diagram

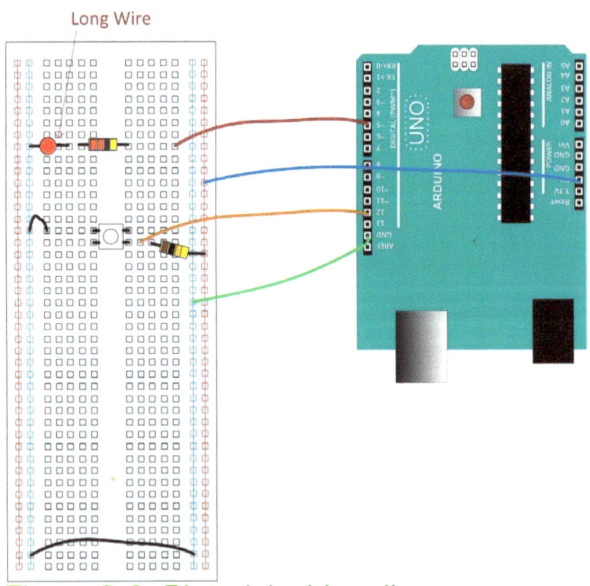

Figure 8-8. Pictorial wiring diagram

2. Connect the Arduino™ to the computer via the USB cable. Start the Arduino™ IDE.
3. Create a new Arduino™ sketch. Name it `Lesson8PushButtons`.
4. Enter the comments and programming statements as shown in Snippet 8-1.

Snippet 8-1.

```
/* Lesson8PushButtons
   <author>
   <date>
*/

#define pinLED 5
#define pinPushButton 12

void setup(){
    pinMode(pinLED, OUTPUT);
    pinMode(pinPushButton, INPUT);
}
```

8

Notice the use of the C-language keyword `define`. The statement that begins `#define` creates a name for a value. That name, then, can be used everywhere the programmer would otherwise have had to use an `integer literal`. This makes programming easier in that, should the programmer decide to use a different pin for one of these, a change need be made in only one place in the sketch.

In a sense, a name created this way is similar to a variable. But a defined value has two important differences:

- The value cannot be changed while the sketch runs.
- The Arduino™ does not set aside memory space to store the value if it isn't referred to anywhere in the sketch.

The latter point is important because it means the programmer pays no memory penalty for defining values she does not actually use. Later lessons will show how this is useful for writing easily understood sketches.

5. Add the `loop()` method that reads the value of the push button pin and use that information to either turn the LED on or off.

Snippet 8-2.

```
...
void loop(){
int pinStatus;
    pinStatus = digitalRead(pinPushButton);
    if(pinStatus == HIGH){
        // button is not pushed
        digitalWrite(pinLED, LOW); // turn LED off
    } else {
        // button is pushed
        digitalWrite(pinLED, HIGH);  // turn LED on
    }
}
```

6. Save the sketch as `Lesson8PushButtons` then upload it to the Arduino.™ Test the sketch by pushing the button. The LED should be on when the button is being pushed and off when it is not being pushed.

Notice that while the logical test is `pinStatus == HIGH` it could just as well be

`pinStatus != LOW`. These are logically the same.

7. Add a second LED and current-limiting resistor to digital pin 6. Then create a name for this pin by adding the `define` statement to the sketch just below the other two `define` statements.

```
#define pinLED2 6
```

8. Next add the `pinMode` statement to the `setup` method to initialize `pinLED2` to `OUTPUT`.

9. The `loop()` method can be modified to set `pinLED HIGH` and `pinLED2 LOW` when the button is pushed and the reverse when it is not. Make these changes, upload the sketch, and test. The completely revised sketch should now look something like Complete listing 8-1.

Complete listing 8-1. `Lesson8PushButtons`

```
/* Lesson8PushButtons
   by W. P. Osborne
   6/30/15
*/

#define pinLED 5
#define pinPushButton 12
#define pinLED2 6

void setup(){
     pinMode(pinLED, OUTPUT);
     pinMode(pinPushButton, INPUT);
     pinMode(pinLED2, OUTPUT);
}

void loop(){
int pinStatus;
    pinStatus = digitalRead(pinPushButton);
    if(pinStatus == HIGH){
        // button is not being pushed
        digitalWrite(pinLED, LOW);    // turn LED off
        digitalWrite(pinLED2, HIGH);  // 2nd LED on
    } else {
        // button is being pushed
        digitalWrite(pinLED, HIGH);  // turn LED on
        digitalWrite(pinLED2, LOW);  // 2nd LED off
    }
}
```

8

Exercise:

Exercise 8-1. Blinking LEDs at two speeds

Create a new Arduino™ sketch named `Lesson8Exercise1.ino` that causes the two LEDs to blink together at ½ second intervals when the button is not being pushed. When the button is pushed, the LEDs blink alternately at 100 millisecond intervals, very fast.

Lesson 9 | Analog IO

The Big Idea:

Computers are *binary*. Everything is on or off, high or low, one or zero. There are no gradations in between. But the real world is *analog*. A light may have an infinite number of brightness settings from off to full on. Sounds range from barely detectable through painfully loud.

In this lesson we learn how to connect the digital Arduino™ to the analog world such that we can detect where an input is within its natural range, and control an analog device by providing an output that matches its natural range.

Background:

Up to now all work with the Arduino™ has been with digital inputs and outputs. A button is either "pushed" or not. An LED is either on or it isn't. The `digitalRead()` statement returns either `HIGH` or `LOW`, while the `digitalWrite()` statement either sets a pin `HIGH` or `LOW`.

But the real world doesn't work that way. States have an infinite number of values. Here are some examples:

- The music was very loud.
- She spoke in a moderate voice.
- The piano played softly.
- Miracle Max, from *The Princess Bride* (1987), says, "It just so happens that your friend here is only *mostly* dead."

Analog input

In input mode a digital pin is either `HIGH` or `LOW`, never anything in between. This characteristic is referred to as binary, meaning it is either one thing or not that one thing. This is sufficient if what is to be measured is itself binary. Examples are a button that has been pushed or not, a sensor that sees a light or doesn't, and a switch that is either on or off.

But what if what needs to be measured is not binary but rather something that can have multiple values between the binary extremes? Examples of this: How far is the knob turned? How loud is the sound? How bright is the light? How salty is the water?

The Arduino™ Uno's analog pins, pin A0 through A5, can each measure a voltage between 0 and +5 volts to an accuracy of about 0.005 volts. This measurement is expressed as a number between 0 and 1023.

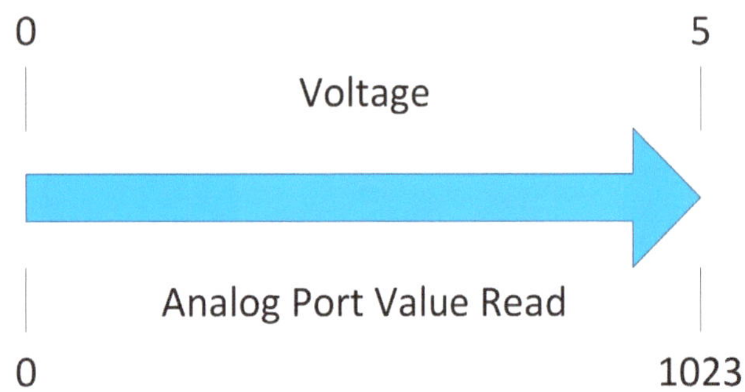

Figure 9-1. Analog port representation of voltage

The C language provides a tool for translating analog readings into other scales, from 0 to 100 for example. This is called *mapping*.

Analog output

While it is true that an analog port can accurately measure any voltage from 0 through +5, the Arduino™ Uno has no way of providing an output voltage in that range. The output voltage of an Arduino™ pin, be it an analog or digital, is +5 volts or zero, and nothing in between.

Yet the C language does provide a way of writing an analog value that approximates the range of 0 through +5 volts. It does this by switching rapidly between 0 volts and +5 volts.

If the output of a pin is at +5 volts half the time and 0 volts the other half, then the average voltage is 2.5 volts. Not only that, but an LED attached to that pin will produce half as much light as when the average voltage is +5 volts.

By modifying the ratio of the time the output pin is at +5 volts to the time it is at 0 volts, the average output voltage can be set to any value from zero through +5 volts.

The process of repeatedly setting an output pin `HIGH` for a fixed time then returning it to `LOW` is called *pulsing*. A single rise, wait, and fall cycle of the output voltage is called a *pulse*. The length of time the pulse is `HIGH` is called the *pulse width*. Finally, using pulses alternating with periods of `LOW` output is called *pulse width modulation*.

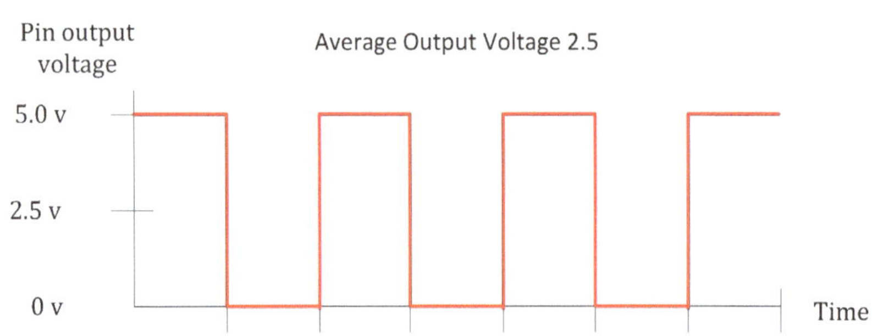

Figure 9-2. Pulse width modulation with average voltage +2.5 v

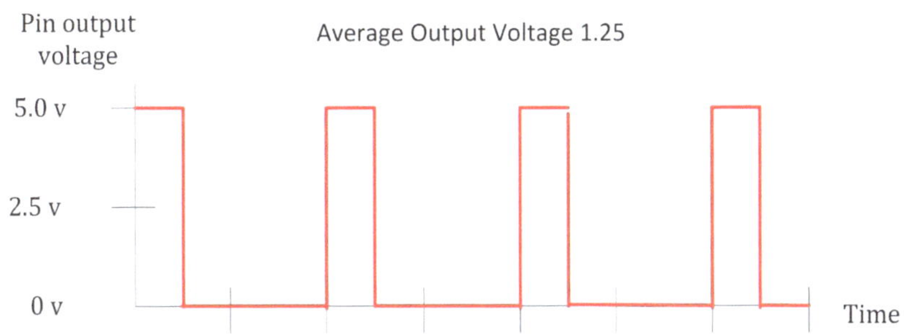

Figure 9-3. Pulse width modulation with average voltage +1.25 v

Not all digital pins of the Arduno Uno can be pulsed. Those that can be are indicated on the Arduino™ by a tilde mark (~) before the pin number. There are six such pins: 3, 5, 6, 9, 10, and 11.

Table 9-1. Vocabulary

Term	Definition
analog	A thing that is representative of the state of another thing. In this lesson, the read value for a potentiometer will be a number between 0 and 1023. The actual number is analogous to the rotation of the shaft of the potentiometer. The farther it is turned the higher the read number.
duty cycle	The length of time that a specified pin is `HIGH` vs. `LOW`; duty cycle is expressed as a percentage.
mapping	The determination of a number within a range based on another number and its range. If the number 8 is between 1 and 12 the mapped number between 100 and 160 is 140. The proportions are the same.
pulse	The setting of a pin from `LOW` to `HIGH` for a specific time then returning it to `LOW`.
pulse width	The length of time a pulse is `HIGH`.
pulsing	Repeatedly setting an output pin `HIGH` for a fixed time then returning it to `LOW`.
pulse width modulation	Using pulses alternating with periods of `LOW` output.
potentiometer	A variable resistor, usually disk shaped with a knob that may be turned to select the resistance.

9

Description:

Although they are related, reading an analog value from an analog pin is different from writing an analog value, which is sent to a digital output pin capable of sending pulses.

Programming statements

The three C-language commands that work with analog input and output are `analogRead`, `analogWrite`, and `map`.

The command `analogRead()` returns a number from 0 through 1023 that is proportional to the voltage from 0 through +5 volts on the read pin. The command `analogWrite()` sets an output pin's average voltage between 0 and +5 volts by writing an integer in the range of 0 through 255.

The command `map()` remaps a number from one range to another.

analogRead

`analogRead(pinNumber)`

value	Integer between 0 and 1023
pinNumber	Integer that specifies which analog port is to be accessed. On the Arduino™ Uno the analog ports are 0 through 5.
example	`int val;` `val = analogRead(A2); // returns 0 to 1023`

analogWrite

`analogWrite(pinNumber, value)`

value	Integer from 0 through 255 that specifies how much time the pin specified by `pinNumber` is `HIGH` vs. `LOW`. Expressed as a percentage of 255, this value is called the *duty cycle*. For example, a value of 153 specifies a duty cycle of 60%, meaning the pin is switching rapidly between `HIGH` and `LOW` in such a way that it is `HIGH` 60% of the time.
pinNumber	Integer that specifies which pin is to be accessed. Use of pins 5 and 6 are not recommended.
example	`analogWrite(3, 100);`

map()

`map ( value, fromRangeLow, fromRangeHigh, toRangeLow, toRangeHigh)`

value	The number to be mapped. It is expected to be between `fromRangeLow` and `toRangeLow`.
fromRangeLow	Integer representing the low end of the range being converted from.
fromRangeHigh:	Integer representing the high end of the range being converted from.
toRangeLow	Integer representing the low end of the range being converted to.
toRangeHigh	Integer representing the high end of the range being converted to.

example	`int new Value;`
	`newValue = map (15, 0, 50, 0, 100);`
	Converts the value of 15 as it appears between 0 and 50 to the equivalent value for the range 0 to 100. `newValue` will be 30.

Electronics

This lesson introduces the *potentiometer*. A potentiometer is a resistor, much like those used to limit current for LEDs and to pull a digital input pin to +5 volts. But it is mechanically different. The resistor itself is a flat, curved surface. A slider controlled by a knob moves across this surface. Pins are connected to each end of the surface with a third pin connected to the slider. The slider, then, becomes a variable resistor.

	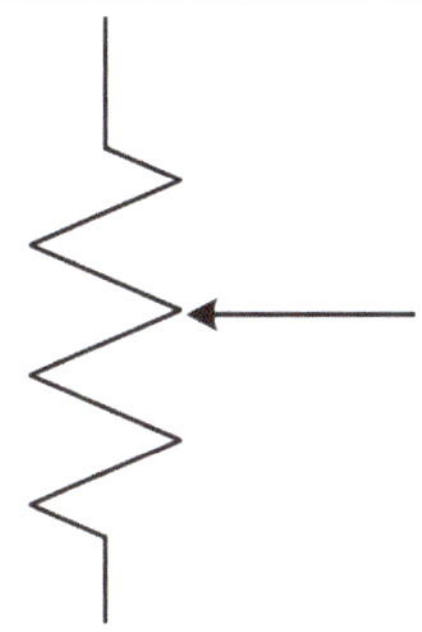
Potentiometer	Schematic Symbol

Figure 9-4. Photograph of and schematic symbol for potentiometer

As Figure 9-5 shows, the total resistance is between pins 1 and 3. The resistance between pin 1 and 2 increases as the potentiometer is turned clockwise and the wiper moves farther away from pin 1. Also, the resistance between pins 2 and 3 decreases as the wiper gets closer to pin 3.

The relationship of R1 and R2 to Rtotal is also true for voltage. If pin 3 is connected to ground and pin 1 is connected to +5 volts, then the voltage at pin 2 will be proportional to the position of the wiper on the resistive material. Translating this into an equation:

$$V_{total} = V_1 + V_2$$

where:

V_1=voltage from pin 1 to pin 2

and:

V_2=voltage from pon 2 to pin 3

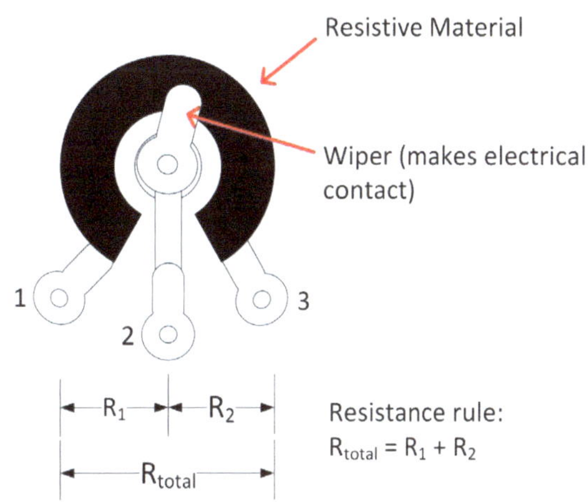

Figure 9-5. Resistance in a potentiometer

9

What this means for this lesson is if pin 1 is connected to +5 volts and pin 3 is connected to ground (GND), then the voltage on pin 2 can be adjusted to any value from 0 through +5 volts.

The potentiometer, in this case, is called a voltage divider. Pin 2 is an ideal input to an Arduino™ analog pin.

Goals:

By the end of this lesson readers will:

1. Be able to identify a potentiometer and know that it is merely a resistor whose value can be adjusted.
2. Write an Arduino™ sketch that can use an analog pin to read the relative position of a potentiometer and translate that into an integer between 0 and 1023.
3. Write a sketch that generates a series of pulses. Use these pulses to set the brightness level of a light-emitting diode (LED).
4. Recognize that the brightness of the LED is proportional to the width of these pulses.
5. Write a sketch that allows a user to control the brightness of an LED by turning a potentiometer.

Materials:

Quantity	Part	Image	Notes	Catalog Number
1	Arduino™ Uno		Single-board computer. This board is delicate and should be handled with care. When you are not using it, keep it in a box or plastic bag.	3102
1	USB Cable		This is a standard USB adapter cable with a flat connector on one end and a square connector on the other.	2301
1	Computer with at least one USB port and access to the Arduino™ website, http://www.arduino.cc.	---	The operating system of this computer must be Windows, Macintosh OS/X, or Linux.	---
1	Light-emitting diode (LED)		Single color, about 0.02 amps rated current, diffused	1301
1	220 ohm resistor		¼ watt, 5% tolerance. Color code: red-red-brown.	0102

Quan-tity	Part	Image	Notes	Catalog Number
1	Potentiometer		10k ohm.	0301
1	Bread-board		Used for prototyping.	3104
As req'd	Jumper wires	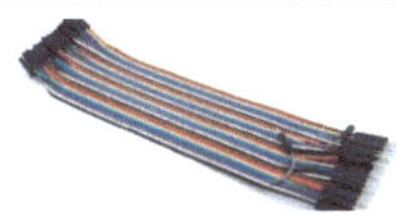	Used with bread-boards for wiring the components.	3105

Procedure:

Part 1: Explore `analogRead()`

In this lesson only schematics are supplied to guide wiring the circuits on the bread-board.

1. Construct the circuit shown in Figure 9-6. Connect the potentiometer to the Arduino™ using clip leads and short jumpers.

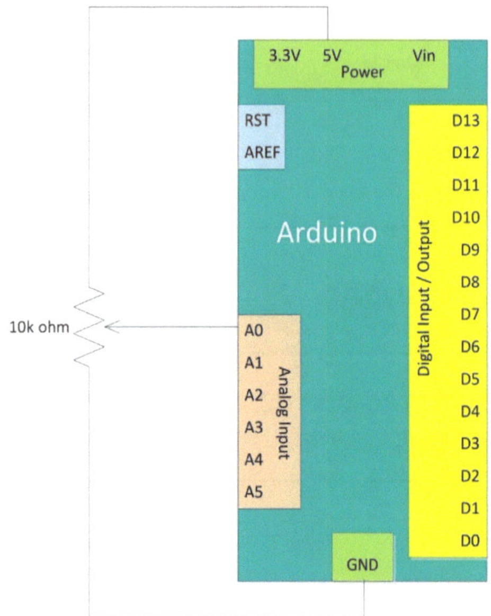

Figure 9-6. Schematic diagram of potentiometer connected to Arduino™ Uno

2. Open the Arduino™ IDE and create a new sketch. Name the sketch `Lesson9AnalogRead`. This sketch will read the value of an analog pin and display the reading on the Serial Monitor.

3. Enter the sketch as shown in Sketch 9-1.

Sketch 9-1. Complete listing for `Lesson9AnalogRead`

```
/* Lesson9AnalogRead
   by W. P. Osborne
   6/30/15
*/

void setup(){
    Serial.begin(9600);
}

void loop(){
    int readValue;
    readValue = analogRead(A0);
    Serial.println(readValue);
}
```

4. Upload the sketch to the Arduino™ and open the Serial Monitor. A number somewhere between 0 and 1023 should appear about 10 times per second. Adjusting the potentiometer should change this number. At one end of the potentiometer rotation the number will be 0. At the other extreme it will be 1023.

5. Map the read value to the range 0 through 255 by adding a `map` programming statement. The new `loop()` method should be as shown in Snippet 9-1.

Snippet 9-1. `loop()` *method demonstrating mapping*

```
...
void loop(){
    int readValue;
    readValue = analogRead(A0);

    int mappedValue;
    mappedValue = map(readValue, 0, 1023, 0, 255);

    Serial.println(mappedValue);
}
```

The numbers displayed now should range from 0 through 255.

6. Save the sketch and close it.

Part 2: Explore `analogWrite()`

The potentiometer can remain connected to the Arduino™, but it won't be used for now.

7. Add an LED and its current-limiting resistor to the Arduino™, connecting it to pin 9. Note the short wire of the LED is going to GND. Also notice pin 9 is capable of generating pulses, as indicated by the tilde ahead of the pin number.

The schematic diagram is now as shown in Figure 9-7.

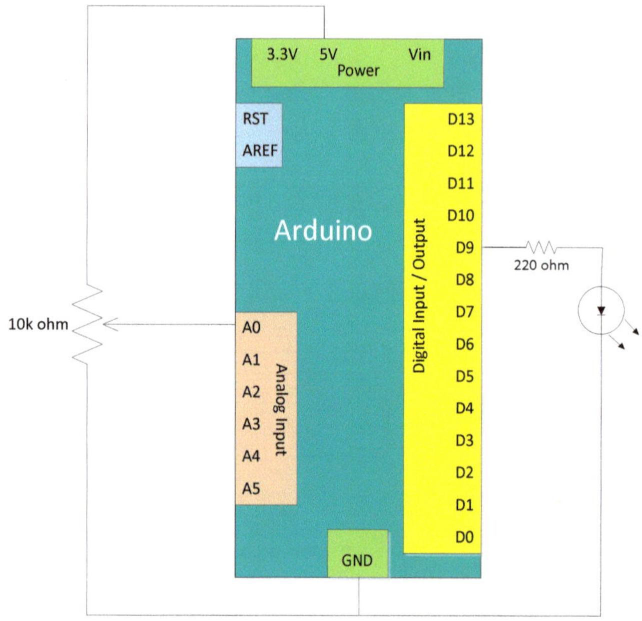

Figure 9-7. Schematic diagram of control of LED by potentiometer

8. Create another Arduino™ sketch. Name it `Lesson9AnalogWrite` and enter the code as shown in Sketch 9-2.

Sketch 9-2. Complete listing for `Lesson9AnalogWrite`

```
/* Lesson9AnalogWrite
   by W. P. Osborne
   based on sample from www.arduino.cc
   6/30/15
*/

#define pinLED 9

int brightness = 0;
int fadeAmount = 5;

void setup(){
    pinMode(pinLED, OUTPUT);
}

void loop(){
    // use analogWrite to set the average output
    // voltage.
    analogWrite(pinLED, brightness);
```

```
    // change the brightness for the next loop
    brightness = brightness + fadeAmount;

    // If brightness is equal to or greater than
    // 255 the diode is as bright as it is going
    // to get because the output voltage is
    // averaging 5 volts. So, start subtracting
    // the fadeAmount.
    //
    // The same is true if the brightness is less than
    // or equal to zero. Start adding the fade amount.

    // The following program statements reverse the
    // sign of fadeAmount by effectively multiplying
    // by -1.

    if(brightness >= 255 || brightness <= 0){
        fadeAmount = -fadeAmount;
    }

    delay(30);
}
```

Note: Sample from www.arduino.cc and modifications to the sample, as used in Sketch 9-2, used under a Creative Commons Attribution ShareAlike 3.0 license (http://creativecommons.org/licenses/by-sa/3.0/).

9. Save the sketch.

10. Notice that a new logical operator is used in the test of the brightness range. It is the pair of vertical lines, `||`. This operator is called `OR`. By putting it between two logical tests a new one is created. This new one evaluates to true if either or both of the logical tests is true.

Part 3: Explore `map`

For this part, no additional components are required. Rather, a new sketch combines `analogRead`, `analogWrite`, and `map` to use a potentiometer to set the brightness of an LED.

11. Create a new Arduino™ sketch. Name it `Lesson9AnalogReadAndWrite`.

12. Enter the sketch as shown in Sketch 9-3.

9

Complete listing 9-1. Using `analogRead`, `analogWrite`, and `map` to set brightness of an LED

```
/* Lesson9AnalogReadAndWrite
   by W. P. Osborne with some content from
   arduino.cc
   6/30/15
*/

#define pinLED 9

void setup(){
    pinMode(pinLED, OUTPUT);
}

void loop(){
    int readValue = analogRead(A0);
    int brightness;
    brightness = map(readValue, 0, 1023, 0, 255);
    analogWrite(pinLED, brightness);
}
```


13. Save the sketch then upload to the Arduino™. Turning the shaft of the potentiometer should now adjust the brightness of the LED from completely off to full brightness.

Exercise:

Exercise 9-1. Controlling two LEDs

Connect a second LED to your Arduino™. Don't forget to include the current-limiting resistor (220 ohms, red-red-brown). Write an Arduino™ sketch that increases the brightness of one while decreasing the brightness of the other as the potentiometer is turned. When the potentiometer is turned fully clockwise, only one LED will be on, and at full brightness. The other will be off. Halfway turned, both LEDs will be at half-brightness. Fully counterclockwise, the pattern will be the opposite of fully clockwise.

Name this sketch `Lesson9Exercise1`.

Note	`AnalogWrite` only works with Arduino™ pins marked with the tilde character (~). For the Arduino™ Uno, these are pins 3, 5, 6, 9, 10, and 11.

Lesson 10 Simple Tones

The Big Idea:

This lesson is about enabling an Arduino™ to play musical tones. This capability will be used in Lesson 17 to turn a common television remote control into a sort of musical instrument that produces different sounds when its buttons are pushed. That lesson, in turn, provides the technical base for using remotes for more sophisticated things and, eventually, creating devices that can generate their own messages.

Background:

A *tone* is nothing more than the turning on and then off of something that moves the air. A violin string, for example, moves back and forth rapidly, moving the surrounding air. The musical note *A* is heard when a violin string moves 440 times per second. The number of vibrations per second is called the *frequency*.

A *speaker* is a device with a coil of wire suspended near a permanent magnet. The wire is glued to a paper cone called a diaphragm. When an electrical current moves through the wire, a magnetic field is set up that pushes against that of the magnet causing the cone to move.

10

Typical speaker. Small earphones are similar but often use a plastic membrane in place of the paper cone.

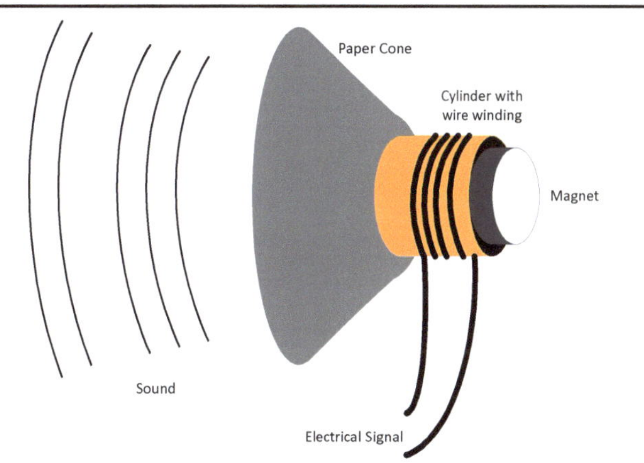

Figure 10-1. Speaker

If a speaker is connected to a digital port on an Arduino™ and that port is turned on and off, the speaker diaphragm will move in and out. As with the violin string, if the port turns on and off 440 times per second, the musical note *A* will be heard coming from the speaker.

As it happens, there is a C-language method that does precisely this. It is `tone()`. The C-language method `noTone()` stops a tone from playing.

Table 10-1. Vocabulary

Term	Definition
coupling capacitor	An electronic component that passes on current that is increasing or decreasing in magnitude but does not allow a steady flow of electrons. For audio it allows only the sound produced by the Arduino™ to reach the speaker.
frequency	The ratio of the number of times some repeating event occurs per unit of time. For audio the most common ratio is cycles per second. The unit name for this is the Hertz.
Hertz	The name of the unit of measure for cycles per second or frequency. Abbreviated as Hz. 1 Hertz = 1 cycle / second.
period	The duration of one cycle. For a frequency of 1000 Hz the period is 1/1000 second, or 1 x 10^{-3} seconds.
sine wave	A repeating event the magnitude of which is sinusoidal. In electronics a sine wave of audio frequency is a pure tone.
speaker	A mechanical device that translates electrical current into the movement of air. Examples include loudspeakers and ear buds. Many technologies are used to perform this translation, but electromagnetism and piezo crystal are the most common.
square wave	A repeating event in which the resulting voltage is a square wave, high for one-half the period and low for one-half the period. The sound produced is not pure, but it is suitable for steady tones, sound effects, and simple melodies.
tone	The turning on and then off of something that moves the air.

Description:

A "pure" tone is a *sine wave.* But an Arduino™ is a digital device. It simply turns on and off. The resulting voltage is then a *square wave,* high for one-half the period and low for one-half the period. The duration of one cycle is called the *period.* The speaker, being a mechanical device that takes time to respond to changes in voltage, is most sensitive to the output frequency, but other frequencies are present as well. As a result, the sound of a square wave is not pure, but the pitch is obvious to the listener. Square wave audio is suitable for steady tones, sound effects, and simple melodies.

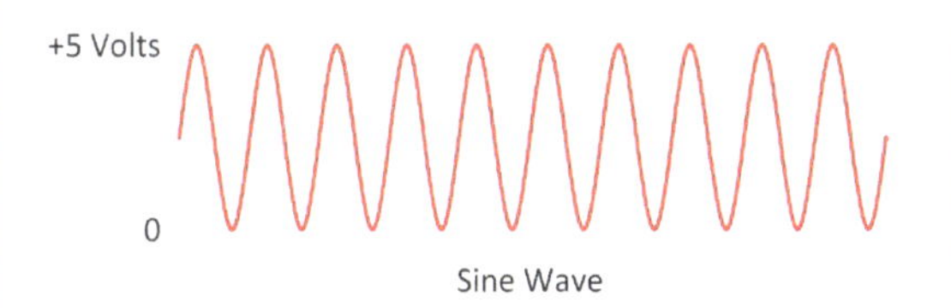	A sine wave in audio frequencies produces a pure, clean, and undistorted tone. The Arduino™ cannot produce a sine wave without added components.
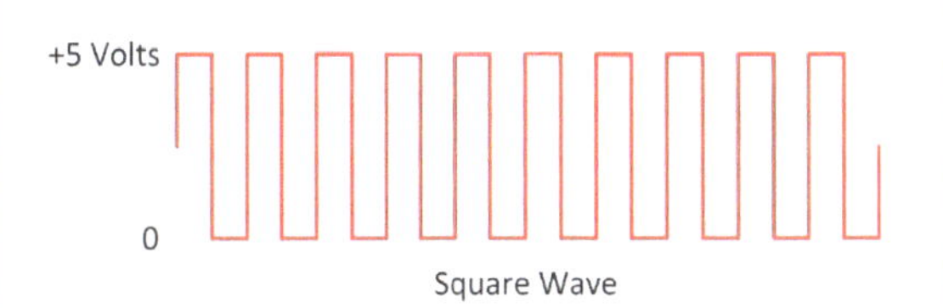	A square wave in audio frequencies produces a clear pitch that is dominant but not pure. Many other frequencies are present in lower volumes. The Arduino™ excels at producing square waves.

Figure 10-2. Sine and square waves

The musical note *A* has a frequency of 440 cycles per second. The unit of frequency is the *Hertz*. So we say an *A* has a frequency of 440 Hertz. The duration of a single pulse, up and down, is the inverse of the frequency, as shown in Figure 10-3.

10

duration = 1 / frequency in Hertz => duration of an *A* = 1 / 440

duration of an *A* = 2.28 milliseconds.

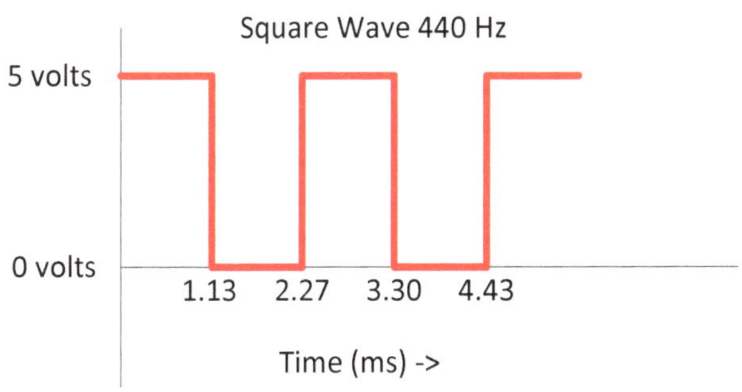

Figure 10-3. Portion of a square wave that produces the musical note A

To make an Arduino™ produce a sound, all that needs to be done is to alternately set a pin `HIGH` then `LOW` for the duration of half a cycle of the desired frequency. Fortunately, the Arduino™ method `tone()` does precisely that.

Table 10-2. Tone-related Arduino™ methods

Method Signature	Description
`tone( pin, frequency)`	Sends a pulse with the specified frequency to the specified pin. The pulse is repeated until the `noTone()` method is called or the `tone()` method is called again. `pin`[1]: Pin number of the digital port. `frequency`: Frequency of the tone.
`tone( pin, frequency, duration)`	Sends a pulse with the specified frequency to the specified pin. The pulse is repeated for the time specified in "duration." `pin`: Pin number of the digital output port. `frequency`: desired frequency of tone. `duration`[2]: duration of tone in milliseconds.
`noTone(pin)`	Stops a tone playing. `pin`: specifies pin where note is to be stopped.

Notes:

1. Even though `noTone` specifies a pin number, the Arduino™ will not play more than one tone at a time. If a tone is started on pin 3 and then another on pin 7, the tone on pin 3 will stop immediately when the tone on pin 7 begins.
2. The duration is observed only if no other tone is started and `noTone` is not called. In the code shown in Example 10-1, the 440 Hertz tone will not be heard because the 1000 Hertz tone begins immediately after the 440 tone was started.

Example 10-1.

```
tone(3, 440, 500);  // won't be heard
tone(3, 1000, 500); // might be heard
```

The code shown in Example 10-2 will, however, play the 440 tone followed one-half second later by the 1000 Hertz tone.

Example 10-2.

```
tone(3, 440, 500);  // will be heard
delay(500);
tone(3, 1000, 500); // will be heard
delay(500);
```

Materials:

Quantity	Part	Image	Notes	Catalog Number
1	Arduino™ Uno		Single-board computer. This board is delicate and should be handled with care. When you are not using it, keep it in a box or plastic bag.	3102
1	USB Cable		This is a standard USB adapter cable with a flat connector on one end and a square connector on the other.	2301
1	Computer with at least one USB port and access to the Arduino™ website, http://www.arduino.cc.	---	The operating system of this computer must be Windows, Macintosh OS/X, or Linux.	---
1	Bread-board		Used for prototyping.	3104
As req'd	Jumper wires		Used with bread-boards for wiring the components.	3105
1	Capacitor		2.2 mfd.	0205
1	Speaker		Magnetic speaker 4, 8, or 16 ohm.	3119

Procedure:

1. Connect a speaker to the Arduino™ as shown in Figure 10-4.

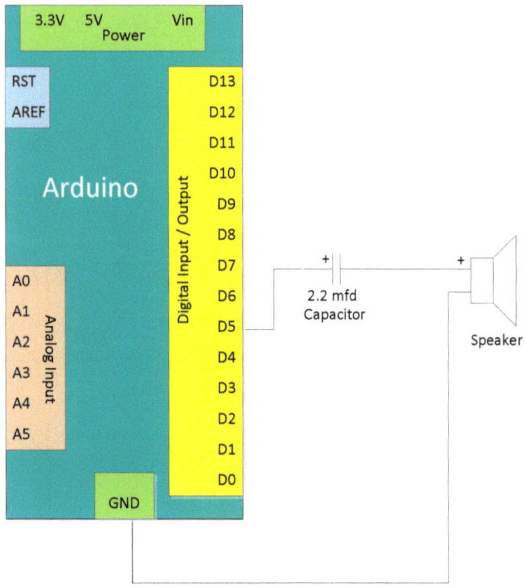

Figure 10-4. Schematic diagram of connection between Arduino™ and speaker

2. Create a new Arduino™ sketch. Name it `Lesson10SimpleTones`. Enter the test program as shown in Snippet 10-1.

Snippet 10-1. `Lesson10SimpleTones` *sketch*

```
// Lesson10SimpleTones.ino
// <author>
// <date>

#include "pitches.h"

#define soundPin 5 // speaker pin

void setup(){ }

void loop(){
  tone(soundPin, NOTE_A4, 50);
  delay(600);
  tone(soundPin, NOTE_E4, 50);
  delay(600);
  tone(soundPin, NOTE_C4, 50);
  delay(600);
```

```
    tone(soundPin, NOTE_E4, 50);
    delay(600);
}
```

3. Save the sketch as `Lesson10SimpleTones`.
4. Close the Arduino™ IDE.
5. Download the file `pitches.h`. Save it to the same folder that contains the `Lesson10SimpleTones.ino` file.
6. Open the Arduino™ IDE.
7. Using File -> Sketchbook open `Lesson10SimpleTones`. Two tabs should appear. One should be labeled `Lesson10SimpleTones`, the other `pitches.h`.
8. Upload the program and listen for the sounds.
9. Experiment with the program until you have some feel for how to use `tone()` and `delay()`.

10

Exercises:

Exercise 10-1. Create sketch to play a recognizable melody

Create a new Arduino™ sketch, `Lesson10Exercise1.ino`, that plays a recognizable melody.

Exercise 10-2. Create sketch to generate sound effects

Create a new Arduino™ sketch, `Lesson10Exercise2.ino`, that uses `for` loops to generate sound effects. Experiment with changing durations of sounds.

Exercise 10-3. Amplify sounds

Use "How to Make Arduino™ Tones Louder" to increase the volume of the tones coming from your Arduino.™

Lesson 11 Standard Servos and Helper Methods

The Big Idea:

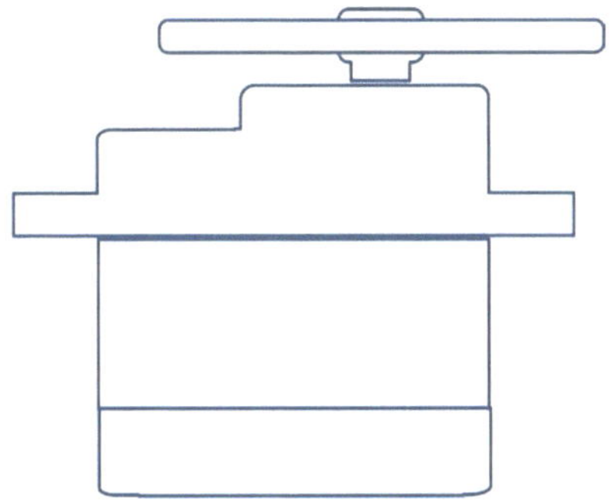

Figure 11–1. Standard servo - side view

A *servo* is an electric motor whose shaft rotation is controlled by an electrical signal called a *pulse*. Servos come in two types: the standard servo and the continuous rotation servo. The standard servo has a shaft that can be positioned at an angle, usually between 0 and 180 degrees. The angle depends on the duration of the pulse. Such servos are often used to position the angle of control surfaces of a model airplane or steer a model car.

The other type, the *continuous rotation servo*, is not discussed in this lesson.

This lesson shows how a standard servo, hereafter referred to as simply "servo," can be connected to and controlled by an Arduino.™ Along the way, the concept of helper methods is introduced.

11

Background:

Servo motors

As was described in Lesson 9, `analogWrite()` sets the output of an Arduino™ pin to an average somewhere between 0 and 5 volts. It does this by rapidly switching the pin on and off. In the Arduino™ C language, these two states are referred to as `LOW` and `HIGH`. The switch from `LOW` to `HIGH` and then back to `LOW` is called a *pulse.*

Once called, the `analogWrite` command sends the pulse repeatedly. The ratio of the duration of `HIGH` to the time between each pulse, `LOW`, determines the output voltage. For example, if the pulse duration is three times the time the pulse is `LOW`, the output voltage is 3/4ths that of the maximum possible voltage. Usually the output voltage ranges from 0 (pulse is never on) to +5 volts (pulse is never off). A pulse that is `HIGH` the same amount of time as that between pulses produces an average output voltage of +2.5. An Arduino™ can be configured to provide voltage higher or lower than +5 volts, but how to do this is beyond the scope of this lesson.

This lesson also focuses on how the pulse is used to control a servo.

A servo motor is similar to other motors in that it has a shaft that rotates, usually up to 180 degrees. How far it moves between 0 and 180 degrees depends on the pulse width. Table 11-1 shows the typical movement of a servo arm for pulses of 600 microseconds, 1500 microseconds, and 2400 microseconds and the resulting rotation of the servo arm.

One often sees pulse width range from 1000 to 2000 microseconds for standard servos. The range shown in this lesson of 600 microseconds to 2400 microseconds is taken from the Arduino™ Servo library.

Table 11-1. Servo direction as a result of pulse width

Duration	Movement	Position
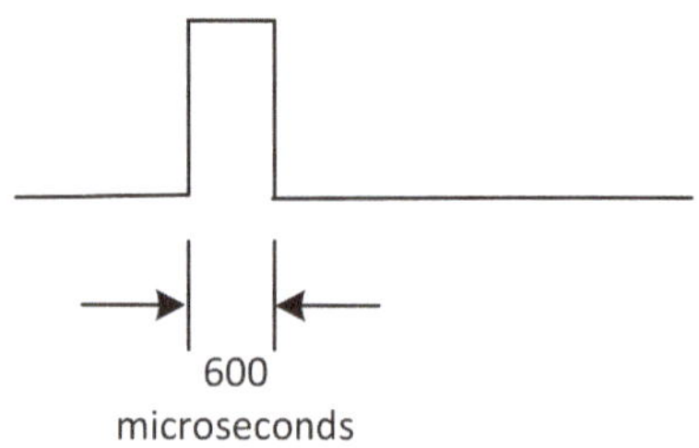	Set servo arm to 0 degrees	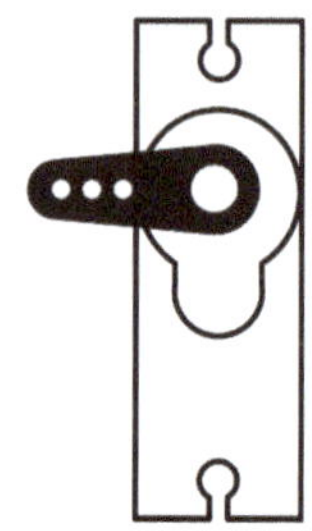
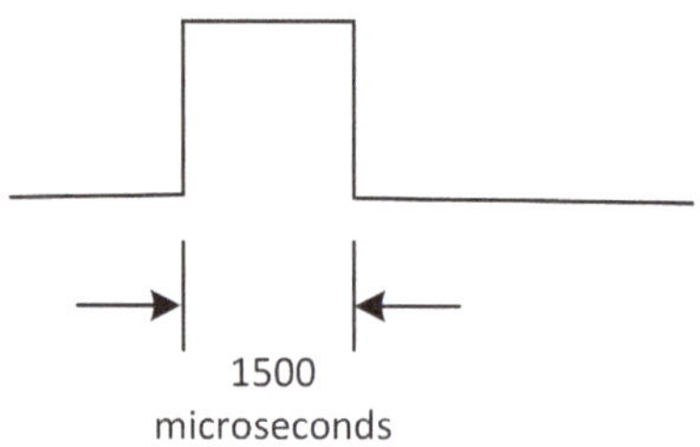	Set servo arm to 90 degrees	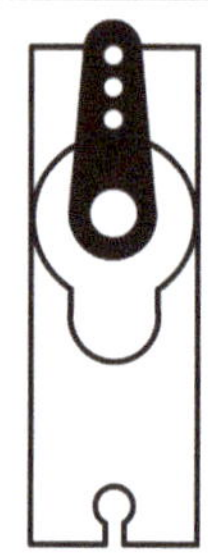
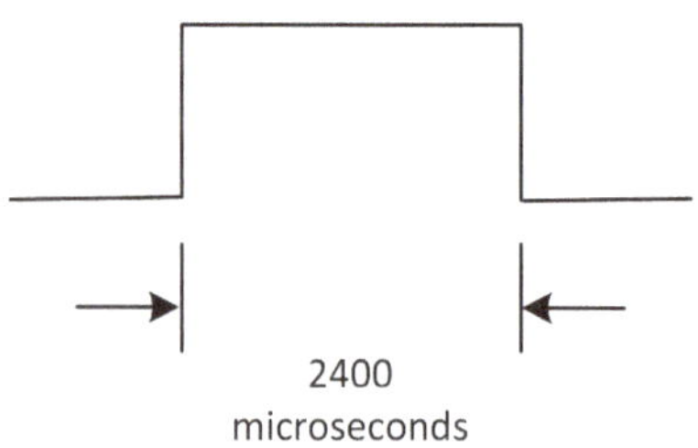	Set servo arm to 180 degrees	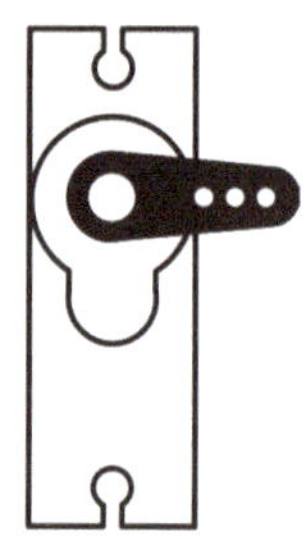

An arm can be attached to this motor to move things. One example is for controlling the ailerons of a radio-controlled airplane.

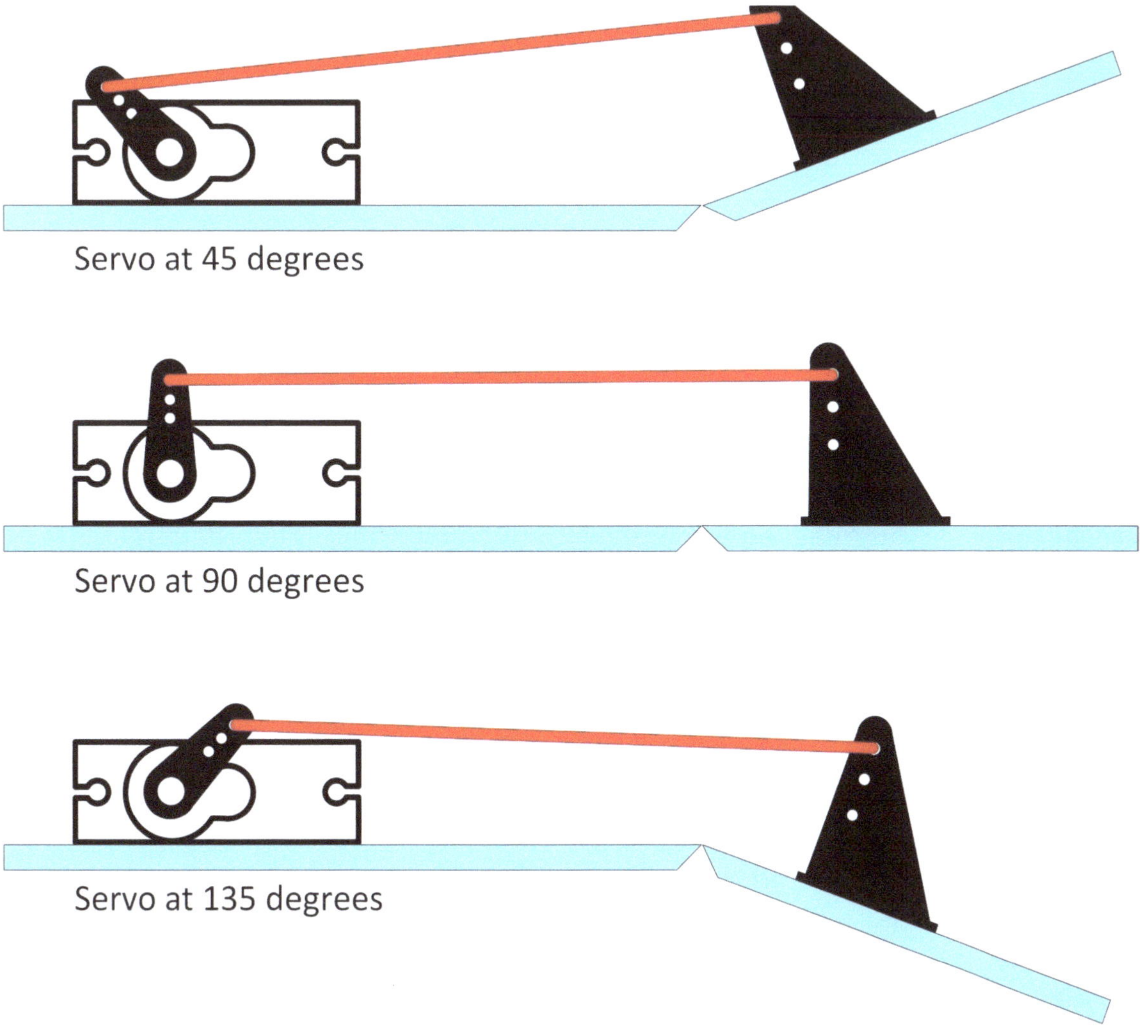

Figure 11-2. Servo used to control aileron of RC airplane

Helper methods

Sometimes a sketch will contain tasks that need to be performed in more than one place in the program code. Good practice calls for these tasks to be placed in their own methods. These are called ***helper methods***.

Helper methods are also appropriate for containing a set of program instructions that perform a specific task that is easily separated from others. Setting a servo pulse width is an example of such a task.

A helper method looks very much like the `setup()` or `loop()` method but with a different name. Helper methods may have parameters and may return a value of some type.

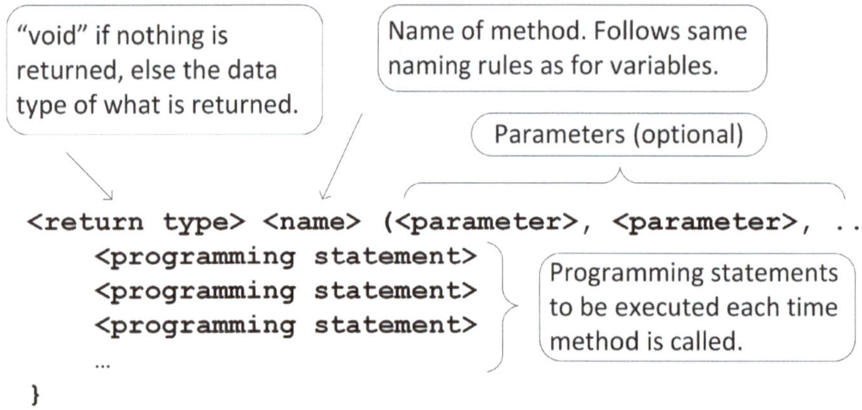

Figure 11-3. General structure of helper method

The programming statements within a helper method should perform a single task. Example 11–1 is a simple helper method that prints the nose cone and the rocket engine in Exercise 2-3 of Lesson 2.

Example 11-1. Simple helper method

```
void drawCone(){
    Serial.println("  /\\");
    Serial.println(" /  \\");
    Serial.println("/    \\");
}
```

The helper method `drawCone()` has no parameters. The return type is `void` because no value is returned. This is a method with parameters that returns the results of a calculation. `drawCone()` can be called by its name from the `loop()` method or from any other method in the sketch.

Example 11-2. Using the helper method `drawCone()`

```
void loop(){
    <some programming statement>
    <some programming statement>
    ...
    drawCone();  // draw the cone

    <some programming statement>
    ...
}
```

The `findPerimeterOfRectangle()` helper method, shown in Example 11–3, by contrast, has both parameters and a calculated return value. Notice that the return type is `int` and that the variable names of `width` and `height` are declared in the parentheses.

Example 11-3. Helper method with parameters and calculated return value

```
int findPerimeterOfRectangle(int width, int height){
    int perimeter;
    perimeter = (2 * width) + (2 * height);
    return perimeter;
}
```

Calling `findPerimeterOfRectangle()` from another method is similar to calling `drawCone()`but with two important differences. First, notice `findPerimeterOfRectangle()` contains two parameters. These are variables that contain data essential for calculation of perimeter. Second, the return type is `int`, meaning the results of the calculation are returned as an integer. Example 11-4 illustrates how the perimeter of a rectangle of width 8 and height 12 is printed from within the `loop()` method. The call to `findPerimeterOfRectangle(8, 12)` is made and returns an integer value. This value is then sent to the Serial Monitor via the `Serial.println()` method.

Example 11-4. Helper method that prints from within `loop()` method

```
void loop(){
    <some programming statement>
    <some programming statement>
    ...
    Serial.println("The perimeter is: ");
    Serial.println( findPerimeterOfRectangle(8, 12));

    <some programming statement>
    ...
}
```

Instead of printing the perimeter, the programmer could have assigned the return value to a variable. Suppose the integer answer has been declared as type `int`. Example 11–5 illustrates how to assign the results of calling the `findPerimeterOfRectangle()` method to the `answer` variable.

Example 11-5. Assigning return value from method to a variable

```
answer = findPerimeterOfRectangle(8, 12);
```

Helper methods are used extensively in Arduino™ sketches.

Servo library

An earlier method referred to Arduino™ libraries as sets of program code written by others that may be accessed from an Arduino™ sketch. The Math library was used as an illustration.

The Arduino™ IDE includes a library specifically for the control of servo motors, the *Servo library*. It is similar to other libraries in that it is prewritten and available for use. But it is different in two important ways.

1. Because most sketches will have no need to control servos, this library must be specifically "included" in the sketch so that the IDE will know to retrieve it when the sketch is uploaded to the Arduino.™ To do this, the programming statement shown in Example 11-6 is placed near the beginning of the sketch.

Example 11-6.

```
#include <Servo.h>
```

Important	The capitalization of the library name is important. Also notice this statement does not include a semicolon at the end.

2. Because the sketch may control more than one servo and have them do different things, a copy of the library must be made for each servo so they can be addressed separately. This is called making an *object* of the library. An object is a data type that must be given a variable name, much as `String` is the type of a `String` variable. Example 11–7 is an example of how to create and name objects, producing two variables of type `Servo`. These are typical of what can be found in an Arduino™ sketch used to control the ailerons of a radio-controlled airplane.

Example 11-7. Creating and naming objects

```
Servo servoLeft;
Servo servoRight;
```

These variables, then, can be used by the sketch to initialize and send pulses to each servo.

Table 11-2. Vocabulary

Term	Definition
helper method	A method, which can be added to an Arduino™ sketch, that contains programming statements that perform a specific task. This method, then, may be accessed by other methods in the sketch, eliminating a need to duplicate sets of programming statements.
object	A date type that must be given a variable name.

Term	Definition
pulse	The setting of a pin from `LOW` to `HIGH` for a specific time, then returning it to `LOW`. A single rise, wait, and fall cycle of the output voltage.
pulse width	The length of time a pulse is `HIGH`.
Pulse Width Modulation	The act of sending information by varying the width of pulses.
Servo library	A set of prewritten methods for communicating with and controlling servos.
servo object	A copy of the Servo library that controls a specific servo. An object is made with a statement of the form `Servo servo_1;` In this example `servo_1` is a variable of type `Servo`.
standard servo	A type of motor that moves in response to a pulse. The pulse width (length of time it is `HIGH`) specifies the direction and angular distance of the turn. The range of 0 through 180 degrees is common.

Description:

Programming and controlling the servo

11

As mentioned, the Servo library makes available a set of methods specifically intended to control servos. The steps for using this library in an Arduino™ sketch are:

1. Connect a servo to the Arduino™.
2. Include the Servo library in the sketch.
3. Create a servo object for each servo to be controlled.
4. Initialize each servo object.
5. Use the methods in the servo objects to position the servos as needed.

Step 1: Connecting a servo to an Arduino™

Servos come with three wires to be connected to the Arduino,™ one to be connected to ground (gnd), one to be connected to a positive voltage (+5 or +6 volts), and one to receive the signal (pulse). Each wire has its own color indicating the type of purpose of the wire.

Table 11-3. Servo wires

	Type of Servo	
Wire connection	**Standard**	**Continuous Rotation**
Signal	Orange	White
Power	Red	Red
Ground	Brown or Black	Black

About the power connection – most servos used with Arduinos™ prefer +6 volts. Further, standard size servos can draw considerably more current than can be delivered by an Arduino™. For these, a regulated source of +6 volts should be provided. One way of doing this is shown in the retired Lesson 11 and is built into the Motor Controller Shield described in How-To #3.

Small servos, as those used on radio-control airplanes, and larger servos lightly loaded will work when connected to the Arduino's™ +5 volts.

Step 2: Including the Servo library

Before an Arduino™ sketch can begin using Servo objects, the library must be included. Notice the word Servo is capitalized and that the statement is not followed by a semicolon.

```
#include <Servo.h>
```

Notice that this statement must appear before any reference to the Servo library can be made. All include statements in an Arduino™ sketch are usually placed near the top, just below introductory comments.

Step 3: Creating the Servo object

Below the include statement but before any methods, global variables are created. Global variables are those that may be accessed by any method. The following statement creates a Servo object and names it `myServo`.

```
Servo myServo;
```

Step 4: Initialize the Servo object

Initialization of an object is the act of telling it to perform any required startup actions. It also provides any required information. In the case of a Servo object, the number of pin to which the servo is connected is provided.

This statement is usually found in the sketch's `setup()` method. In this case, the sketch is telling the `myServo` object to initialize and that the servo to be controlled is connected to pin number 9 on the Arduino.™

```
void setup(){
...setup statements
myServo.attach(9); // init servo at pin 9
...maybe more statements
}
```

Important	Servos may only be controlled through pins capable of sending pulses. The act of sending information by varying the width of pulses is called *Pulse Width Modulation* (PWM). Not all Arduino™ digital pins are PWM-capable. Those that are have a tilde mark beside the number. Pin 9 on the Arduino™ Uno, for example, is marked ~9.

Step 5: Using the Servo object methods

The Servo library provides each object with the following methods:

`attach( int pinNumber)` Initializes the servo

pinNumber: Integer. The pin to which the pulse wire of the servo is connected. The pin must be capable of `AnalogWrite()`. This is indicated by the tilde character in front of the pin number. Example: ~9.

example:

```
Servo myServo;    // declared above setup method
void setup(){
  myServo.attach(9);

}
```

11

Sending the pulse is pretty simple with the `writeMicroseconds()` function.

`writeMicroseconds(int duration)` returns the position of the servo. Actually, this is the value of the most recent write statement.

`duration`: integer that specifies the width of the pulse to be written to the servo.

example:

```
myServo.writeMicroseconds( 1500);
// places servo arm at 90 degrees
delay(15);
```

Caution	A servo is a mechanical device. The programmer must allow time for the servo to respond when it receives a pulse. It cannot change position instantly. A delay of about 15 milliseconds is recommended by Arduino.cc.

```
write(int degrees)
```

degrees: Integer. Position, in degrees, to which the servo arm is to move. Most servos are limited to 180-degree motion.

example:
```
myServo.write(45);
// positions servo arm at 45-degree angle
```

`int read()` returns the position of the servo.

example:
```
int position = myServo.read();
// get value of most recent write
```

Goals:

By the end of this lesson readers will

1. Know how to connect a servo to an Arduino.™
2. Know that a servo has three wires: one is for power; one is ground, and the third is to receive the pulse.
3. Know how to declare variables of type `Servo` and that each such variable refers to a particular servo attached to the Arduino.™
4. Know how to program an Arduino™ to set a servo to any position from 0 through the end of its range.

Materials:

Quantity	Part	Image	Notes	Catalog Number
1	Arduino™ Uno		Single-board computer. This board is delicate and should be handled with care. When you are not using it, keep it in a box or plastic bag.	3102
1	USB Cable		This is a standard USB adapter cable with a flat connector on one end and a square connector on the other.	2301
1	Computer with at least one USB port and access to the Arduino™ website, http://www.arduino.cc.	---	The operating system of this computer must be Windows, Macintosh OS/X, or Linux.	---
1	Bread-board	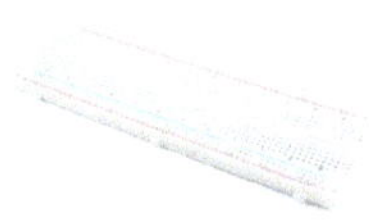	Used for prototyping.	3104
1	Servo		Standard Micro Servo.	3137
1	Potentiometer		10k ohm.	0301
As req'd	Jumper wires		Used with bread-boards for wiring the components.	3105

11

Procedure:

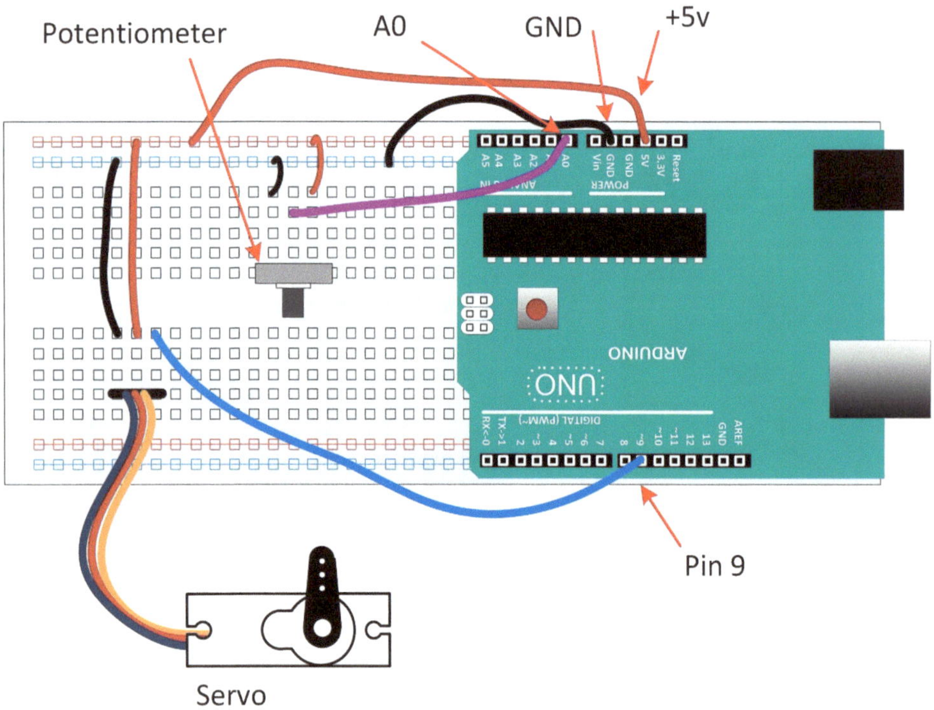

Figure 11-4. Servo wiring pictorial

Caution	The orange wire from the servo must ultimately connect to pin 9 of the Arduino.™ Do not reverse this. The servo could be damaged if you wire incorrectly.

1. Construct the electronic circuit shown in Figure 11-2. Take care to wire the servo and the potentiometer correctly. A mistake can cause damage. Also, a rubber band to hold the Arduino™ on the solderless bread-board makes the circuit easier to handle.

   The diagram shows a 3-pin header (parts catalog number 2303) connecting the servo to the bread-board. Three jumper wires may be used instead, which are less prone to becoming unplugged.

2. Connect the Arduino™ to the computer and open the Arduino™ IDE. Create a new sketch. Name it `Lesson11StandardServo`.

3. Enter the following programming statements into this sketch. Notice you will be replacing the default `void setup()` and `void loop()` methods automatically created for you by the Arduino™ IDE.

```
/* lesson11StandardServo
   by <your name here>
   date
*/

#include <Servo.h>

#define pinServo 9  // servo's white or orange wire
#define pinPotentiometer A0

Servo myServo;  // Servo variable declared

void setup(){
  myServo.attach(pinServo);
  pinMode(pinPotentiometer, INPUT);
}

void loop(){
  // match the position of the servo to that of
  // the potentiometer
  setServoToPotentiometer();

  // Exercise 2 begins here
  // Set brightness of an LED to represent the inverse of the
  // position of the servo
  setLEDToServoPosition();
}

// Helper method
void setServoToPotentiometer(){
  // get position of potentiometer
  int myPosition = analogRead(pinPotentiometer);

  // Position will be between 0 and 1023.
  // Map to servo 0 to 180 degrees.
  // Activity 1 modifies this programming statement
  int degreePosition = map(myPosition, 0, 1023, 0, 180);
```

11

```
// Move the servo
  // Activity 1 modifies this programming statement
  myServo.write(degreePosition);
  delay(15);
}

void setLEDToServoPosition(){
  // Activity 2 programming statements go here.


}
```

As the knob of the potentiometer is turned, the servo should move to follow. The arm of the servo should be at 0 degrees when the potentiometer is fully counterclockwise and 180 degrees at fully clockwise.

Exercises:

Exercise 11-1. Verify `writeMicroseconds()` method

Recall that the servo is actually controlled by pulses sent at regular intervals by the Arduino,™ and that the angle of the servo is specified by the width in microseconds of that pulse.

Modify the `setServoToPotentiometer()` method of the sketch to use the `writeMicroseconds()` method in place of the `write()` method. Keep in mind the following:

- The pulse width range is 600 microseconds to 2400 microseconds, representing 0 degrees through 180 degrees of the servo.
- The `map()` statement parameters will have to be modified.

Exercise 11-2. Increase and decrease LED brightness according to degree

Add an LED that increased brightness as the servo angle approaches 0 degrees and dims as the angle approaches 180 degrees. The LED should be dark at 180 degrees and full brightness at 0 and fade evenly over the values in between.

Keep in mind the following:

- An LED must be added to the circuit. Be sure to use a current-limiting resistor of 220 ohms.
- The pin the LED connects to must be PWM-capable. Look for the tilde mark.
- Good programming practice requires a `#define` statement to specify the pin number for the LED. The identifier of PIN_LED is sufficient. The following is for connecting the LED to pin 5:

  ```
  #define PIN_LED 5
  ```

- Do not read the value of the potentiometer again. Instead, use a method from the Arduino™ Servo library that returns the position of the servo.
- Use the `map()` method to translate the servo position to a value between 0 and 255 for the LED.

Lesson 12 Infrared Sensors

The Big Idea:

With the addition of a small electronic device called the infrared sensor, we can add to an Arduino™ the ability to detect infrared radiation. This, in a sense, brings eyes to an Arduino.™ Infrared is simply light, although it is light outside the frequency range visible to humans. Future lessons will use infrared two ways: first, to detect objects and, later, to detect and decode messages. This lesson is about detection. Detection of objects is one of the first exercises with the rolling robot of Lesson 15 and decoding messages of Lesson 16.

Background:

Previous lessons introduced the Serial Monitor, the push button, and the potentiometer as means for bringing information into an Arduino™ sketch. This lesson introduces *infrared*, the first of two wireless technologies used in these lessons to connect the Arduino™ to the surrounding world. The second technology, to be addressed later, is radio.

Infrared

Infrared (IR) is a particular frequency range of electromagnetic radiation, similar to that of visible light. IR, in fact, sits just before the red end of the visible light.

12

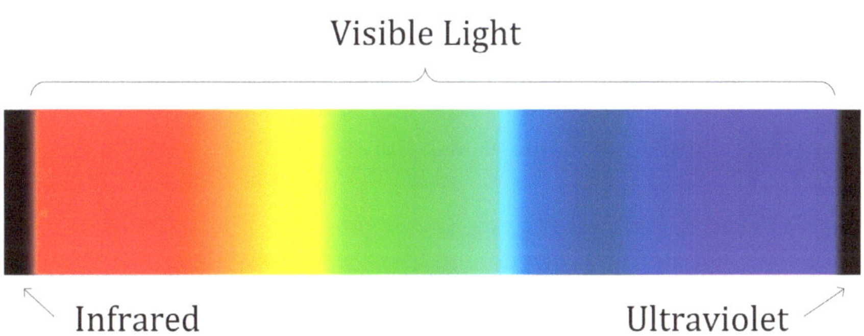

Figure 12-1. Visible light spectrum

Infrared is ubiquitous. It is present in sunshine and is generally associated with objects radiating heat, which is everything from a human body to freshly baked bread. And it is by far the most commonly used technology for remote control of electronic devices, including home entertainment systems.

This presents a problem. How is it that the television receiver can respond instantly to an infrared message from a remote control but is somehow able to ignore a warm chocolate chip cookie?

The answer is that infrared radiation as it is used in common remote controls and will be used in these lessons is *modulated*. In other words, when it is on it is actually being turned on and off 38,000 times per second. The infrared receivers used in this lesson are specially designed to detect only infrared that is flashing on and off at this frequency. The infrared from the cookie, which is not modulated, is ignored.

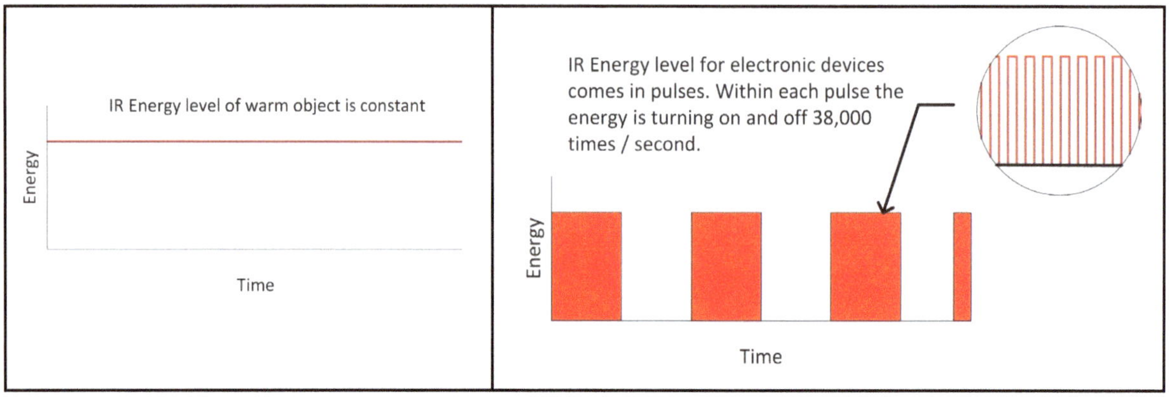

Figure 12-2. Unmodulated vs. modulated infrared radiation

This lesson deals only with detection of infrared energy being transmitted by an electronic device. But note that actual messages can be encoded into the transmitted infrared by changing the lengths of the pulses and the times between them. This is how a television remote is able to perform specific tasks. Message encoding will be used in later lessons to remotely control a rolling robot and play a sort of musical instrument.

The rate at which some signal is turned on and off is called the *frequency*. One on and off pair is called a *cycle*. Frequency is the number of cycles per some unit in time, in this case cycles per second. The unit for cycles per second is the *Hertz*, named after Heinrich Hertz, a German physicist generally credited with proving the existence of electromagnetic waves. The abbreviation for the Hertz is Hz. For convenience, frequency is usually referred to in thousands of cycles per second, for which the abbreviation is kHz.

Table 12-1. Vocabulary

Term	Description
cycle	A single pulse followed by a period of no pulse just before another pulse.
frequency	The number of times the pulse is turned on and off per second. Infrared used for control of electronic devices is typically modulated at a frequency of 38,000 cycles per second.
Hertz	The unit of measure for frequency. One Hertz is equal to one cycle per second. The abbreviation is Hz.

Term	Description
infrared	The frequency of electromagnetic radiation just below light visible to humans. The first visible color is red, hence the name infrared (infra means below).
infrared sensor	Electronic component with an output pin that is normally at +5 volts. When this device detects modulated infrared, this output voltage drops to zero.
modulate	The process of turning a pulse on and off very rapidly when that pulse is in the ON, or HIGH, state.

Description:

The *infrared sensor* is a small electronic component with three wires. One is connected to the Arduino™ +5, one to ground (GND), and the third is the device output, typically connected to an Arduino™ digital pin configured for INPUT mode.

The output pin is HIGH when no modulated infrared is detected (or sensed). When the receiver detects infrared modulated at 38 kHz, the voltage on its output pin drops to LOW.

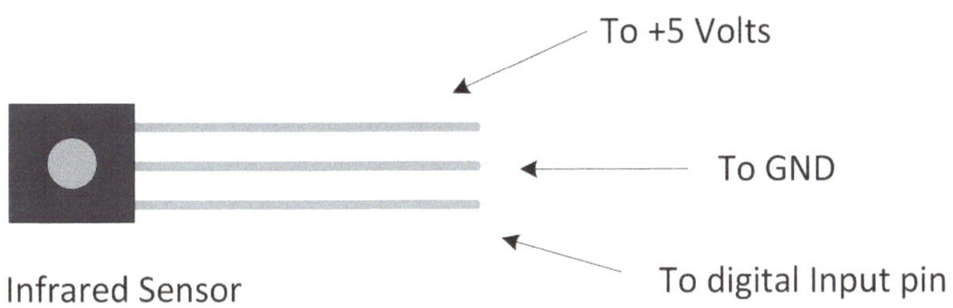

12

Table 12-2. Pin 1 status and meaning

Pin 1 status	Meaning
HIGH	No modulated infrared detected.
LOW	Modulated infrared is detected.

Caution	Generally speaking, pin 1 of the IR sensor may be connected to any Arduino™ Uno digital port configured for INPUT. But the Uno also has a built-in LED and current-limiting resistor connected to pin 13. As a result, special care must be taken before using it for INPUT. See http://arduino.cc/en/Tutorial/DigitalPins for specifics. These lessons do not attempt to use this pin for input.

This lesson does not decode incoming infrared messages. It merely detects them. Refer to Lesson 15 for decoding of messages.

Goals:

By the end of this lesson readers will:

1. Be able to identify an infrared detector and the individual pins by pin number.
2. Know how an infrared detector is wired for power and how to feed its output to an Arduino™ digital pin.
3. Know how to configure an Arduino™ digital pin for reading the infrared sensor signal.
4. Write a sketch that detects and responds to an infrared signal from a remote control.

Materials:

Quantity	Part	Image	Notes	Catalog Number
1	Arduino™ Uno		Single-board computer. This board is delicate and should be handled with care. When you are not using it, keep it in a box or plastic bag.	3102
1	USB Cable		This is a standard USB adapter cable with a flat connector on one end and a square connector on the other.	2301
1	Computer with at least one USB port and access to the Arduino™ website, http://www.arduino.cc.	---	The operating system of this computer must be Windows, Macintosh OS/X, or Linux.	---
1	Bread-board	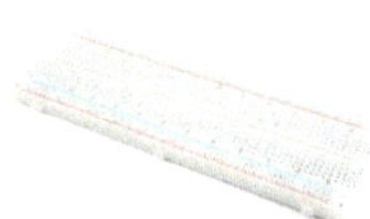	Used for prototyping.	3104
2	Light-emitting diodes (LEDs)		Single color, about 0.02 amps rated current, diffused.	1301
2	Resistors, 220 ohm		1/4 watt, 5% tolerance, red-red-brown-gold.	0102
1	Television remote control		Any Sony-compatible remote	---

Quan-tity	Part	Image	Notes	Catalog Number
1	Infrared sensor		3-pin, 38kHz.	1302
As req'd	Jumper wires		Used with bread-boards for wiring the components.	3105

Procedure:

1. Construct the circuit as shown in Figure 12-4.

Using a bread-board, wire the infrared sensor, LEDs, and current-limiting resistors.

Figure 12-4 is a schematic. The IR sensor's pin 1 is NOT the center pin. It just sort of looks that way because a schematic is drawn for a simple diagram of the electronic components.

2. Connect the Arduino™ to the computer via the USB cable and start the Arduino™ IDE.
3. Create a new Arduino™ sketch. Name it `Lesson12IRSensor`.
4. Enter the header comments and define the pins to be used

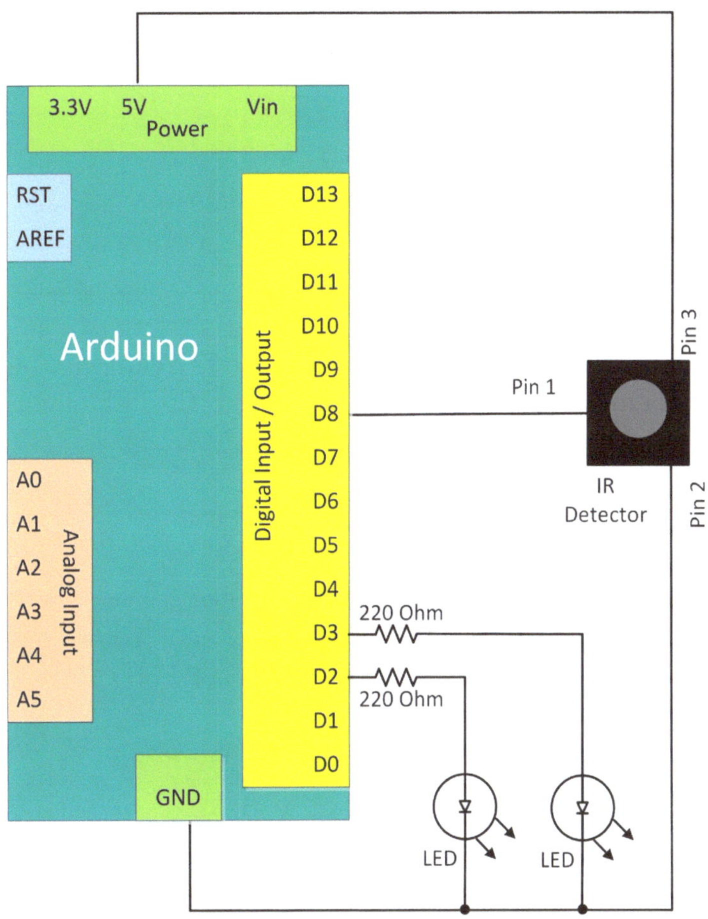

Figure 12-4. Schematic Diagram

Snippet 12-1.

```
/* Lesson12IRSensor
   by W. P. Osborne
   6/30/15
*/

#define pinLED1 2
#define pinLED2 3
#define pinIRSensor 8
...
```

5. Add the `setup()` method and use it to initialize the three digital pins. Notice that the pins being used for the LEDs must be initialized as `OUTPUT`, while the pin for sensing the infrared must be `INPUT`.

Snippet 12-2.

```
...
void setup(){
    pinMode(pinLED1, OUTPUT);
    pinMode(pinLED2, OUTPUT);
    pinMode(pinIRSensor, INPUT);
}
...
```

6. Finally, add the `loop()` method. Use an `if-else` pair to either light or put out the first LED depending on if the sensor detects infrared. The LED should light when infrared is present.

Snippet 12-3.

```
...
void loop(){
    if( digitalRead(pinIRSensor) == LOW){
        // infrared is detected. Light the LED
        digitalWrite(pinLED1, HIGH);
    } else {
        digitalWrite(pinLED1, LOW);
    }
    delay(10);
}
```

7. Save the sketch then upload it to the Arduino.™ Neither LED should be lit.

8. Point the remote control at the infrared sensor, then press a button. The LED should flash.

Notice that the LED isn't on all the time. The remote control is sending the command message associated with the button being pushed. This message is composed of pulses. The LED is lighting in response to these pulses.

Experiment with the remote control to see how far away it can get and still be detected. Determine if one side of the sensor is more sensitive than the other.

Exercises:

Exercise 12-1. No infrared detected

Modify the `Lesson12IRSensor` sketch to have the second LED light when no infrared is detected but go out when infrared is detected. The two LEDs, then, will be exact opposites. When one is on the other is off. Save the sketch as `Lesson12Exercise1`.

Note: This second diode will be on most of the time.

Exercise 12-2. Smooth infrared detected

Modify the sketch from Exercise 12-1 to keep the IR detected LED on for one second each time infrared is detected. Ask yourself if this this makes the sensor easier to use. That is,

- Does the sensor seems to respond immediately when infrared is detected?
- Does the detection LED go out in a timely manner when infrared is no longer detected?

12

Exercise 12-3. Distance front and back

Infrared sensors have a front, where the raised area of plastic is found, and a back, which is flat. Measure how far the remote control can be taken from the sensor and still have detection occur reliably. Record these differences:

Distance from front: ____________ meters / feet

Complete listing 12.1. Lesson12IRSensor

```
/* Lesson12IRSensor
   by W. P. Osborne
   6/30/15
*/

#define pinLED1 2
#define pinLED2 3
#define pinIRSensor 8

void setup(){
    pinMode(pinLED1, OUTPUT);
    pinMode(pinLED2, OUTPUT);
    pinMode(pinIRSensor, INPUT);
}

void loop(){
    if( digitalRead(pinIRSensor) == LOW){
        // infrared is detected. Light the LED
        digitalWrite(pinLED1, HIGH);
        digitalWrite(pinLED2, LOW);
    } else {
        digitalWrite(pinLED1, LOW);
        digitalWrite(pinLED2, HIGH);
    }
}
```

Lesson 13 Infrared Transmitters

The Big Idea:

In Lesson 12 the ability to detect infrared radiation modulated at 38,000 Hertz was added to the Arduino.™ This lesson brings the ability to generate modulated infrared. The two can be used in combination to make a system that can detect nearby objects and obstacles. IR is transmitted, and the IR sensor looks for reflections.

Lesson 15 uses a pair of generators and sensors to add the ability to turn away from (or toward) an obstacle. But this has many other uses. Model railroad enthusiasts, for example, can detect trains. Elevators use such combinations to determine the precise position of the door relative to the floor.

Figure 13-1 shows a pair of infrared transmitter/receivers used by some Sears garage door openers to detect the presence of small children and pets.

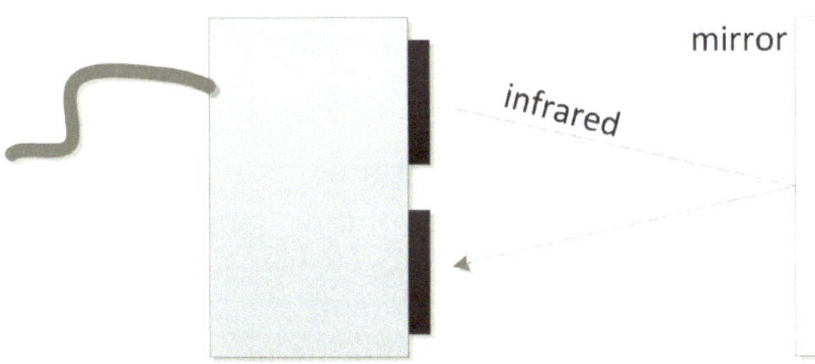

Figure 13-1. Garage door obstacle detectors

13

Background:

About infrared transmission

By now the light-emitting diode (LED) is familiar. It is simply a semiconductor device that can emit electromagnetic radiation in the frequencies of visible light. Semiconductor technology makes up most of what is referred to as electronics. In addition to diodes, this family of devices includes transistors and integrated circuits, the building blocks of computers including the ATmega 328 that is the heart of the Arduino™ Uno.

An infrared transmitter is almost exactly the same as an LED. It, too, is a diode that emits electromagnetic radiation. But the frequencies of this radiation are just below the red end of the visible light spectrum. This is the range named infrared. The term "infra" is Latin meaning "below."

Because of the similarity to the LED, the infrared diode is referred to as an IRED.

The human eye does not respond to infrared. But some inexpensive digital cameras of the type found in older cell phones can. The circuit shown in Figure 13-2 will produce infrared light easily seen by one of these cameras.

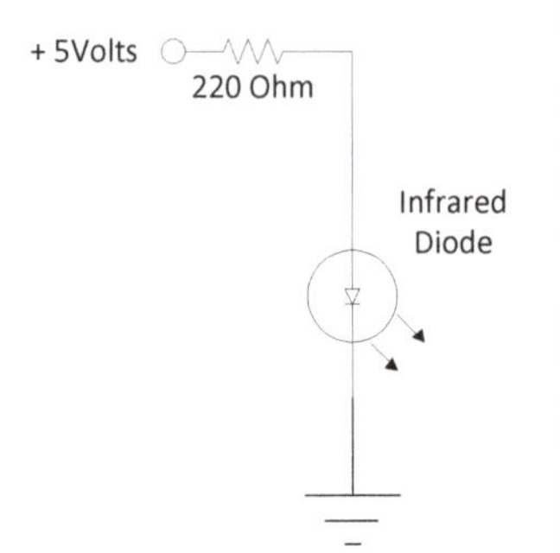

An infrared diode is electrically almost the same as a light-emitting diode. The difference is that the light emitted is not visible to the human eye. This is why infrared diodes are used for television remote controls.

To accurately mimic what the eye can see, better digital cameras filter out infrared light. But older cell phone cameras lacked this filter.

Figure 13-2. IRED circuit diagram

Recall from Lesson 12 that infrared is very common. For this reason, infrared used in remote control electronics is modulated at 38,000 Hz. This modulation is unlikely to be found in nature.

About modulation

Lesson 12 introduced the terms modulation, frequency, and the Hertz. This lesson will show how an Arduino™ can be programmed to transmit modulated pulses of infrared via an IRED. To do so, however, a little more needs to be understood about this modulation.

The IRED must be turned on for a short time and then turned off for a short time; this must happen 38,000 times per second. This pair of events is called a *cycle*. The length of time consumed by one cycle is called the *period*.

The units of time used for the Arduino™ are the second, the millisecond, and the microsecond. The relationships are: 1000 microseconds equals one millisecond, and one thousand milliseconds equals one second.

Table 13-1. Arduino™ C-language time units

Unit	Symbol	Relation to second	Programming example
second	s	1:1	none
millisecond	ms	1 ms = 10^{-3}	delay(<ms>)
microsecond	µs	1 µs = 10^{-6} seconds	delayMicroseconds(<µs>)

Figure 13-3 shows a few of the cycles within a portion of a pulse. One of these cycles is identified; the duration in microseconds shown.

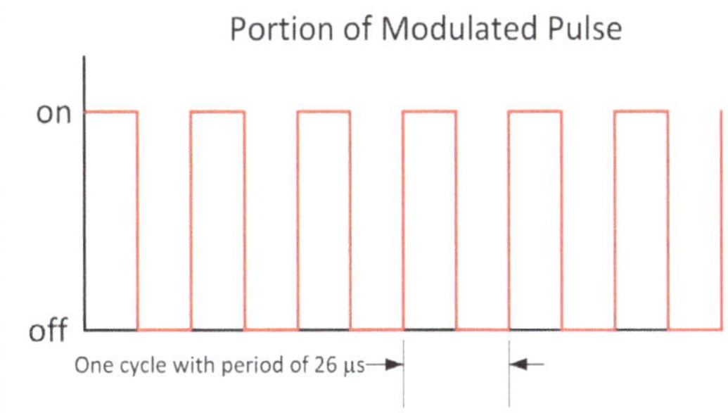	One cycle of a pulse modulated at 38,000 Hz is composed of the IRED being set on for 13 microseconds then off for 13 microseconds. The period of one cycle is 26 microseconds.

Figure 13-3. Cycle within a portion of a pulse

Important	These modulation cycles may be thought of as pulses within pulses. The IR pulse itself is the time the IRED is on. When it is on it is actually turning on and off very rapidly. This rapid on and off is the modulation.

Why 13 microseconds on, followed by 13 microseconds off? It's math.

Step 1: Calculate the time for one cycle:	tcycle = 1 / 38000 cycles / second = 2.6×10^{-5} seconds / cycle = 26×10^{-6} seconds / cycle = 26 µs / cycle
Step 2: Assume a symmetrical cycle. This means the time on must equal the time off.	t_{on} = 13 µs and t_{off} = 13 µs

13

Table 13-2. Vocabulary

Term	Description
boolean	A data type that may have only two states: true and false. First encountered in the lesson on input from the serial port as the result of a test of the number of characters waiting to be read.
cycle	A single pulse followed by a period of no pulse just before another pulse. With infrared the period of one cycle is 26 microseconds.
flow chart	A method of diagramming process flow, frequently used by programmers to describe how a portion of an Arduino™ sketch is to work.

Term	Description
infrared-emitting diode (IRED)	A semiconductor device similar to an LED except that the electromagnetic radiation frequency is just below visible red light.
period	The elapsed time of one cycle. With infrared, the period of one cycle is 26 microseconds.
second, millisecond, microsecond	Measures of time, each 1/1000 of the preceding measure.
programming statement execution time	The time taken by the Arduino™ to perform a programming statement. Execution time must be allowed for in portions of a sketch where timing is important, such as generating a pulse.

Discussion:

This lesson implements an IRED in combination with an infrared sensor to construct an obstacle sensor, much as might be used by a rolling robot to find its way through a maze. The programming statements to do this fit neatly into a helper method. This method has three basic steps: light the IRED for a short time; determine if the IR sensor saw any infrared reflections from an obstacle; and return the results to the method that called it.

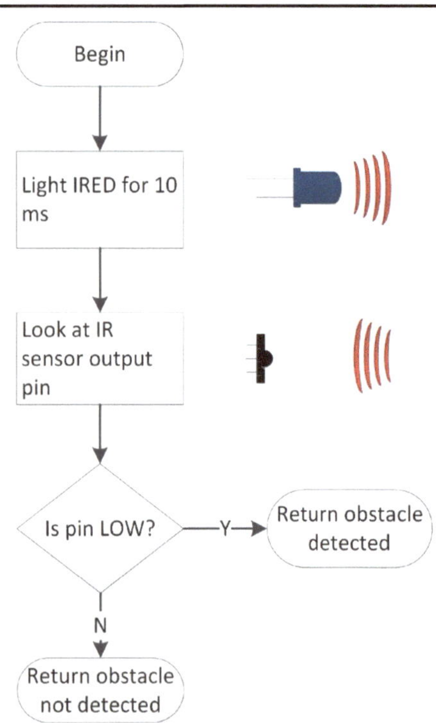

If an obstacle is present, some of this infrared light will be reflected where it can be seen by the IR sensor.

After flashing the infrared light, the program code reads the digital pin to which the output of the IR sensor is attached.

If that pin is `LOW`, then infrared was detected. Otherwise, infrared was not detected.

Figure 13-4. Flow chart of helper method that detects obstacles by flashing modulated infrared light

About flow charting

The chart in Figure 13-4 is an example of flow charting, a process commonly used by engineers to diagram processes. Figure 13-4 shows how the IR transmitter and sensor can be used together to detect an obstacle. It also serves to guide the writing of the C-language program to make this happen. Each shape has a specific meaning.

Table 13-3. Shapes used in flow charting in this lesson

Symbol	Name	Description
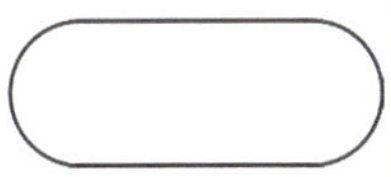	Start / End	Identifies the beginning of a process and the end. A process may have more than one end but not more than one beginning. In C, the beginning might be the name of a method.
	Process	A specific task. In C, this is a collection of programming statements that do one thing. An example is using a `for` loop to light and modulate an IRED.
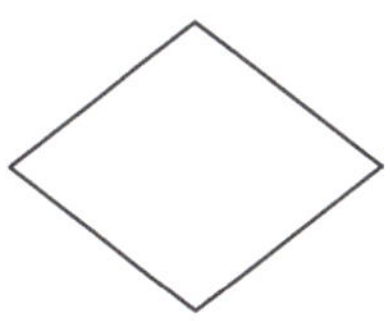	Decision	Selects what is to happen next based on the state of some variables. In C, this is usually represented by `if` and `if-else`.

Program code

Because the task of attempting to detect an obstacle is self-contained, it fits well into its own method. For illustration, suppose that method is named `lookForReflection()`. The flow chart says either an obstacle is detected or it is not. This is a true or a false, where a returned value of true means yes, an obstacle reflected some infrared light.

Boolean data type

C has a data type called *boolean*. A `boolean` variable is one that can have as a value only true or false. These are, in fact, the words used to represent these values. Example 13-1 shows the declaration of a variable of type `boolean` and the setting of the value of true.

Example 13-1. Declaring variable type of `boolean` and value of true

```
boolean gameOver;  // declares variable of type boolean
gameOver = true;  // gameOver is now true
```

The helper method `lookForReflection()` is to return true if an obstacle reflects infrared. Otherwise it is to return false. So, for this reason, the variable is written as having a return type of `boolean`.

Example 13-2.

```
boolean lookForReflection(){
      // programming statements
      // go here
}
```

Generating one pulse cycle

One single infrared pulse is `HIGH` for 13 microseconds, then `LOW` for 13 microseconds. Assume `IRTransmitterPin` is initialized to the pin number of the digital port to which the IRED is attached. The programming statements shown in Example 13-3 generate one period of an infrared pulse.

Example 13-3.

```
digitalWrite(IRTransmitterPin, HIGH);
delayMicroseconds(13);
digitalWrite(IRTransmitterPin, LOW);
delayMicroseconds(13);
```

Generating a modulated infrared pulse

The period of one cycle is 26 microseconds. To generate an IR pulse of a specific duration a `for` loop is used. The number of times the loop runs is determined by the duration of the pulse. Typically, an infrared pulse is one millisecond. The general formula for the number of periods is shown in Example 13-4.

Example 13-4.

```
numberOfPeriods = (38,000 periods / sec) * (duration in seconds)
```

One millisecond is 10^{-3} seconds. The number of periods, then, is as shown in Example 13-5.

Example 13-5.

```
numberOfPeriods = (38,000 periods / sec) * (10-3 sec)
numberOfPeriods = 38 periods
```

So, the final `for` loop to generate a modulated pulse of 1 millisecond duration is shown in Example 13-6.

Example 13-6.

```
// not quite correct. Does not account for the time of
// execution of the for loop statements
for(int counter = 0; counter < 38; counter++){
        digitalWrite(IRTransmitterPin, HIGH);
```

```
        delayMicroseconds(13);
        digitalWrite(IRTransmitterPin, LOW);
        delayMicroseconds(13);   // too long
    }
```

As precise as this is, the code is still not quite right because of *programming statement execution time.* This is the program delay caused by the execution of program `for` statement, where the loop is ended, the counter incremented, and the test performed. So, the IRED is off longer than 13 microseconds.

> `timeOff` = 13 milliseconds + the statement execution time of processing the `for` loop. For the Arduino™ Uno, this is about 4 microseconds.

The corrected code subtracts this from the second delay. The revised loop is shown in Example 13-7.

Example 13-7.

```
    // includes latency for Arduino™ Uno
    for(int counter = 0; counter < 38; counter++){
        digitalWrite(IRTransmitterPin, HIGH);
        delayMicroseconds(13);
        digitalWrite(IRTransmitterPin, LOW);
        delayMicroseconds(9);  // adjusted for statement
                                // execution time
    }
```

Reading the IR Receiver and Returning the Result

13

Programming statements for reading an infrared sensor are covered in Lesson 12. To these are added the statements to return true or false. `IRDetectorPin` is assigned the number of the Arduino™ pin to which the output of the IR sensor is attached.

Example 13-8.

```
    boolean result;
    if(digitalRead(IRDetectorPin) == LOW){
        result = true;
    } else {
        result = false;
    }
    return result;
```

Putting all this together the completed helper method is shown in Example 13-9.

Example 13-9.

```
boolean lookForReflection(){
    // Send IR for 1 ms
    int halfPulse = 13;
    for(int counter = 0; counter < 32; counter++){
        digitalWrite(IRTransmitterPin, HIGH);
        delayMicroseconds(halfPulse);
        digitalWrite(IRTransmitterPin, LOW);
        delayMicroseconds(halfPulse - 4);
    }

    boolean result;
    if( digitalRead(IRDetectorPin) == LOW){
        result = true;
    } else {
        result = false;
    }
    return result;
}
```

The final six lines of program code can be simplified as shown in Example 13-10.

Example 13-10.

```
    if( digitalRead(IRDetectorin) == LOW){
        return true;
    }
    return false;
}
```

Goals:

The goals of this lesson are:

1. Know that infrared diodes are connected to digital ports and are wired and programmed exactly the same way.
2. Be able to write an Arduino™ sketch that generates infrared light that can be detected by an infrared detector. This means that when on, the IRED is modulated at 38,000 Hz.
3. Be able to write an Arduino™ sketch that pairs an IRED with an IR sensor to form a system capable of detecting obstacles that reflect infrared light.

Materials:

Quan-tity	Part	Image	Notes	Catalog Number
1	Arduino™ Uno		Single-board computer. This board is delicate and should be handled with care. When you are not using it, keep it in a box or plastic bag.	3102
1	USB Cable		This is a standard USB adapter cable with a flat connector on one end and a square connector on the other.	2301
1	Computer with at least one USB port and access to the Arduino™ website, http://www.arduino.cc.	---	The operating system of this computer must be Windows, Macintosh OS/X, or Linux.	---
1	Bread-board		Used for prototyping.	3104
As req'd	Jumper wires		Used with bread-boards for wiring the components.	3105
1	Light-emitting diode (LED)		Single color (color doesn't matter), about 0.02 amps rated current, diffused.	1301
2	Resistors, 220 ohm		1/4 watt, 5% tolerance, red-red-brown.	0102
1	Infrared headlight	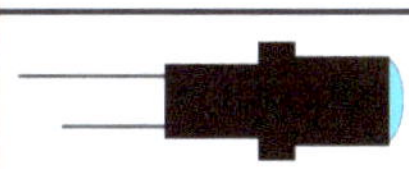	Infrared-emitting diode with light-proof shrink wrap.	See Note 1
1	Infrared sensor		3-pin, 38kHz.	1302

Note 1: Headlight is constructed from an infrared LED and two 1/2-inch sections of heat-shrink tubing. See How-To #6 on LearnCSE.com for instructions.

Procedure:

1. Using the Arduino™ Uno and bread-board, construct the circuit shown in Figures 13-5 and 13-6.

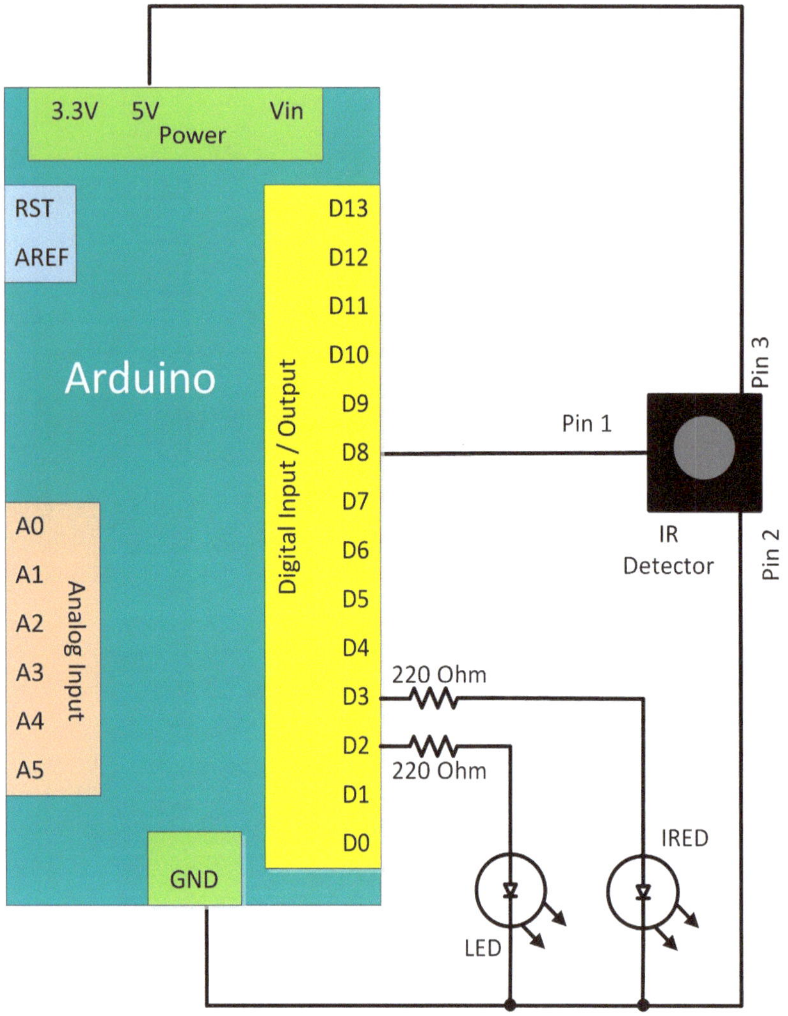

Figure 13-5. IR transmitter / receiver schematic

When used together, as in this lesson, the headlight is placed in front or alongside of the receiver, as shown in Figure 13-6. This is to prevent the receiver from responding to the light source itself.

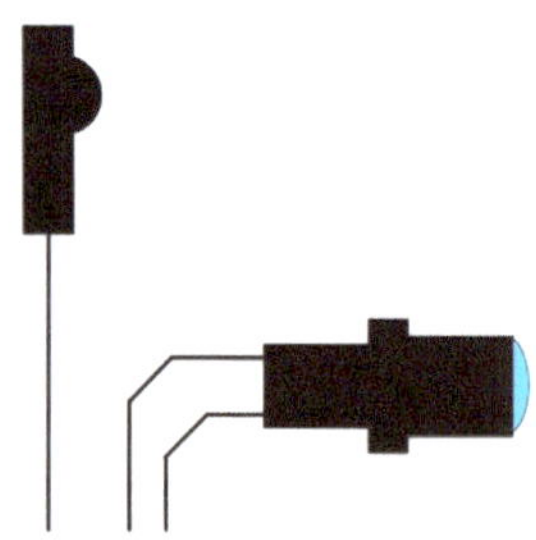

Figure 13-6. Proximity of headlight to receiver

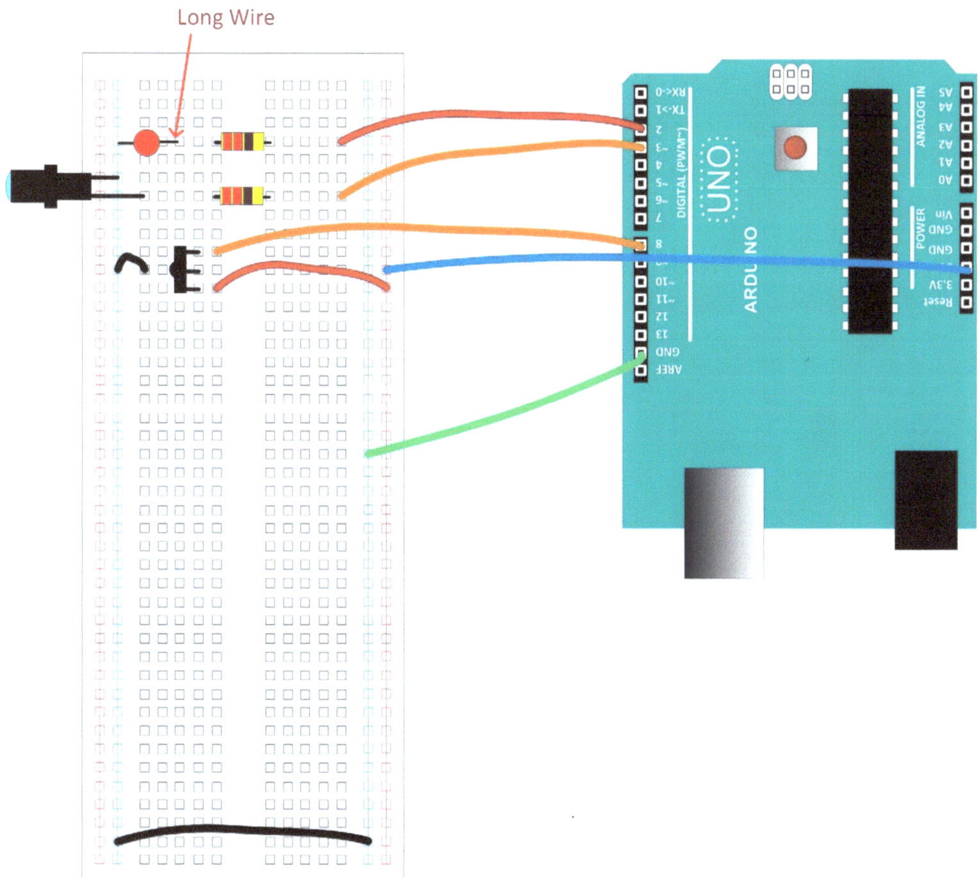

Figure 13-7. IR transmitter / receiver pictorial

13

1. Connect the Arduino™ to the computer and bring up the Arduino™ IDE.
2. Create a new Arduino™ sketch to be named `Lesson13IRTransmit`.
3. Enter the heading and the defined values as shown in Snippet 13-1.

Snippet 13-1.

```
/* Lesson13IRTransmit
   <author>
   <date>
*/

// define the pins to be used
#define pinLED 2         // for LED
#define pinIRED 3        // for IRED
#define pinIRDetect 8    // for IR Sensor
...
```

4. Initialize the pins in the `setup()` method.

Snippet 13-2.

```
...
void setup(){
    pinMode(pinLED, OUTPUT);
    pinMode(pinIRED, OUTPUT);
    pinMode(pinIRDetect, INPUT);
}
```

5. Add the `loop()` method to light the LED while an obstacle is detected.

Snippet 13-3.

```
...
void loop() {
    boolean obstacle;
    obstacle = lookForReflection();

    if(obstacle){
        digitalWrite(pinLED, HIGH);
    } else {
        digitalWrite(pinLED, LOW);
    }
    delay(10);
}
```

6. Finally, add the helper method that lights the IRED then looks at the IR sensor for evidence of a reflection.

Snippet 13-4.

```
...
boolean lookForReflection(){
    // Send IR for 1 ms
    int halfPulse = 13;
    for(int counter = 0; counter < 32; counter++){
        digitalWrite(pinIRED, HIGH);
        delayMicroseconds(halfPulse);
        digitalWrite(pinIRED, LOW);
        delayMicroseconds(halfPulse - 4);
    }
```

```
    if( digitalRead(pinIRDetect) == LOW){
        return true;
    }
    return false;
}
```

1. Save the sketch. Upload it and test by moving a hand or other obstacle in front of the IRED and removing it. When an obstacle is directly in front of the IRED the LED should light. Otherwise, the LED should be dark.

Exercises:

The range of the detector is influenced by three factors. These exercises explore each factor.

Exercise 13-1. Reflectivity of the obstacle

Begin with a flat, white surface for the obstacle. What is the maximum distance the surface can be from the sensor and still light the LED? How does the LED respond to other colors? Complete Table 13-4.

Table 13-4. Observations on reflectivity of the obstacle

Color	Maximum distance (inches)
White	
Black	
Warm color	
Cool color	

13

Exercise 13-2. Brightness of IRED

The IRED's current-limiting resistor influences how much current passes through the diode. Increasing this resistance will reduce the brightness. Experiment with different resistors and record the maximum distance from which a white surface can be detected. Complete Table 13-5.

Table 13-5. Observable maximum distance as function of IRED brightness

Resistor	Maximum distance to white surface (inches)
150 ohm brown-green-brown	
220 ohm red-red-brown	
1000 ohm brown-black-red	
2000 ohm red-black-red	

Exercise 13-3. Frequency of modulation

Replace the IRED's current-limiting resistor with the original 220 ohm (red-red-brown). Change the modulation frequency by modifying the value assigned to the integer variable `halfPulse` in the `lookForReflection()` method. Complete Table 13-6.

Table 13-6. Observed distance as function of pulse width

Value of `halfPulse`	**Maximum distance (inches)**
7	
9	
11	
13	
15	
17	
20	

Complete listing 13-1. `Lesson13IRTransmit`

```
/* Lesson13IRTransmit
   by W. P. Osborne
   6/30/15
*/
// define the pins to be used
#define pinLED 2        // for LED
#define pinIRED 3       // for IRED
#define pinIRDetect 8   // for IR Sensor

void setup(){
    pinMode(pinLED, OUTPUT);
    pinMode(pinIRED, OUTPUT);
    pinMode(pinIRDetect, INPUT);
}

void loop() {
    boolean obstacle;
    obstacle = lookForReflection();

    if(obstacle){
        digitalWrite(pinLED, HIGH);
    } else {
        digitalWrite(pinLED, LOW);
    }
}

boolean lookForReflection(){
    // Send IR for 1 ms
    int halfPulse = 13;
    for(int counter = 0; counter < 32; counter++){
        digitalWrite(pinIRED, HIGH);
        delayMicroseconds(halfPulse);
        digitalWrite(pinIRED, LOW);
        delayMicroseconds(halfPulse - 4);
    }

    if( digitalRead(pinIRDetect) == LOW){
        return true;
    }
    return false;
}
```

13

Lesson 14 DC Motors

The Big Idea:

The *DC motor* is a simple device, requiring only a connection to a source of direct current of voltage capable of delivering the current the motor requires. This simplicity, however, brings with it three potential liabilities. First, these motors have electricity-conducting brushes that produce electrical interference. This can cause problems with sensors and other devices that work by watching for and interpreting pulses.

Figure 14-1. DC motor with gear box

Second, to develop much power DC motors turn at speeds too high for directly driving wheels for cars or propellers for boats. Gearing is used to reduce the revolutions per minute to values more appropriate for such purposes. The motor shown in Figure 14-1 is attached to a set of gears for just this purpose. The gears are in the yellow housing. The motor is the attached silver and black cylinder.

Third, DC motors are difficult to control precisely and, thus, are unsuitable for fine work such as driving the head on a 3D printer. This can be compensated some by adding components for detecting the speed and direction of the motor. The disc on the motor in Figure 14-1 contains magnets that are part of an encoder, a device for just this purpose.

Despite their limitations DC motors are useful because they are easy to control, respond quickly to changes in speed, make a satisfying whirring sound when spinning, and are inexpensive.

In this lesson we learn how to provide appropriate power to a motor and control its direction and speed from an Arduino.™

Background:

This lesson refers to brushed DC motors. Other types are also in common use, particularly brushless motors and servo motors. The theory of operation is not discussed here. Wikipedia offers an explanation and animated illustrations of the operation of DC motors at https://en.wikipedia.org/wiki/DC_motor.

Voltage regulation

One characteristic of the DC motor that is very important for the purposes of this lesson is the motor's electrical resistance. The slower the motor turns the lower its electrical resistance and, therefore, the greater its demand for electrical current.

The reason this is important is that in these lessons the motors are powered by batteries. Batteries, in turn, have an internal resistance. As the resistance of a motor goes down, the voltage across the motor also drops as the proportion of the battery's internal resistance to total resistance increases. The result is all motors being driven by the batteries slow. To the observer, the DC motors just seem to be running rather poorly.

To minimize that effect, this lesson uses a battery with a higher voltage than what was intended for the motor and a voltage regulator to maintain the voltage delivered to the motor at a lower but constant value. This approach works because the internal resistance of the battery impacts the voltage being delivered to the regulator, not to the motor.

Electrical noise

The DC motor turns because a magnetic field generated by coils of wire switches polarity frequently. This switching is accomplished by brushes that are constantly breaking and then making electrical connections. Each make and break generates a tiny spark that can be picked up inductively by nearby wiring, possibly contaminating whatever electrical messages are being conveyed by these wires.

This interference cannot be completely eliminated, but we do take two suppression steps to reduce the interference to an acceptable level.

One step is the soldering of a 0.1 microfarad capacitor across the electrical terminals of each motor.

The other is the careful preparation and dressing of the wires that bring the electricity to each motor. In particular, these wires are:

1. made just long enough to reach the power source,
2. twisted tightly together, and
3. routed in a way that keeps them away from the wiring of devices that are sensitive to interference.

H-bridge

The direction a DC motor turns is dictated by the polarity of the electricity delivered to the motor terminals. Unlike the servo motor described in Lesson 11, with a DC motor, specifying a pulse width cannot control the motor's direction and speed. However, the digital pins of an Arduino™ can operate an electronic switch capable of controlling the motor's direction and speed.

This device is called an *H-bridge.* Its internal operations aren't described here, but Figure 14-2 shows how one is configured for use with an Arduino.™ The direction of the attached motor is the result of the values written to the Arduino™ pins.

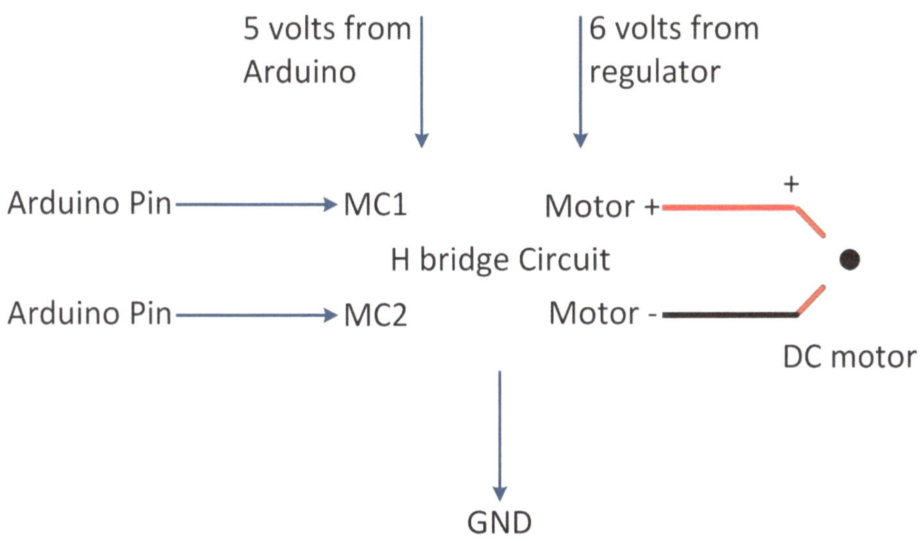

Figure 14-2. H-bridge configured for use with Arduino™ Uno

The H-bridge is an integrated circuit. The five-volt connection to the Arduino™ powers the circuit's logic. The six volts from the voltage regulator is power for the motor. The Arduino™ pins are set to `OUTPUT` mode. If and which direction the DC motor turns depends on the values written to those pins, as shown in Table 14-1.

Table 14-1. Results of Arduino™ pin values

Pin connected to MC1	Pin connected to MC2	Motor
`HIGH`	`HIGH`	`Stops`
`HIGH`	`LOW`	`Turns counterclockwise`
`LOW`	`HIGH`	`Turns clockwise`
`LOW`	`LOW`	`Stops`

14

Speed

Any pair of Arduino™ digital pins can control the direction of a DC motor. If the digital pin connected to MC1 is set to `HIGH` and the digital pin connected to MC2 to `LOW`, the motor will turn clockwise, at full speed. One way to control the speed of a DC motor is to reduce the average voltage. This can be done if one of the digital pins is capable of analog output. Analog output and how it can result in a lower average voltage is discussed in Lesson 9.

For the example just given, the clockwise rotation of the motor can be controlled by setting the pin connected to MC1 to send a series of pulses instead of being set to `HIGH`.

Suppose the motor has connections as seen in Table 14-2.

Table 14-2. Arduino™ pin connections to H-bridge

Arduino™ Pin	H-bridge connection	Notes
3	MC1	Analog-capable
4	MC2	Not analog-capable

The programming statements that cause the motor to turn full-speed counterclockwise are:

```
digitalWrite( 3, HIGH);  // full-speed counterclockwise
digitalWrite( 4, LOW);
```

The following programming statements will also cause the motor to turn full-speed:

```
analogWrite( 3, 255);    // full-speed counterclockwise
digitalWrite( 4, LOW);
```

The speed of the motor can now be reduced by reducing the average output of pin 3. This is accomplished by reducing the second parameter to a value less than 255.

```
analogWrite( 3, 200);  // less than full-speed
digitalWrite( 4, LOW);
```

Note: if the analog-capable pin is set to `LOW` instead of `HIGH`, the speed control process is similar, but instead of reducing the parameter from 255 it is increased from 0. The following statements cause the motor to turn clockwise at full speed:

```
analogWrite( 3, 0);  // Clockwise at full speed
digitalWrite( 4, HIGH);
```

and at reduced speed:

```
analogWrite( 3, 100); // Clockwise at reduced speed
digitalWrite( 4, HIGH);
```

Table 14-3. Vocabulary

Term	Definition
DC motor	A type of motor that uses brushes to cause changes in a magnetic field in order to turn. Requires a two-wire connection, one positive and one negative. Speed is controlled by changing the supplied voltage.
H-bridge	An electronic circuit that can be used to control the polarity of the voltage delivered to a DC motor.

Term	Definition
pinout	A description or cross-reference of each pin of an electrical component and its function. It typically takes the form of a table or diagram.

Description:

The amount of current drawn by a DC motor can be quite high. Further, the speed of a DC motor changes as the supply voltage changes. For these reasons a voltage regulator is used to supply a constant 6 volts from a 9-volt battery pack.

Programming and controlling the DC motor

The programming to control a DC motor is discussed in Background. Unlike working with servo motors (Lesson 11) no library need be imported. The only statements required in the `setup()` method are those for initializing the digital pins to be used to `OUTPUT`. Defining the pin numbers at the beginning of the sketch is simply good practice.

Example 14-1. Initializing sketch for control of DC motor connected to Arduino™ pins 3 and 4

```
#define pinMC1 3
#define pinMC2 4

void setup(){
  pinMode(pinMC1, OUTPUT);
  pinMOde(pinMC2, OUTPUT);
}
```

H-bridge integrated circuit

The actual H-bridge used for this lesson is the L293 integrated circuit from Texas Instruments. The *pinout* of this circuit is shown in Figure 14-3.

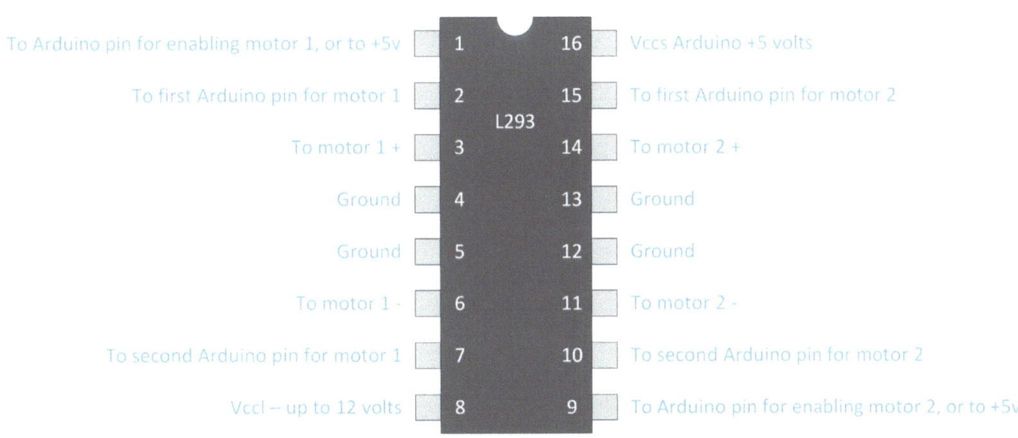

Figure 14-3. Pinout of H-bridge integrated circuit used in this lesson

This circuit is capable of delivering up to one amp per motor, though at such levels a heat sink should be attached. These lessons do not make such demands on the H-bridge, so no heat sink is required.

Goals:

By the end of this lesson readers will

1. Know how to wire a DC motor in such a way as to protect the motor pins and reduce electrical noise.
2. Know how an H-bridge works and how to connect one to a power source, an Arduino™ and to a DC motor.
3. Know how to program an H-bridge to control a motor's direction and speed.

Materials:

Quantity	Part	Image	Notes	Catalog Number
1	Arduino™ Uno		Single-board computer. This board is delicate and should be handled with care. When you are not using it, keep it in a box or plastic bag.	3102
1	USB Cable		This is a standard USB adapter cable with a flat connector on one end and a square connector on the other.	2301
1	Computer with at least one USB port and access to the Arduino™ website, http://www.arduino.cc.	---	The operating system of this computer must be Windows, Macintosh OS/X, or Linux.	---
1	DC motor		DC motor attached to gears.	3132
1	Battery holder		Holds 6 AA cells for a total of +9 volts.	3114

Quan-tity	Part	Image	Notes	Catalog Number
1	Voltage regulator		6-volt regulator capable of delivering up to 1 amp.	1104
1	Capacitor	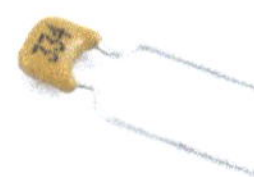	0.33 mfd	0202
1	Capacitor		0.1 mfd	0203
1	Bread-board		Used for prototyping.	3104
As req'd.	Jumper wires	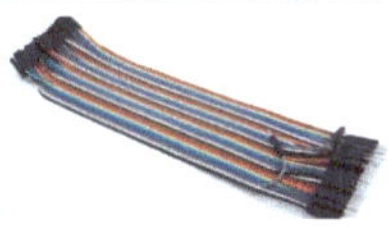	Used with bread-boards for wiring the components.	3105
1	Plug	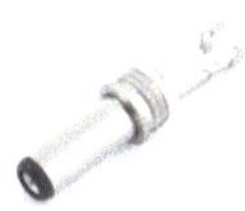	Fit Arduino™ power jack. 2.1mm.	3109
6	Alkaline cells		1.5 volt, AA to fit battery holder.	3118
1	H-bridge		Can be used to control one or two DC motors.	1307

14

Procedure:

1. Attach the power plug to the wires of the battery holder. The red wire solders to the center tab of the holder and the black to the outside tab, as shown in Figure 14-4.

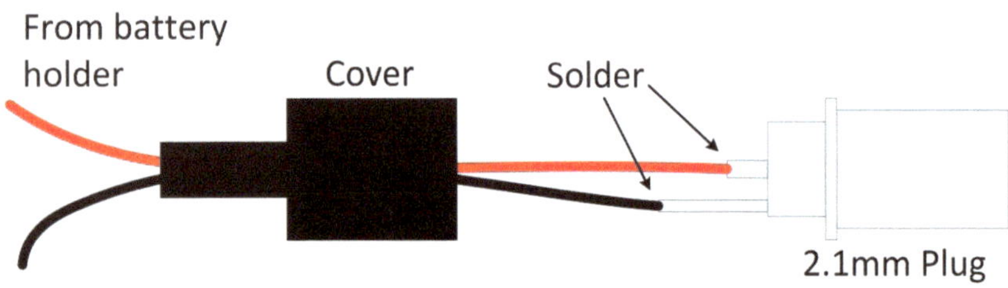

Figure 14-4. Power plug assembly

2. Prepare the DC motor for connection to the H-bridge.

Caution	The terminals of the DC motor are delicate and easily broken. The wiring technique shown here will protect these terminals.

   a. Begin by attaching the 0.1 microfarad capacitor across the motor terminals. Do not solder the connections yet.

Figure 14-5. Attaching capacitor to terminals of DC motor

   b. Cut 12-inch lengths each of red and black #24 solid copper hookup wire. Bare approximately ¼ inch of wire at each end of each wire. Solder the wires to the motor terminals, taking care to solder the capacitor leads as well.

   c. Route each wire under the plastic motor retainer and tie a knot over the top. The purpose of this knot is to protect the motor terminals from flexing when the red and black wires are moved.

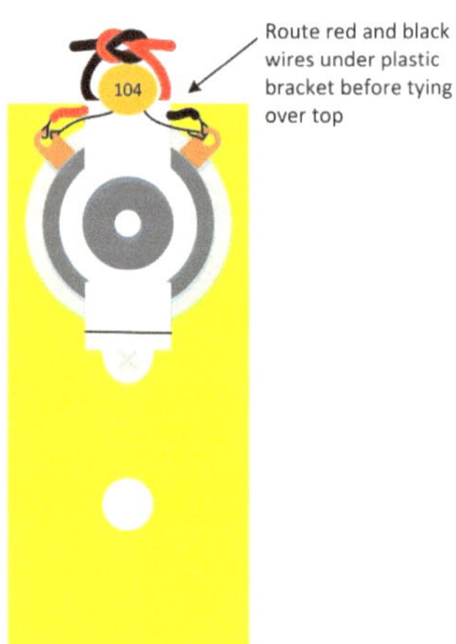

Figure 14-6. Wire routing on DC motor with square knot

d. Twist the remainder of the red and black wire tightly together.

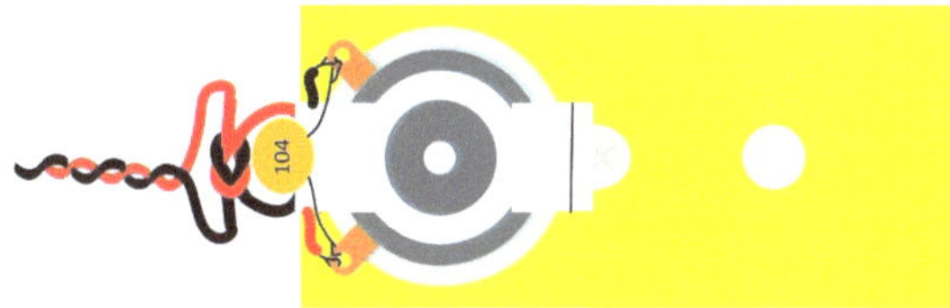

Figure 14-7. Twisted wire routing on DC motor

Together, the capacitor and wire twisting act to reduce the electrical interference caused by the motor's brushes.

3. Connect the DC motor and the H-bridge integrated circuit to the Arduino™ as shown in Figure 14-8. Notice how the voltage regulator is used to supply the H-bridge with 6 volts.

Caution	A mistake in wiring that shorts the output of the voltage regulator to ground can cause the regulator to become very hot, hot enough to raise a blister if touched. Take care with the wiring.

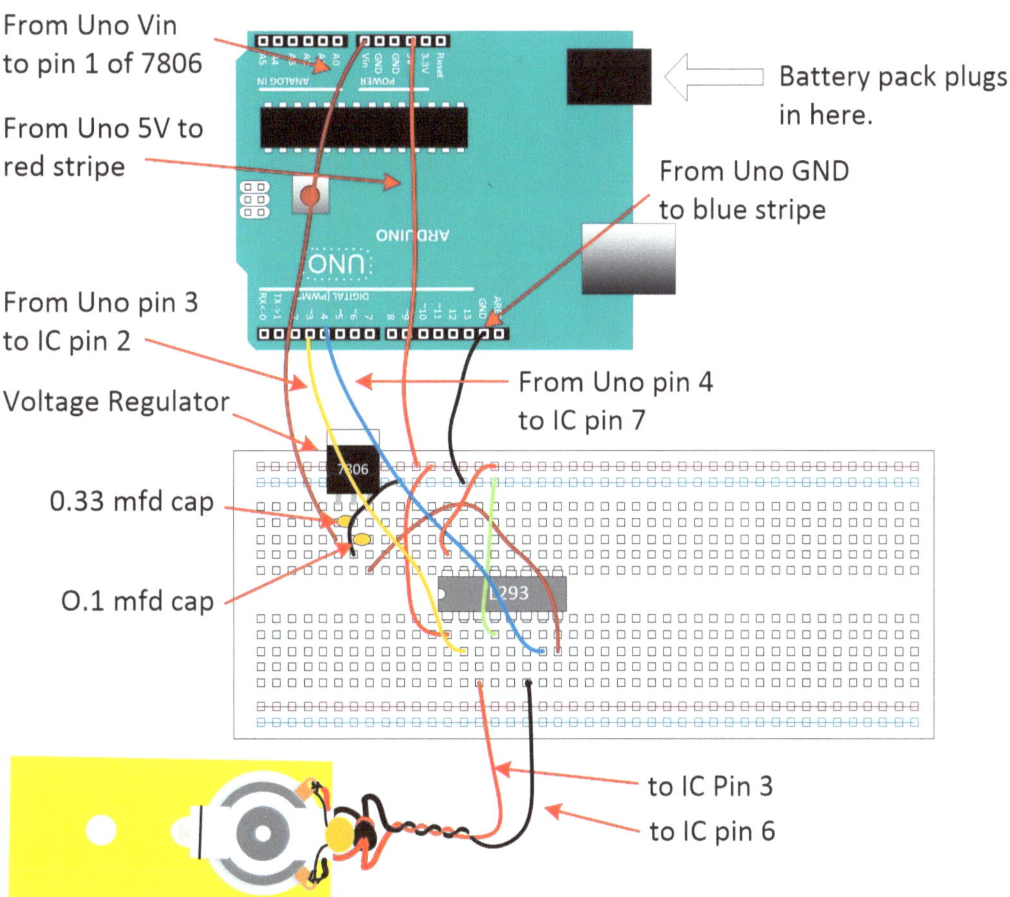

Figure 14-8. Wiring diagram for control of DC motor by Arduino™ via H-bridge

14

4. Place the six AA cells in the battery holder and plug it into the Arduino.™ The green "ON" light on the Arduino™ should be lit. The motor might or might not start to turn. This depends on the state of pins 3 and 4 from whatever sketch was uploaded to the Arduino.™

5. Connect the Arduino™ to the computer and open the Arduino™ IDE. Create a new sketch. Name it `Lesson14DCMotorTest`.

6. Enter the following programming statements into this new sketch. This sketch can also be downloaded from LearnCSE.com.

Complete listing 14-1. `Lesson14DCMotorTest`

```
/* Lesson14DCMotortest.ino
 * by W. P. Osborne
 * 7/5/15
 */

#define MC1 3   // pin to connect to MC1
#define MC2 4   // pin to connect to MC2
#define CW 1    // motor to turn clockwise
#define CCW 2   // motor to turn counterclockwise
#define STOPMOTOR 3   // motor to stop


void setup() {
  // Initialize the pins sending the control
  // signals to the h bridge IC
  pinMode(MC1, OUTPUT);
  pinMode(MC2, OUTPUT);
}

void loop() {
  // run counterclockwise for five seconds
  runMotor(CW);
  delay(5000);

  // stop for one second
  runMotor(STOPMOTOR);
  delay(1000);

  // run counterclockwise for five seconds
  runMotor(CCW);
  delay(5000);


  // stop for three seconds
  runMotor(STOPMOTOR);
  delay(3000);
}

// PRECONDITION: direction is set to CW, CCW, or
// STOPMOTOR. Other values are ignored.
// POSTCONDITION: if the value of direction is recognized
```

14

```
// the MC1 and MC2 pins of the Arduino™ are set to the
// values required to set the direction of the motor
// attached to the h-bridge.
void runMotor(byte direction){
  if(direction == CW){
    digitalWrite(MC1, LOW);
    digitalWrite(MC2, HIGH);
  } else if(direction == CCW){
    digitalWrite(MC1, HIGH);
    digitalWrite(MC2, LOW);
  } else if(direction == STOPMOTOR){
    digitalWrite(MC1, LOW);
    digitalWrite(MC2, LOW);
  }
}
```

Notice the following about this sketch:

- It makes use of definitions at the top to create constants that can be referred to in the programming code. This improves the readability of the statements.
- The actual commands are sent to the H-bridge via a helper method, `runMotor`.

Exercise:

Exercise 14-1. Changing turning direction and speed

Create a new sketch named `Lesson14Exercise1` that is identical to the sketch called `Lesson14DCMotorTest.ino` except that the `loop()` method in the new sketch is modified so that after turning counterclockwise for five seconds the motor pauses one second, turns clockwise at a noticeably slower rate for five seconds, pauses for one second, turns counterclockwise at the same slower rate for five seconds, then pauses three seconds.

Lesson 15 | Infrared Navigation

The Big Idea:

The content of the previous lessons can be combined to make something new. Such combinations are called *integrating projects*. This lesson's integrating project is a rolling robot that combines infrared-emitting diodes (IREDs), infrared sensors, resistors, and servos. This robot can detect and turn away from or toward obstacles. With a different sketch, described in Lesson 18, this robot can be operated from an ordinary remote control.

Background:

This is the first lesson about integration, the combining of the contents of the previous lessons to make a device that actually does something new. By the end of the lesson, you will have assembled completely from scratch a rolling robot capable of detecting and avoiding obstacles. The robot motors are a pair of DC motors of the type explored in Lesson 14. The infrared headlights of Lesson 13 illuminate the robot's path ahead, and the infrared sensors of Lesson 12 identify the presence and location of obstacles. The programming of all the previous lessons is used in the creation of a sketch that operates the infrared devices, interprets what is seen, decides what to do, and executes the decision with commands to the motors.

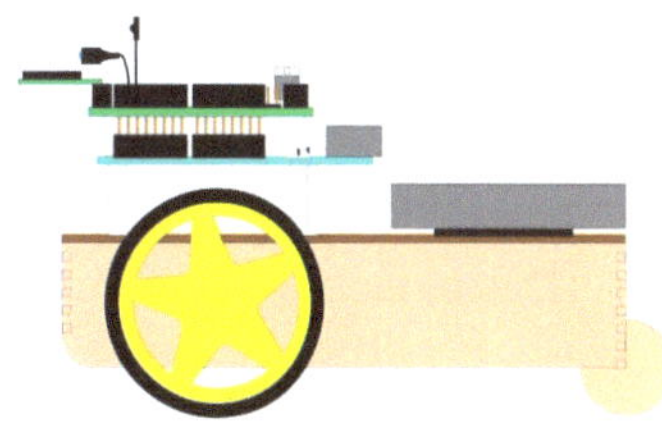

Figure 15-1. Rolling robot side view

The principles of the starting sketch are pretty simple. If no obstacles are detected, the robot moves forward. If an obstacle is detected ahead and to one side or the other, the robot turns away from that side. If obstacles are seen ahead on both sides, the robot backs up. One of the exercises calls for adding sufficient sophistication to this sketch to allow the robot to find its way through a maze.

Because this is a project that results in a working device, some compon,ents need to be procured or fabricated. These are:

1. A *chassis*, the box that serves as the robot body. The Arduino,™ the motors, and the rear wheels are attached to the chassis.

2. A navigation circuit board to which the electronic components are connected. The motor controller shield or *Arduino™ shield* described in "How-To #3" works well for this project. Because it is a "shield," it plugs neatly into the top of the Arduino,™ adding a solderless connection prototyping board and full access to all the pins and voltages of the Arduino.™ Instructions can be found in the How-To section of this book and at LearnCSE.com.

3. An H-bridge circuit board to enable the Arduino™ to control power delivered to the motors. Instructions for this device are in the How-To section of LearnCSE.com.
4. DC motors with gearing appropriate for a small rolling robot.
5. Wheels to be attached to the DC motors.
6. Infrared headlights. These are simply two of the IR headlights assembled for Lesson 13. Instructions can also be found in "How to Make an Infrared Headlight" on LearnCSE.com.

As first constructed, the robot will behave much as any other IR-guided rolling robot, such as the Parallax Boe-Bot. But the design allows for some important differences. Among these are:

1. The robot's dimensions allow for adoption of other motors, including the popular VEX model 393. However, these motors mount and attach to their wheels differently, requiring the maker to modify the side panels.
2. The choice of wood as the building material provides a solid base that is easily modified and extended with inexpensive hand tools and common materials.
3. The surface has mounting holes specifically for the Arduino™ Uno, although other single-board computers can be accommodated.
4. In addition to the Arduino,™ the surface provides sufficient room for a battery holder containing six AA alkaline cells or a rechargeable battery if more powerful motors are used.
5. The top surface has unallocated space suitable for additional circuit boards. One such board is for power regulation and distribution for the VEX motors.

About bread-boards

None of the lessons leading up to this one has required a circuit board. Rather, a bread-board and jumper wires have been used to connect all electronic components. This project, however, does not offer an opportunity to use a bread-board.

Certainly the circuit could be prototyped on a bread-board. But that option has been omitted because of the complexity of the circuit. The number of jumper wires required to connect a voltage regulator, two capacitors, two resistors, two infrared sensors, two infrared headlights, and two motors is just too great to have a reasonable expectation of correct wiring or of the wiring staying in place, even when correctly done.

In place of the bread-board, two circuit boards are constructed using the parts from earlier lessons. These are the motor controller shield and the H-bridge. The motor controller shield includes a small bread-board for prototyping the IR sensing components and, later in Lesson 18, the components necessary to capture the messages from a remote control.

About power

This rolling robot is powered by six AA batteries, producing approximately +9 volts. The motor controller shield uses a voltage regulator to provide a stable +6 volts to the DC motors.

Table 15-1. Vocabulary

Term	Definition
Arduino™ shield	A printed circuit board configured in such a way as to plug directly into a full-sized Arduino™ single-board computer and, by doing so, add capability. The Arduino™ shield is also called the motor controller shield.
chassis	The rigid body of the rolling robot, although the term is also used to refer to the rigid container of components in many devices, including cell phones and automobiles.
integrating project	A project that uses material learned in previous lessons and applies them to something new, in this case a rolling robot that can sense and respond to its environment.
pivot	A turn in which the inside wheel of the spin is stationary while only the outside wheel turns.

Description:

The robot constructed here is using infrared sensors and headlights to enable writing sketches for the following behaviors:

- Detecting and turning away from obstacles: useful for maze navigation.
- Following a wall: a common strategy for escaping a maze.
- Detecting and turning toward an obstacle: useful for robot "combat."
- Closing in on but maintaining a distance from an obstacle. This has been used for follow-the-leader activities in which one robot leads several others.

Materials:

Quantity	Part[1]	Image	Notes	Catalog Number
1	Arduino™ Uno		Single-board computer. This board is delicate and should be handled with care. When you are not using it, keep it in a box or plastic bag.	3102
1	USB Cable		This is a standard USB adapter cable with a flat connector on one end and a square connector on the other.	2301
1	Computer with at least one USB port and access to the Arduino™ website, http://www.arduino.cc.	---	The operating system of this computer must be Windows, Macintosh OS/X, or Linux.	---
1	Chassis and related hardware[2]		Rolling robot chassis for two DC motors, including Arduino™ mounting hardware and rear wheel assembly.	3110
2	DC Motors		Geared DC motors, six volts.	3132
2	Wheels		Rubber-tired wheel to fit DC motor.	3133
1	Battery Holder		For six AA cells, flat, with power connector.	3131
6	Alkaline Cells, AA		1.5 volt.	3118

Notes:

1. Part numbers refer to the Parts Catalog on LearnCSE.com. The catalog identifies possible sources.
2. LearnCSE.com offers plans for making this body from scratch. A kit that includes all mounting hardware is also available from the website.

Goals:

By the end of this lesson readers will:

1. Understand that in order to perform predictably a robot must have some means of detecting and responding to its surroundings.
2. Know how infrared-emitting diodes and infrared sensors can be used by an Arduino™ sketch to detect nearby objects.
3. Know how to assemble a rolling robot powered by two DC motors and to mount on that robot an Arduino,™ an Arduino™ motor controller shield, and a nine-volt power supply.
4. Be able to program the robot to avoid obstacles and to find its way out of a maze.

Procedure:

Mechanical Assembly

1. Assemble the robot chassis by following the instructions of "How To Assemble a Rolling Robot Chassis" found on LearnCSE.com. With the Arduino™ attached to the standoffs, the robot should look like Figure 15-2.

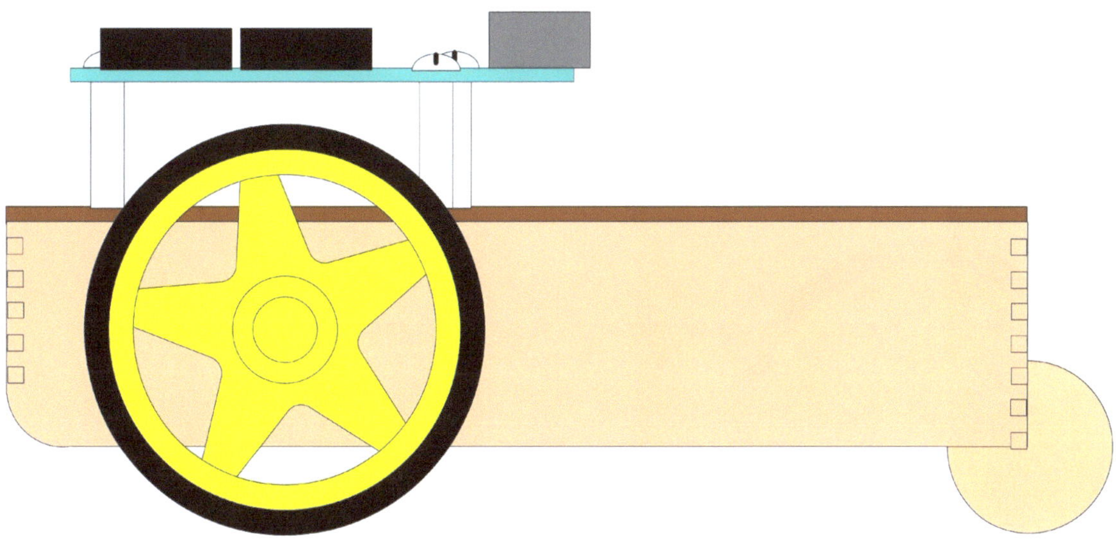

Figure 15-2. Assembled rolling robot chassis with Arduino™ attached

2. Assemble the motor controller shield by following the instructions in "How To Make and Assemble a Motor Controller." Viewed from the top, this shield will look like Figure 15-3.

15

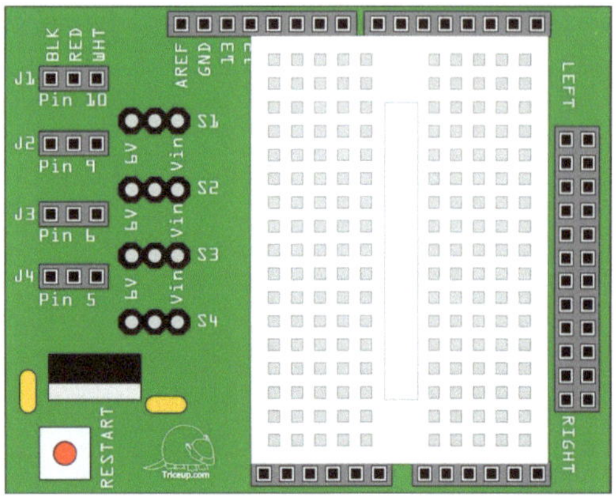

Figure 15-3. Arduino™ motor controller shield

Note	The circuit board shown in Figure 15-3 is green, but the actual color of your circuit board may be different. Circuit boards manufactured by OSH Park, for example, are purple.

3. Plug the shield into the Arduino™ on the top of the robot chassis.

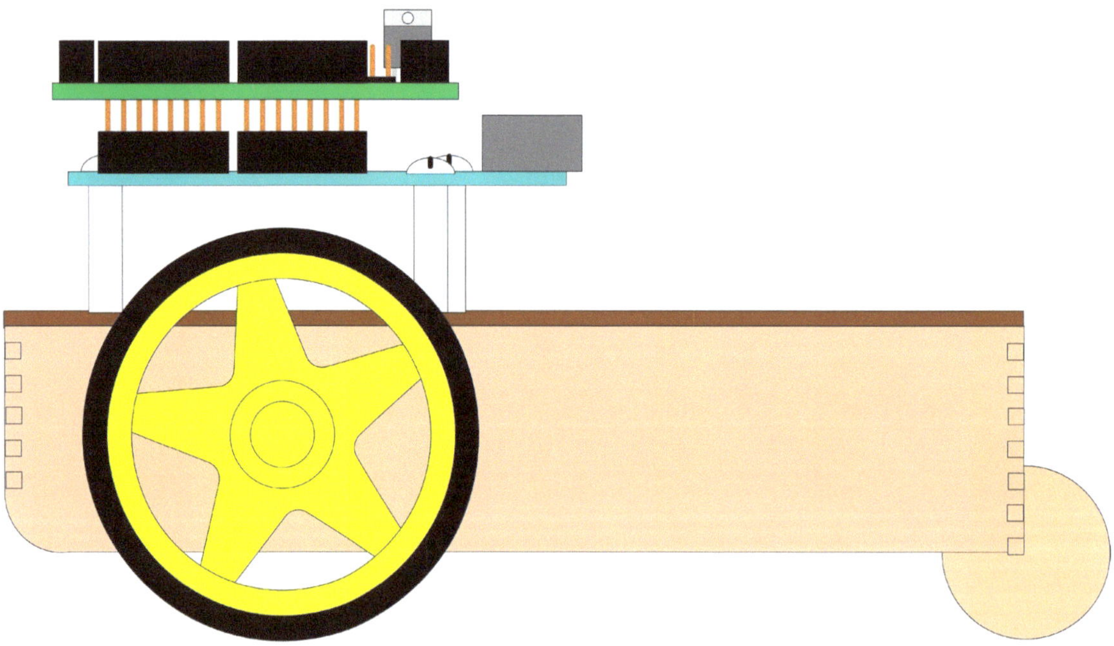

Figure 15-4. Rolling robot chassis with motor controller shield attached to Arduino™

4. Apply the hook half of a 1"-long strip of Velcro ribbon to the top of the robot deck for securing the battery holder.

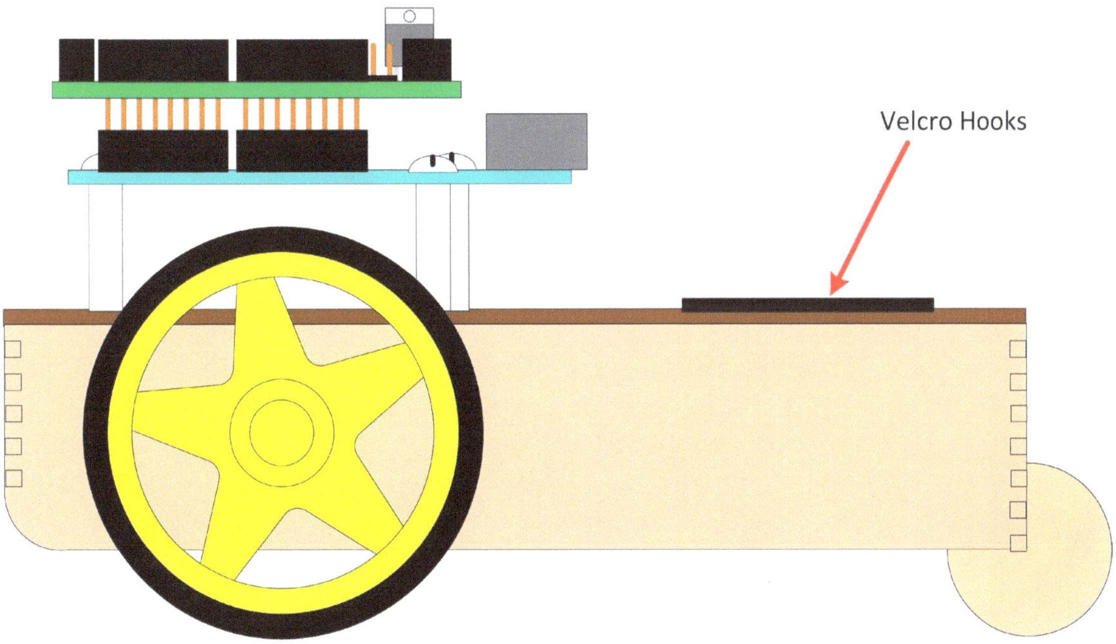

Figure 15-5. Velcro hook placement on rolling robot chassis

5. Solder the power plug that comes with the battery holder to the holder's red and black wires. The red wire is soldered to the center pin and the black to the outside pin, as shown in Figure 15-6.

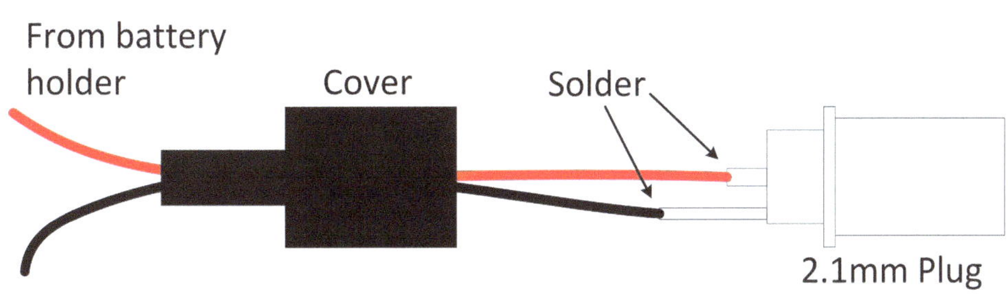

Figure 15-6. Power plug wiring

6. Holding the battery holder crossways on the rear deck of the robot chassis, determine where to put the eye (soft) half of the 1-inch-long strip of Velco ribbon such that it can secure the battery holder. Attach the strip to the bottom of the battery holder.

15

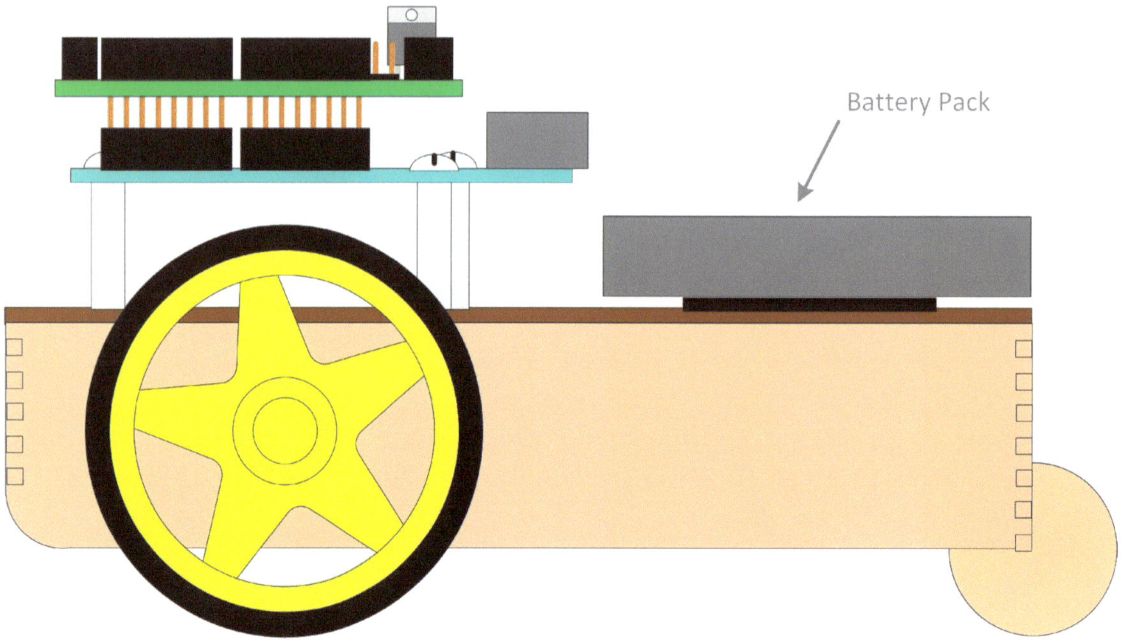

Figure 15-7. Securing battery pack to Velcro

7. Plug the H-bridge circuit board into the outside row of connectors in J9, the double-row female header.

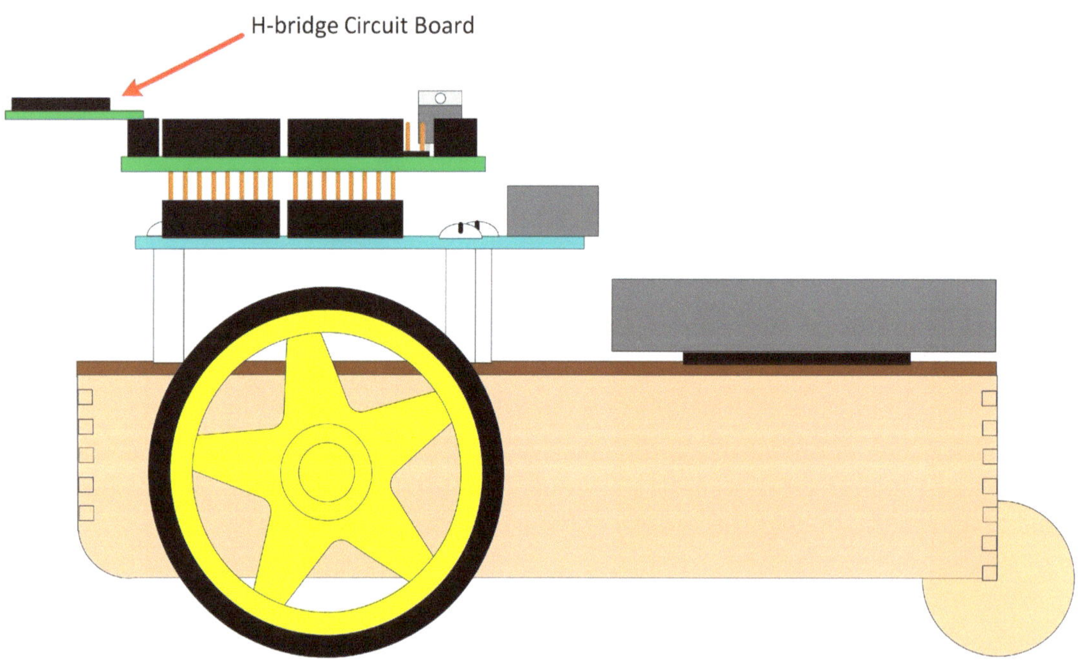

Figure 15-8. Plugging H-bridge into female header

8. Insert the red and black wires from each of the DC motors into the female header holding the H-bridge circuit board as shown in Figure 15-9. Be sure to insert the red wires opposite the M1+ and M2+ pins; insert the black wires opposite the M1- and M2- pins.

Figure 15-9. Inserting the red and black wires into female header

9. Stop and test the robot:

    a. Connect the Arduino™ to your computer. Check to make sure the green power light on the Arduino™ is lit. If it is not a wiring or soldering error has occurred shorting 5 volts to GND. The cause must be found and resolved before proceeding. The most common cause is solder bridging two pins on either the Motor Controller shield or the H-bridge breakout board.

    b. Upload Lesson15MotorTest.ino. This sketch may be downloaded from LearnCSE.com. Save the zip file to your Arduino™ sketchbook folder and unzip in place. Start, or restart, the Arduino™ IDE. The sketch should now appear in your sketchbook.

    c. Insert six AA batteries in the battery holder. Be sure to get the + / - orientation correct. A single cell placed in the holder backwards will prevent the motors from turning or cause them to turn very slowly.

    d. Plug the battery pack plug into the Arduino™.

Caution	At no time should anything on the Arduino,™ the motor controller shield, or the H-bridge become hot. Nor should the batteries become warm. But if +6 volts is somehow shorted to GND, the voltage regulator can become hot enough to raise a blister on a finger. And if Vin is shorted to ground the AA cells can get hot enough to melt the battery holder, although this doesn't happen instantly.

    e. The robot wheels should begin to turn. Place the robot on the floor and observe. The pattern should be:

i. Go forward 3 seconds

ii. Pause 2 seconds

iii. Reverse 3 seconds

iv. Pause 2 seconds

v. Spin clockwise (right) for 3 seconds

vi. Pause 2 seconds

vii. Spin counterclockwise (left) for 3 seconds

viii. Stop and remain still for 5 seconds.

If the robot does not move in precisely this pattern check for wiring errors. If it moves but the order of events is wrong then one or both of the motors has its wires reversed. A simple fix is simply to reverse them where they plug into the header connected to the H-bridge.

If the robot does not move at all then a soldering error of some sort has occurred. Check for pins on the H-bridge and motor controller that are not properly soldered to their circular pads.

10. Use the bread-board of the motor controller shield to wire the infrared headlight and sensor circuit shown in Figure 15-10.

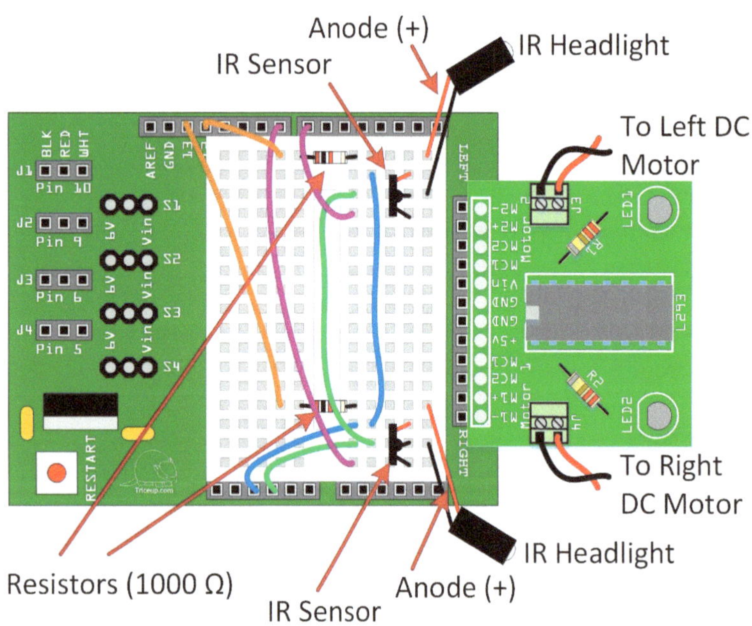

Figure 15-10. Infrared headlight and sensor circuit pictorial

Your rolling robot is now complete.

11. Download the sketch `Lesson15HBridgeIRNav.ino` from the Learn To Program page of LearnCSE.com. Unzip the file in place in your Arduino™ folder, then upload the sketch to your robot. Put six AA cells in the battery pack and plug it into the Arduino.™ Your robot should move forward unless reflected infrared light is detected. The robot should turn away from obstacles, even backing up if the obstacle is directly ahead.

Exercises:

Exercise 15-1. Robot corner

At some point you will want your robot to find its way through a simple maze. Currently the DC motors turn rather quickly and can overcompensate for a detected obstacle. Slow this process down to make obstacle detection more graceful without slowing the straight-ahead speed. Notice that the speed of each motor is specified by a variable declared near the top of the `Lesson15HBridgeIRNav.ino` sketch, `speedMotorLeft` for the left motor and `speedMotorRight` for the right motor.

These values are interpreted by the sketch as the percentage of full speed each motor is to turn. A percentage of 100 means full speed, while 0 means stop. (Values set at over 100 are treated as 100, and values set at less than 0 are treated as 0.) In practice you need to be careful with values less than 30. This is because, as learned in Lesson 9, what is really happening is the motor is being turned on and off several times a second. The slower it appears to be turning, the longer the off periods are compared with the on periods. And, each time the motor is turned on, it must overcome the inertia of being off. If this inertia is great, such as when a robot is at rest, the on period might not be long enough to overcome the inertia and result in movement.

Save the sketch with the new name `Lesson15Exercise1.ino`. Then modify this new sketch so that the robot spins left, spins right, moves forward at full speed, and reverses slowly when responding to detection of an obstacle.

Exercise 15-2. Robot combat

The default sketch for this robot has the robot moving away from obstacles. Save a copy of the `Lesson15HBridgeIRNav.ino` sketch as `Lesson15Exercise2.ino`. Then modify this copy to do the following:

1. run at half speed or slower when no object is detected directly ahead
2. turn toward a detected object instead of turning away
3. increase the robot's speed to 100 percent in an attempt to hit an object that is directly ahead, as detected by both IR sensors.

Exercise 15-3. Pivot instead of spin

Make a copy of the sketch `Lesson15HBridgeIRNav.ino` and save it as `Lesson15Exercise3`. Modify `Lesson15Exercise3.ino` such that instead of having your robot spin away from a detected obstacle, the robot pivots smoothly. In a pivot, the inside wheel of the spin remains stationary while only the outside wheel turns. Modify the method `spinRight()`, then, such that the left wheel turns counterclockwise while the right wheel is stationary. The method `spinLeft()` holds the left wheel stationary while the right wheel turns clockwise. Slowing the turning motor as it turns tends to make the movement more graceful.

Lesson 16 | Sony IR Protocol

The Big Idea:

The common television remote control encodes messages in infrared light. These messages can be received and decoded with an infrared sensor (Lesson 12) and an Arduino.™ Being able to decode these messages enables two possibilities. The first is that remote controls can be used to control devices, such as robots and musical instruments, operated by the Arduino.™ The second is that by understanding how messages are encoded, you can program an Arduino™ to transmit its own messages via an infrared headlight, as used in Lesson 13. This combination of being able to receive and decode infrared messages, along with the ability to encode and transmit messages, enables an entire class of Arduino™ devices, such as communicators and laser tag.

Background:

Infrared used in Lessons 12, 13, and 15 was limited to the illumination and detection of obstacles. No actual information is exchanged. But by turning the infrared light on and off in patterns, actual information can be conveyed. And this is precisely what entertainment remote controls do. Pressing a button on a remote control causes a message to be sent. This message has two parts—the address and the command (Figure 16-1).

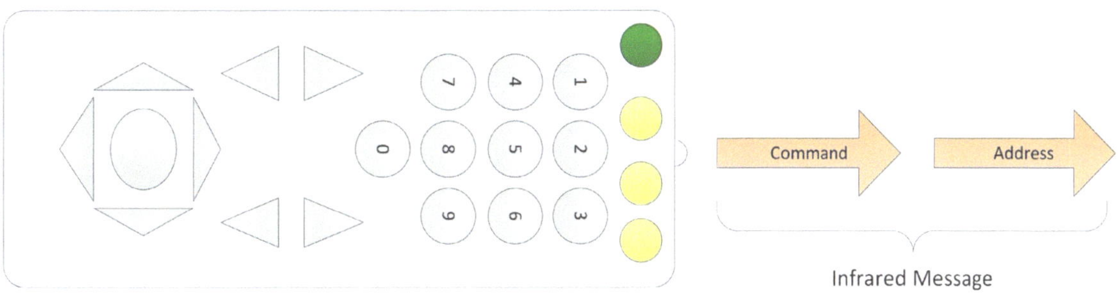

Figure 16-1. Infrared remote control and message

Table 16-1. Parts of an infrared message

Command	The action the device is to take. Examples are: increase volume, switch to a different channel, start playing.
Address	The identification of the device that is to respond to the command. Examples are: television, DVD player, satellite box.

The message is encoded by turning the infrared transmitter on and off in a pattern of pulses. Different manufacturers have different methods of encoding messages. In these lessons we use the method employed by the Sony Corporation and refer to it as the *Sony Infrared (IR) Protocol.*

Table 16-2. Vocabulary

Term	Definition
carrier signal	The base frequency of the infrared as it comes from the diode. In this class this frequency is 38,500 Hertz (cycles per second).
communications protocol	The set of rules used to encode and decode the information imposed with PWM on the carrier signal.
pulse width modulation (PWM)	The encoding of the carrier signal by turning it on and off in a pattern.
resting states	A period of no IR signal of a specific length that indicates the start of an encoded message.
Sony Infrared (IR) Protocol	The method of encoding infrared messages transmitted between remote controls and the Arduino™ that is used by Sony and other manufacturers and has become a de facto standard.

Description:

Recall that the output of the infrared sensor is `HIGH` when no infrared is detected and that this drops to `LOW` when infrared is detected. This is illustrated in Figure 16-2.

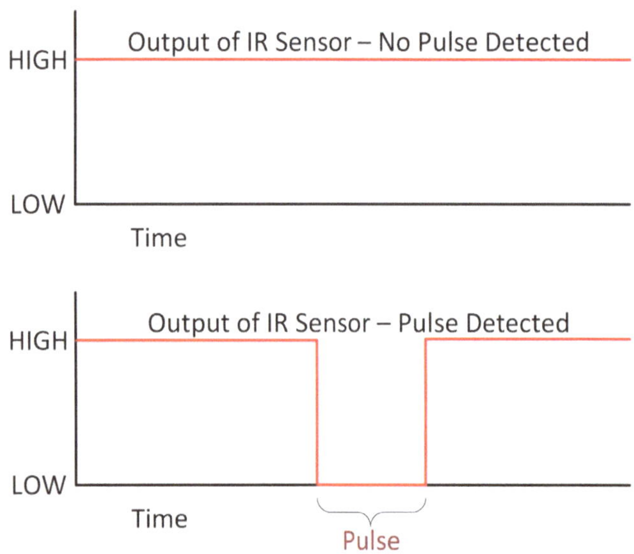

Figure 16-2. Pulse as it appears on the output of an infrared sensor

With this in mind, consider the format of a Sony-protocol infrared message as it appears on the output pin of an infrared sensor. This message has three parts, as shown in Table 16-3.

Table 16-3. The three parts of a Sony-protocol infrared message

Start	A pulse of unusual length that follows a period of no pulse. The start pulse indicates the beginning of a message.
Command	A set of seven pulses that indicates a pattern of seven ones and zeroes. This is a number in binary form. The value of that number indicates the action to be taken.
Address	A set of five pulses that indicates a pattern of five ones and zeroes. This, too, is a number in binary form. The value of this number identifies which device is to respond to the command.

Figure 16-3 is a diagram of a typical Sony-protocol infrared message. Notice that pulses are separated by so-called resting states. The duration of a data pulse indicates its value. A pulse duration of 0.6 milliseconds, for example, indicates that the bit's value is zero. A bit of one is indicated by a pulse duration of 1.2 milliseconds. The start pulse is 2.4 milliseconds.

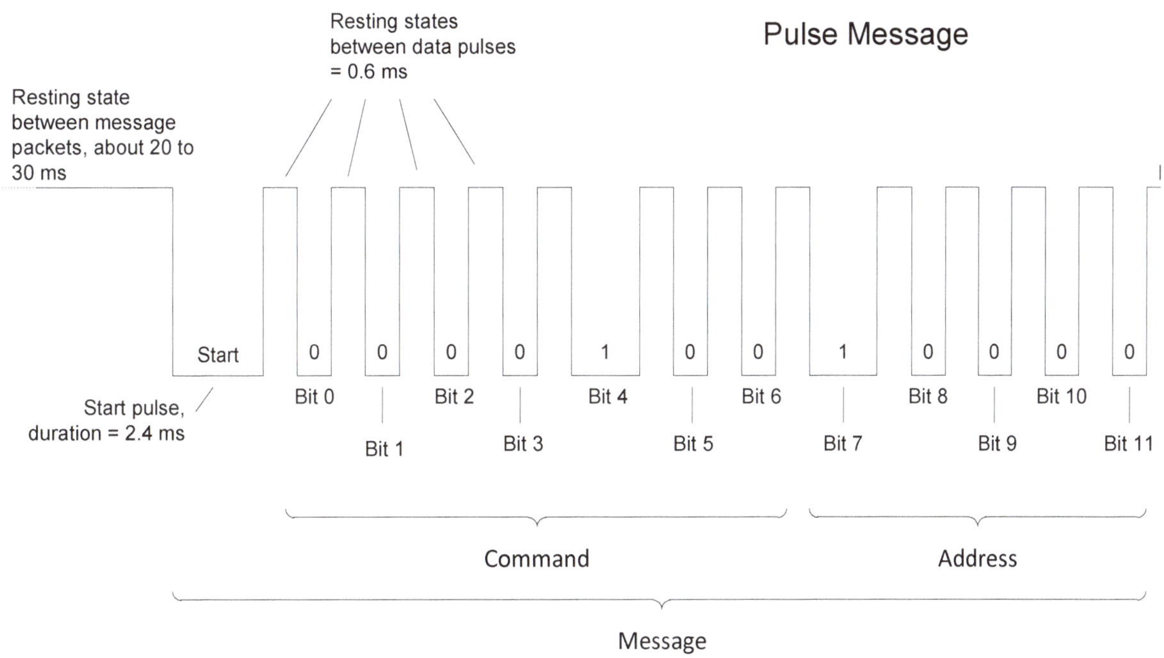

Figure 16-3. Format of a Sony-protocol infrared message

16

Detecting and decoding a Sony-protocol IR message is a four-step process, as shown in Table 16-4.

Table 16-4. Steps for detecting and decoding a Sony-formatted message

Step 1:	Wait for the beginning of a message. In this step the Arduino™ program waits for the output of the infrared sensor to drop to zero. If this doesn't happen within the time expected for a rest period, then we stop and return without doing anything more. There's no message. But, if the output does drop, then IR is detected.
Step 2:	Measure the duration of this first pulse. If it is not about 2.4 ms, then the pulse is not a Start pulse. Return without doing anything more. But if the duration is about 2.4 ms, then a start pulse has been detected. The next 12 pulses are the command and message.
Step 3:	Get the next 12 pulses and determine the command and address. If there are fewer than 12 detected pulses or if a pulse exceeds 1.2 ms or if a rest period is longer than 0.6 ms, then return without doing anything more.
Step 4:	If all 12 pulses are detected and are either 1.2 ms or 0.6 ms, then decode the message into its command and address; then return. Detection is a success.

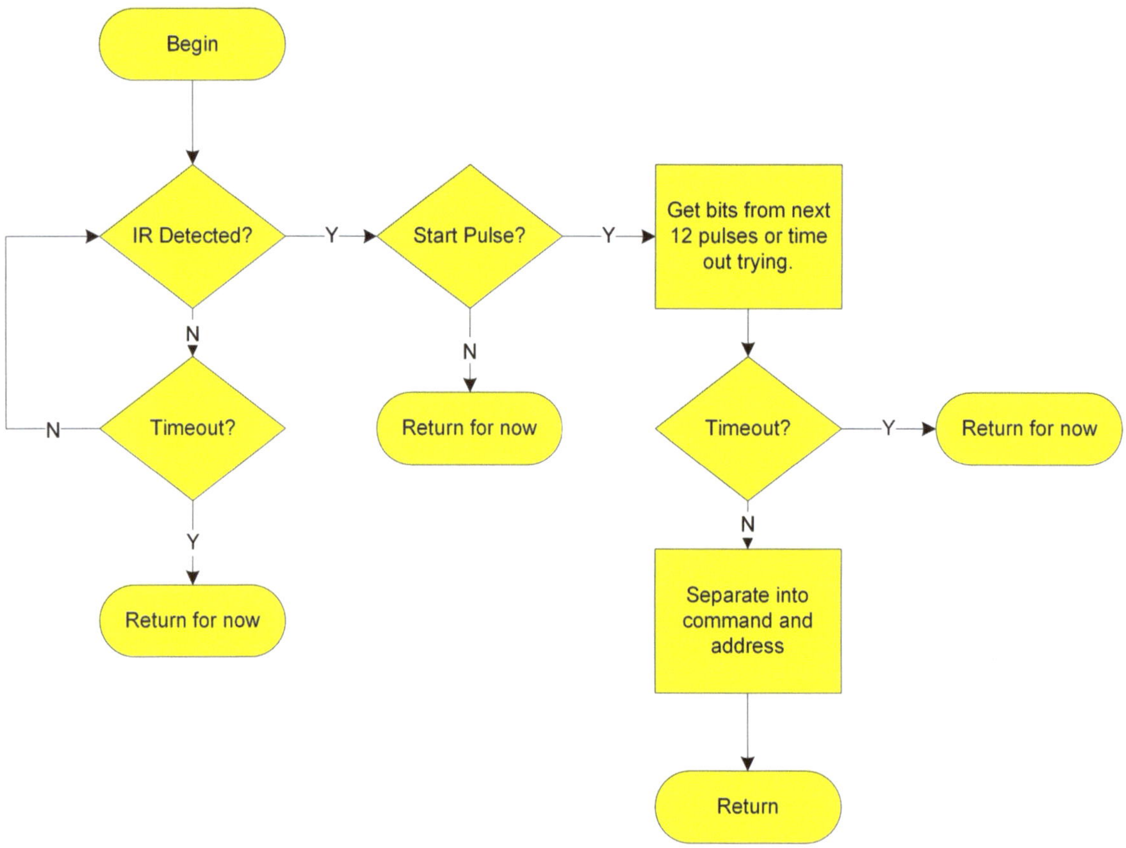

Figure 16-4. Flow chart of detecting and decoding Sony-protocol infrared message

Goals:

By the end of this lesson readers will:

1. Know that an ordinary television remote control uses infrared technology to send commands.
2. Know that each button on the remote sends different information identifying which button is being pushed. Further, this information is conveyed by turning the infrared light on and off in a pattern.
3. Know the definitions of:
   a. Pulse width modulation (PWM)
   b. Carrier signal
   c. Communications protocol
   d. Resting time between messages
4. Know that each time a button is pushed on a Sony remote control, an infrared message is transmitted and that this message has two components: the address of the device to be controlled and the actual command.
5. Extend your knowledge of the new C-language commands used with the Arduino.™
   a. PIND: a special variable that reflects the input status of Arduino™ ports 0 through 7 in a single byte.
   b. << : a special operation on a byte that shifts all the bits to the left.
   c. DEC: a formatting command used with Serial.print and Serial.println to display binary data as decimal.
6. Be able to write a C-language program that can detect and decode a Sony-protocol message, yielding both the command and address.

16

Materials:

Quan-tity	Part	Image	Notes	Catalog Number
1	Arduino™ Uno		Single-board computer. This board is delicate and should be handled with care. When you are not using it, keep it in a box or plastic bag.	3102
1	USB Cable		This is a standard USB adapter cable with a flat connector on one end and a square connector on the other.	2301
1	Computer with at least one USB port and access to the Arduino™ website, http://www.arduino.cc.	---	The operating system of this computer must be Windows, Macintosh OS/X, or Linux.	---
1	Infrared sensor		3-pin, 38kHz.	1302

IR Sensor	Connection on Arduino™	
Pin 1	Pin 5	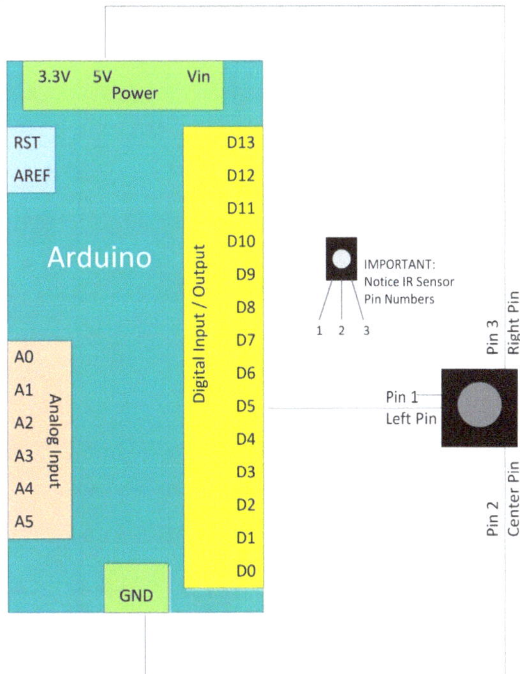
Pin 2	GND	
Pin 3	+5 volts	

Figure 16-5. Schematic of connection between IR sensor and Arduino™

Procedure:

1. Connect an infrared sensor to an Arduino™ as shown in Figure 16-5.

Important	Remember this is a schematic, not a pictorial. Pin 1 is NOT the center pin of the IR sensor!

2. Create a new folder inside the Arduino™ sketch folder. Name it `Lesson16SonyIRProtocol`. THE NAME IS IMPORTANT, both the upper- and the lowercase letters.
   a. Download the Arduino™ sketch Lesson16SonyIRProtocol.ino. Save it in the folder created in step 2. This sketch is available from Lesson 16 at LearnCSE.com.
3. Open the Arduino™ IDE. Then, from the menu, select File -> Sketchbook and open `Lesson16SonyIRProtocol.ino`.
4. Run the program to verify it works.
5. Complete Table 16-5, which lists for each button on the remote control the address and command code it transmits for each of the types of devices it can control.

16

Table 16-5. Sony-protocol remote control addresses and commands

	Television		Satellite/Cable		DVD		Other: ______	
Button	**Ad-dress**	**Com-mand**	**Ad-dress**	**Com-mand**	**Ad-dress**	**Com-mand**	**Ad-dress**	**Com-mand**
1	1	0						
2	1	1						
3	1	2						
4	1	3						
5								
6								
7								
8								
9								
Vol up								
Vol dn								
Ch up								
Ch dn								
Stop								

	Television		Satellite/Cable		DVD		Other: ________	
Button	Ad-dress	Com-mand	Ad-dress	Com-mand	Ad-dress	Com-mand	Ad-dress	Com-mand

Exercises:

Exercise 16-1. Draw a flow chart of `Lesson16SonyIRProtocol` sketch

Look at the flow chart in this lesson; then look at the code in your sketch. Draw a flow chart that reflects how the sketch actually works. Is it different from the flow chart? If yes, in what ways?

Exercise 16-2. Modify `PrintFull()` to print device addresses and names of buttons

Modify the `PrintFull()` method to print in text the device for the address and the name of each button pushed.

16

Lesson 17 | Control Tone with IR Remote

The Big Idea:

The ability to detect and decode Sony-protocol infrared messages, which was explored in Lesson 16, can be added to any Arduino™ sketch. This means that with the addition of an infrared sensor, an Arduino™ sketch can be made to respond to the buttons being pushed on a remote control.

This lesson combines this remote controllability with the techniques for generating musical notes explored in Lesson 10 to transform a television remote into a sort of musical instrument.

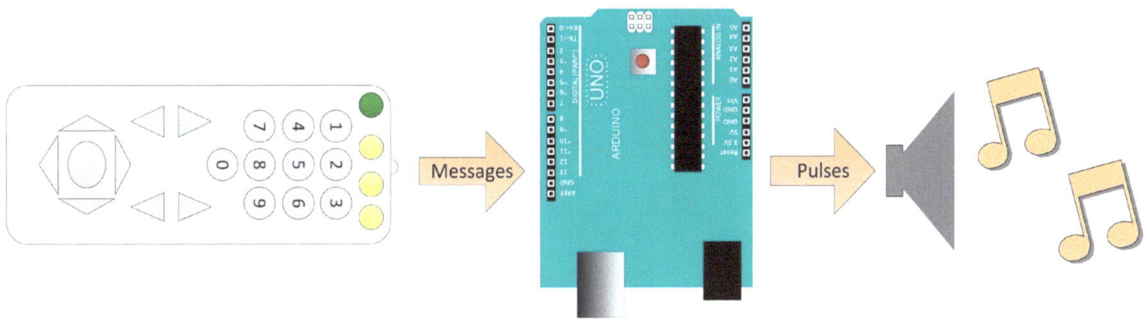

Figure 17-1. Create musical instrument using remote control, Arduino™ and speaker

Background:

Clearly a television remote control does not make a good musical instrument. But that's not really the purpose of this lesson. The next lesson, Lesson 18, adapts the infrared remote to the rolling robot built in Lesson 15. The purpose of this lesson is to introduce adding the ability to detect and decode infrared messages to a sketch intended to do something else, in this case play a musical note. The final sketch will play eight different notes in response to pressing the numbers 1 through 8 of the remote control.

This lesson also introduces the *array*, a programming tool for managing a group of values. In this case the array holds the values of the eight notes the remote can play. Arrays are extremely useful in programming and, therefore, very common.

Table 17-1. Vocabulary

Term	Definition
array	A set of values, in this case integers that represent different musical notes.
array declaration	The programming statement that creates and initializes an array.
array type	The type of data that a cell may contain. In this lesson the array is of type `int`, meaning each cell may store only an integer. But arrays can be of other types, including `boolean`, `double`, and `String`.
cell	An individual location within an array. A value is stored in a cell.
index	The address of a cell within an array. These are assigned in order, beginning with zero. The index of the first cell is always 0, the second is 1, the third is 2, and so on. A cell of length 5, for example, has the index numbers of 0, 1, 2, 3, and 4.
value	The contents of a cell.

Description:

The `Lesson17IRPlayTones.ino` sketch

The Arduino™ sketch in Lesson 16 is `Lesson16SonyIRProtocol.ino`. A reminder here: the approach and much of the code in this sketch is from a LadyAda tutorial, as is noted in the heading comments. Contained in this sketch is the method `printFull()`, which abstracts and prints the address and command components of the message.

The sketch for this lesson is `Lesson17IPlayTones.ino`. It is essentially a copy of the Lesson 16 sketch but with the following changes:

1. An array of eight integers is added to identify the eight different musical notes that are to be played in correspondence with the buttons 1 through 8 on the remote control. The actual values contained in each cell of this array are defined by the file `pitches.h`, which was introduced in Lesson 10. This file is also included in this sketch.
2. The `printFull()` method is renamed `playNote()` and its contents modified as follows:
    a. The command is evaluated to see if it is one of the buttons 1 through 8. If not, then any tone currently being played is stopped.

    b. If a button 1 through 8 is being pushed, then the note corresponding to the array positions of the button is played.

But this only works because of that array of integers.

Arrays

An array is a collection of like values. In that sense, it can be considered a list and be given a name. To be used, an array must first be created, then filled with the desired values, and finally accessed by the sketch.

Creating an array of integers

Suppose there is need for a list of numbers three long. The list needs a name. That name is a variable. As with any variable it has an *array type*, in this case an integer array, and a name. The act of creating it is called *array declaration*. The C statement in Example 17-1 declares a variable of type `integer array`. The resulting array has room for three integers.

Example 17-1. Declaring an array

```
int myNumbers[3];  // create int array of length 3
```

Setting the values of each cell in the array

Important	Each location in an array is called a *cell*. The array in Example 17-1 has three cells. Cells are numbered beginning with the number 0. The number of the last cell in an array is always the length of the array minus 1.

The programming statements in Example 16-2 set the value of the first cell to -27, the second cell to 45, and the third cell to 14.

Example 17-2. Setting the value of a cell

```
myNumbers[0] = -27;        // first cell is now -27
myNumbers[1] = 45;         // second cell is now 45
myNumbers[2] = 14;         // third cell is now 14
```

An array can be created and initialized in a single step, as shown in Example 17-3.

17

Example 17-3. Initializing an array

```
int myNumbers[] = { -27, 45, 14};  // same result
```

Accessing the values of each cell in the array

Suppose there is need for assigning the contents of the third cell to another variable. The contents of the third cell is the name of the array with the index in square brackets. Example 17-4 assigns the value 14 to the variable `aNumber`.

Example 17-4. Assigning the value to a variable

```
int aNumber;     // declare int variable
aNumber = myNumbers[2]; // the value 14 is assigned to aNumber
```

One advantage of the cells in an array each having an index number is that a `for` loop can be used to access the values in order. The following prints the values of the array to the serial port.

Example 17-5. Printing values of the array to the serial port

```
...
for(int i = 0; i < 3; i++){
     Serial.print("Index " + i);
     Serial.println(" has the value of: " +
          myNumbers[i]);
}
```

If this code snippet were run, the following would appear on the computer monitor:

```
Index 0 has the value of: -27
Index 1 has the value of: 45
Index 2 has the value of: 14
```

In this lesson, the array is named `myNotes`, and it is declared and initialized as shown in Example 17-6.

Example 17-6. Declaring and initializing an array

```
...
int myNotes[] = {NOTE_C5, NOTE_D5, NOTE_E5, NOTE_F5,
                 NOTE_G5, NOTE_A5, NOTE_B5, NOTE_C6};
```

The values of each of the cells, in turn, are integers. `NOTE_C5`, for example, is declared in `pitches.h` as the integer value 523. If a speaker were connected to pin 5 of an Arduino,™ the C-language statement shown in Example 17-7 would result in the note C5 being heard.

Example 17-7. Playing first note in an array

```
...
     tone( 3, myNotes[0]);  // plays C5 tone
```

Materials:

Quantity	Part	Image	Notes	Catalog Number
1	Arduino™ Uno		Single-board computer. This board is delicate and should be handled with care. When you are not using it, keep it in a box or plastic bag.	3102
1	USB Cable		This is a standard USB adapter cable with a flat connector on one end and a square connector on the other.	2301
1	Computer with at least one USB port and access to the Arduino™ website, http://www.arduino.cc.	---	The operating system of this computer must be Windows, Macintosh OS/X, or Linux.	---
1	Infrared sensor		3-pin, 38kHz.	1302
1	2.2 microfarad capacitor		Actual value is not critical. Any capacitor of values between 1.0 and 10.0 microfarads will serve.	0205
1	Speaker		Magnetic speaker 4, 8, or 16 ohm.	3119

Procedure:

Important	The sketches in this lesson require a file named `pitches.h`. This file can be found on the Arduino™ website at http://arduino.cc/en/Tutorial/tone.

1. Using a bread-board, wire the parts as shown in Figure 17-2.

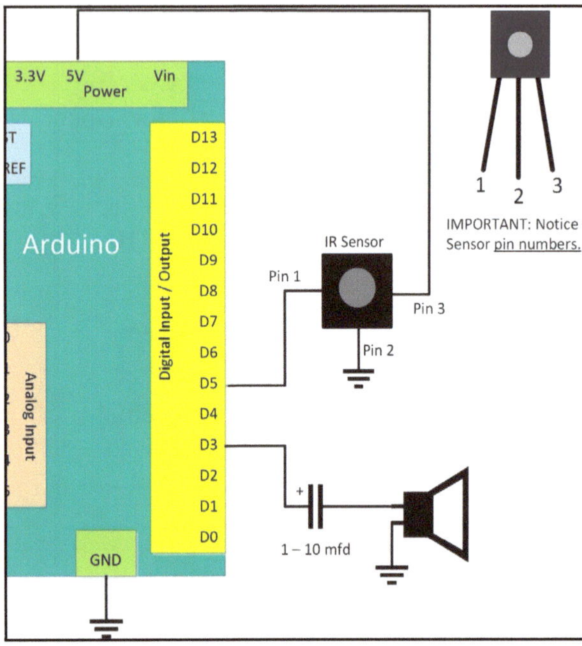

Caution

This is a schematic diagram, not a pictorial diagram. This means the physical locations of the various pins may be different from those shown here.

The IR sensor is an example. This diagram implies the center pin is pin 1. But it is not. The pins on the IR sensor are numbered 1, 2, 3, left to right when the round button is facing the observer.

Figure 17-2. Schematic diagram of Arduino™ Uno wired to IR sensor and speaker

2. Make a copy of the `Lesson16IRSonyProtocol` sketch to use as a base for this lesson. Rename it `Lesson17IRPlayTones.ino`. The steps are:
   a. From within the Arduino™ IDE open the `Lesson16IRSonyProtocol` sketch you used for preparing the remote control command code spreadsheet.

   b. From the Arduino™ File menu select Save As. Then, save the sketch as `Lesson17IRSonyDecodeToTone`. This is the sketch you will modify, leaving the `Lesson16IRSonyProtocol.ino` sketch unchanged.

Before making any changes to `Lesson17IRSonyDecodeToTone` run it to make sure it works exactly the same as `Lesson16IRSonyProtocol`.

3. If necessary, add the file `pitches.h` to this sketch. The file may be found on the Arduino™ website at http://arduino.cc/en/Tutorial/tone. Add it to the sketch by:
   a. placing a copy of the file in the Lesson17IRSonyDecodeToTone folder.

   b. closing and then reopening the Arduino™ IDE to the `Lesson17IRSonyDecodeToTone.ino` sketch. The `pitches.h` file should appear in the IDE with its own tab as shown in Figure 17-3.

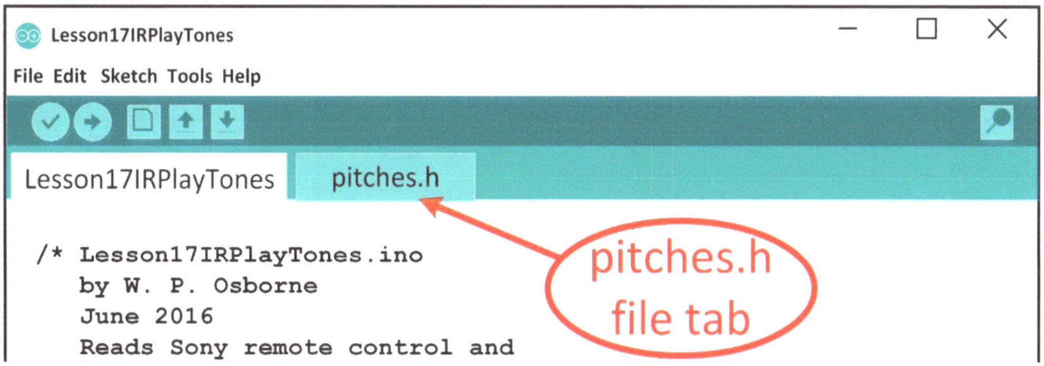

Figure 17-3. Portion of Arduino™ IDE showing tab for `pitches.h` *file*

c. adding two lines to the very top of the `Lesson17IRSonyDecodeToTone` sketch, just after the introductory comments and before DEFINITIONS AND GLOBAL VARIABLES, as shown in Snippet 17-1.

Snippet 17-1. Modification of `Lesson17IRSonyDecodeToTone` *sketch to include* `pitches.h`*. (Added lines are highlighted.)*

```
...
// INCLUDE FILES
#include "pitches.h"

//////////////// DEFINITIONS AND GLOBAL VARIABLES
///////////////
// DEFINE the allowed input pins. These are the pins to which
// pin 1 of the IR Receiver may be connected
#define IRInputPin0 1
#define IRInputPin1 2
#define IRInputPin2 4
#define IRInputPin3 8
#define IRInputPin4 16
#define IRInputPin5 32
#define IRInputPin6 64
#define IRInputPin7 128
```

17

In the next few steps we will be testing the ability of this circuit and sketch to play and stop a tone by direction from a Sony-protocol remote control.

4. Locate the `printFull()` method in the `Lesson17IRSonyDecodeToTone` sketch. It will be near the bottom of the sketch and can be identified by the comments just above that say, "Prints the components of the detected message. This method, as written, sends the command

and address of a received message to the Serial Monitor. We are going to replace this method with a new one of the same name that plays a tone instead. We do this by:

a. Replacing the comments above the method so that they look like Snippet 17-2:

Snippet 17-2. Modifications to `printFull()` comments

```
//////////PRINTFULL//////////
// isolates the address and the command from the message, then
// plays a tone
```

b. Replacing the programming statements within the method so that they play a note when the number 5 is pressed on the remote and stops playing it when any other number is pressed.

The resulting `printFull()` method should look as shown in Snippet 17-3, Modifications to `printFull()` to play tone. Delete the code that does the printing and replace it with code that will play an *A* note when button number 5 is pushed and stop playing whenever any other button is pushed.

Snippet 17-3. Modifications to `printFull()` to play tone

```
//////////////// PRINTFULL //////////////
// isolates the address and the command from the message,
// then plays a tone
void printFull(uint16_t n)
{
  // break into command and address
  uint8_t command = n & 127;
  uint16_t address = (n >> 7);

  if(command == 4){
    tone(3, NOTE_A4);
  }
  else {
    noTone(3);
  }
}
```

5. Upload the program and test. A tone should start playing when button number 5 is pressed and stop when any other button is pressed.

Notice how simple these changes are. Now, one by one, the pieces necessary to make playing a simple melody possible will be added.

6. So far, these changes have "hard coded" the sound pin into the `printFull()` method. This is not good practice. A constant that identifies the pin should be created at the top of the program, and the name of that constant should replace the number 4 inside the `printFull()`method. To do this:

   a. At the top of the sketch and, within that, at the bottom of the declarations of constants, add the highlighted statements, as shown in Snippet 17-4.

Snippet 17-4. Adding the definition of `soundPin`
(Added statements are highlighted.)

```
// Variable to hold the collection of incoming low pulses
// that contain the address and message.
// For those who don't remember, uint means unsigned integer.
// 16 means sixteen bits. This variable is used to contain
// the 12 bits of the incoming message.
uint16_t currMessage = 0;

// TONE related variables and definitions
#define SOUND_PIN 3
```

   b. Inside the `printFull` method, replace the number 4 with the constant `soundPin`.

Snippet 17-5. Replacing a variable with the constant `soundPin`

```
///////////////// PRINTFULL //////////////
// isolates the address and the command from the message,
// then plays a tone
void printFull(uint16_t n)
{
  // break into command and address
  uint8_t command = n & 127;
  uint16_t address = (n >> 7);

  if(command == 4){
    tone(SOUND_PIN, NOTE_A4);
  }
  else {
    noTone(SOUND_PIN);
  }
}
```

Again, test the program to make sure it still works.

7. Recall that the intent is to play different notes by pressing different buttons on the remote. For this, an array of integers is added to the sketch. The array is eight cells long, and each cell contains the frequency for a musical note. These frequencies are defined in `pitches.h`.

   a. Create an array variable to hold the eight notes. Call it `myNotes`. The declaration should go just below the declaration of `soundPin`; see Snippet 17-6.

Snippet 17-6.

```
// TONE related variables and definitions
#define SOUND_PIN 3


//Array of notes
int myNotes[] = {NOTE_C5, NOTE_D5, NOTE_E5, NOTE_F5, NOTE_G5
                 NOTE_A5, NOTE_B5, NOTE_C6};
```

   b. The indexes of this array are 0, 1, 2, 3, 4, 5, 6, 7. As with any array, the index of the first cell is 0, and the last is the cell length minus one. By happy coincidence, the commands generated by the number buttons on a Sony-protocol remote also begin with 0 and are always one less than the number of that button, as shown in Table 17-2.

Table 17-2. Commands sent by remote number button

Button Number	1	2	3	4	5	6	7	8
Command Sent	0	1	2	3	4	5	6	7

Because the commands of the buttons exactly match the indexes of the array, to play different notes the only modification needed to `PrintFull()` is to replace `NOTE_A4` with the `myNotes` cell corresponding to the button command. This is shown in Snippet 17-7.

Snippet 17-7. Modification of `PrintFull()` to play note from `myNotes` array

```
//////////////// PRINTFULL //////////////
// isolates the address and the command from the message,
// then prints them to the serial port.
void printFull(uint16_t n) //prints first 12 bits (starting
from MSB)
{
  // break into command and address
  uint8_t command = n & 127;
  uint16_t address = (n >> 7);
```

```
    if(command >= 0 && command < 8){
   view ban, myNotes[command]);
  }
  else {
    noTone(SOUND_PIN);
  }
}
///////////////// END PRINTFULL ////////////////////////
```

The Arduino™ should now play a different note for each of the first eight buttons of the Sony-protocol remote control.

Exercises:

Exercise 17-1. Play a simple melody

Show working numbers by playing a simple melody.

Exercise 17-2. Shift scale, play sharp or flat

Put some of the other remote control buttons to work for shifting scale or playing sharps or flats, or some other music-related purposes.

Complete listing 17.1. `Lesson17IRSonyDecodeToTone.ino`

This sketch may be downloaded from LearnCSE.com.

```
// Lesson17IRSonyDecodeToTone.ino
// by W. P. Osborne
// 6/30/15
// Reads Sony remote control and
// displays the encoded 12 bits. The first seven bits are the
// "command", the remaining 5 bits are the device being
// addressed.
//
// Based on code from LadyAda tutorial as edited,cut,
// enhanced, and generally changed by Luke Duncan,
// Preetum Nakkarin, and W. P. Osborne.

// PIND is an Arduino™ command that gets a byte containing
// the input status of bytes 0 through 7. In our case we want
// the bit corresponding to pin 2.
// NOTE: If you are seeking input from ports 8 - 15 use
// PINDB. For analong pins 0 - 5 use PINC
//
// Modified from IRSonyDecodeToDecimal to match the flow
// charts used for the lesson. By W. P. Osborne.


// INCLUDE FILES
#include "pitches.h"

//////////////// DEFINITIONS AND GLOBAL VARIABLES
///////////////
// DEFINE the allowed input pins. These are the pins to which
// pin 1 of the IR Receiver may be connected
#define IRInputPin0 1
#define IRInputPin1 2
#define IRInputPin2 4
#define IRInputPin3 8
#define IRInputPin4 16
#define IRInputPin5 32
#define IRInputPin6 64
#define IRInputPin7 128
```

```
// Assign the pin to be used for the IR sensor
#define IRpin_PIN  PIND
#define IRpin      IRInputPin5

// Sony protocol has 12 data bits in its message.
#define NUMBITS 12

// RESOLUTION is how finely we can measure the length of a
// pulse. Any measurement is a multiple of RES
#define RES 50  // resolution

// A low pulse of length LOWUS is a binary zero
// A low pulse of length HIGHUS is a binary one
#define LOWUS 600
#define HIGHUS 1200

// Maximum amount of time we'll wait for a pulse.
#define MAXPULSE 5000 // longest pulse we'll accept

// Maximum amount of time we'll wait to see if there
// are any pulses coming in. Used to find the end
// of the rest period between messages.
#define MAXREST 20000 // longest we'll wait for a pulse

// Define variables to be used to tell the wait() method
// if it is timing a high pulse or a low pulse.
#define HIGHP true
#define LOWP false

// Variable to hold the collection of incoming low pulses
// that contain the address and message.
// For those who don't remember, uint means unsigned integer.
// 16 means sixteen bits. This variable is used to contain
// the 12 bits of the incoming message.
uint16_t currMessage = 0;

// TONE related variables and definitions
#define soundPin 4

// Array of notes
int myNotes[] = {NOTE_C5, NOTE_D5, NOTE_E5, NOTE_F5, NOTE_G5,
                 NOTE_A5, NOTE_B5, NOTE_C6};
```

17

```
/////////////// END OF DEFINITIONS AND GLOBAL VARIABLES
///////////

/////////////// SETUP (Light yellow on flow chart) ///////////
// All we set up is the serial port so we can see the
// commands and addresses
void setup()
{
  Serial.begin(9600);
  Serial.println("Ready to decode IR!");
}
/////////////// END OF SETUP METHOD //////////////////


///////////////// LOOP (Dark yellow on flow diagram) /////////
// Remember, loop is run over and over and over and over ////
and....
void loop()
{
  if(readIR())
  {
    printFull(currMessage);
  }
}
////////////////// END OF LOOP METHOD //////////////////////


////////////////// READIR (Blue on flow chart) //////////////
// Attempts to read a message. First, it looks for a rest
// period.
// Remember, the IR Sensor output is HIGH when there is no
// IR detected.
// If it goes LOW sooner than the length of a rest period
// then we have a message. A Sony remote sends messages in
// groups of three. The rest period is the time between two
// messages.
//
// If a candidate rest period is found then IRRead looks to
// see if the input then drops long enough to be a start
// pulse, but not too long.
//
// Finally, if the rest period and start pulse are detected,
```

```
// the 12 data bits are collected and put into an unsigned
// integer for later decoding.
//
// Notice how readIR() makes extensive use of the wait()
// method.
boolean readIR()
{
  currMessage = 0;

  if( wait(HIGHP, MAXREST) == -1)
  {//timeout ( before sees a low pulse)
    return false;
  }

  if(wait(LOWP, MAXPULSE) == -1) //start pulse
  {
    return false; //timeout
  }
  //start decoding message

  for(int i = 0;i<NUMBITS;i++)
  {
    if(wait(HIGHP, MAXPULSE) == -1)
     {return false;}
    int data = wait(LOWP, MAXPULSE);
    if(data == -1)
    { return false; } //timeout

    // Here the pulse is put in its
    // appropriate bit position.
    if(data * 2 > LOWUS + HIGHUS)
    {
      currMessage = currMessage | (1 << i);
    }
    else
    {

      //It's a zero, do nothing
    }
  }
  return true;
}
```

17

```
///////////// END IRREAD Method ///////////////////////
////////////// WAIT (Green on flow diagram)
////////////////////////
// In the following the (IRpin_PIN & (1 << IRpin)) test is a
// bit tricky. We named setthe value of IRpin to 2 because
// that is the pin to which the output of the sensor is
// attached.
// But, that pin in IRpin_PIN is actually in the third
// position.
// So, to do the test IRpin value must be shifted to the left
// one bit. The (1 << IRpin) results in a "mask", that limits
// testing to the desired pin(s). In this case, it is Pin 2.
//
// A visual example may help:
//     Assume the only HIGH is on Pin 2, to which the output
//     of the IR sensor is connected.
//     The bit pattern of IRpin_PIN is:  00000100
//
//     But, the bit pattern of IRpin is: 00000010 because
//     this is decimal 2.
//     To make the "AND" test meaningful the IRpin pattern
//     must be shifted left 1 bit.
//     This is done with the (1 << IRpin) command.
//     Then, the pattern is:
//                                       00000100
//
// This trick works with pins 1, 2, and 4 but none of the
// others.
// Pin 3, for example, resolves to the decimal value of 8.
// If the input were connected to Pin 3 the test would be:
//     (IRpin_PIN & 8)







// A better way to do this may be as follows:
//      Pin to be tested  Mask in binary  Mask in DEC
//      0                  00000001        1
//      1                  00000010        2
//      2                  00000100        4
```

```
//       3                          00001000        8
//       4                          00010000        16
//       5                          00100000        32
//       6                          01000000        64
//       7                          10000000       128

//wait until the pulse of type TYPE ends. returns -1
// if timedout, otherwise returns length of pulse
int wait(boolean type, int timeout)
{
  int num = 0;  // we wait in increments of RES in
microseconds.
  while( ( type == HIGHP && (IRpin_PIN & IRpin) )
          ||
         ( type == LOWP && !(IRpin_PIN & IRpin ) ) )
  {
    // pin is still HIGH
    delayMicroseconds(RES);
    num++;
    // if the pulse is too long we 'timed out'
    if(num*RES >= timeout)
    {
      return -1;
    }
  }
  return num*RES;  // return the duration of the pulse
}
///////////////// END WAIT METHOD ////////////////////////////


/////////// PRINTFULL ///////////////////////////
// Plays the tone selected by the button pushed
// on the Sony-compatible remote control
void printFull(uint16_t n) //prints first 12 bits (starting
from MSB)
{

  // break into command and address
  uint8_t command = n & 127;
  uint16_t address = (n >> 7);

  if(command >= 0 && command < 8){
```

17

```
    noTone(soundPin);
    delay(60);
    tone(soundPin, myNotes[command]);
  }
  else
    noTone(soundPin);
}
///////////////// END PRINTFULL ////////////////////////
```

Lesson 18 | IR Robot Remote Control

The Big Idea:

This lesson uses DC motors controlled by an H-bridge. The result is a quick and agile robot that responds to an infrared remote control.

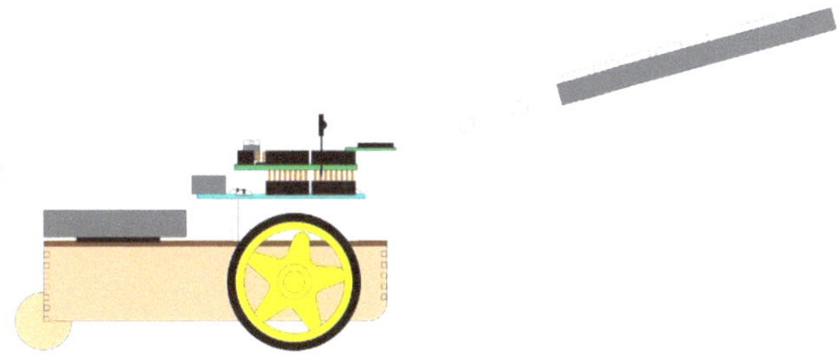

Figure 18-1. Rolling robot with remote control

Background:

This lesson makes use of the rolling robot constructed for Lesson 15. All the components plugged into the small solderless bread-board in the center of the motor controller shield should be removed. Of these, one infrared sensor and three male-to-male jumpers will be needed for this lesson. In Lesson 15 the sensors were programmed to detect infrared light reflected from obstacles.

In this lesson, one of those sensors is repurposed to detect messages from the common infrared remote control introduced in Lesson 16. The detection and decoding of these messages was used in Lesson 17 to make a sort of musical instrument. In this lesson we combine the robot and an infrared sensor from Lesson 15 with what we know of infrared messages from Lessons 16 and 17 to make a robot that can be controlled remotely.

How-To #1 contains instructions for assembling a complete rolling robot powered by DC motors.

How-To #7 shows how to assemble an H-bridge circuit board suitable for connection to an Arduino.™

Finally, this lesson provides a sketch for controlling that rolling robot. The result is an attractive and nimble little robot.

Description:

This lesson results in a rolling robot that responds to infrared messages from a common infrared remote control. The components and wiring of the robot are identical to those used in Lesson 15 with the exception that the solderless bread-board contains only an infrared sensor used to detect messages.

18

The focus of this lesson is on the actual programming of this robot. The sketch must detect, decode, and act upon infrared messages. *Act* in this case means first determining if a message is intended for this robot and, if so, the command is translated into speed and direction instructions for the DC motors.

A starter sketch is provided that can perform these tasks but is limited to having the robot move forward, reverse, spin left, spin right, and stop. Further, when moving, the motors are at top speed. Although these commands may work, they do not provide sufficiently subtle control of the robot to allow the operator to perform tasks such as playing robot soccer with grace, parallel parking the robot, or allowing the variety of approaches necessary to win at robot sumo.

At the least, the programmer needs to enhance this starter sketch by adding the ability to turn right and left while moving forward and to change the robot's overall speed. An understanding of this sketch is essential in order to make these enhancements.

Recall that every Arduino™ sketch requires at least two methods—`setup()` and `loop()`.

The `setup()` method

This method is run only once, when the robot is first started. As shown in Figure 18-2, the mode of the diginal pin used for the IR sensor is set to `INPUT`.

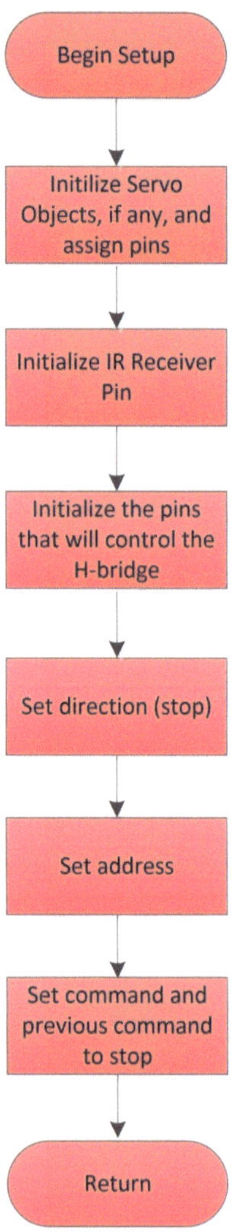

The `setup()` method goes on go initializes the digital pins that control the H-bridge, which, in turn, controls the two DC motors that provide propulsion.

The basic robot does not use any servos, but the motor controller shield can accommodate up to three. Programmers sometimes find servos useful for adding features to their robots such as grasping the ball in robot soccer and lowering a blade in robot sumo. If servos are present, they are initialized here and assigned to Arduino pins.

Although they are not reflected in Figure 18-2, any other initializations a programmer might use belong in `setup()` as well. Examples are a digital pin used for sound effects or music or another pin to light an LED to indicate the robot is powered and ready to use.

Incoming messages contain the address for the type of device to be controlled. This could be a television, a DVD player, a cable box, or a recorder. `Setup()` identifies which device address the sketch will respond to.

Finally, the robot motors are set to "stop," meaning the robot is not moving but is ready to respond to commands.

Figure 18-2. Flow chart of the `setup()` method

The `loop()` *method*

Figure 18-3 illustrates the program flow of the `loop()` method. This method appears deceptively simple. The `loop()` method looks for a message and, if it finds one, takes action.

The `loop()` method performs only two tasks. Each time it is run it calls another method, `checkForMessages()`, to see if an incoming infrared message has been detected and decoded. If such a message has been sent, then the `loop()` method acts on that message by calling `processMessage()`.

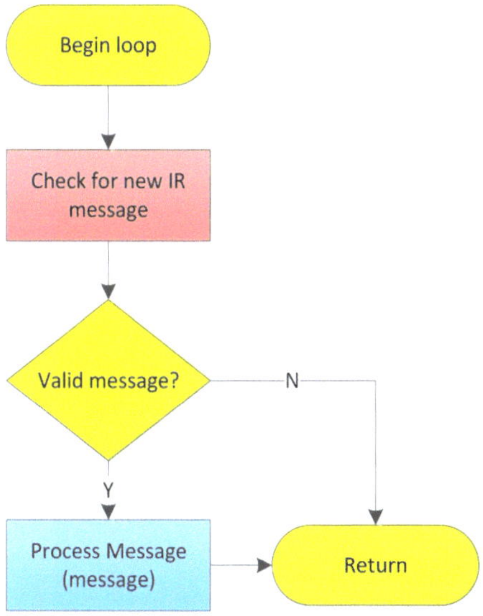

Figure 18-3. Flow chart of the `loop()` *method*

The `checkForMessages()` *method*

Called by the `loop()` method, `checkForMessages()` uses the program code from Lesson 12, Infrared Sensors. Details of how this method works and the methods it calls, in turn, are contained in that lesson.

The `processMessage()` *method*

The `processMessage()` method is called by the `loop()` method only if a valid message has been detected and decoded. Recall from Lesson 12 that an incoming message contains two pieces of information— the device for which the message is intended, called the address, and the button pushed, called the command. The `processMessage()` method first looks at the address. If it does not match the address assigned by the `setup()` method then no action is taken. If, however, there is a match then `processMessage()` examines the command portion of the message to determine what action to take. This starter sketch, `Lesson18IRControlRollingRobot.ino`, provides only five possible actions: go forward, reverse, spin left, spin right, and stop. Exercise 18-2 extends this set. Note that the exercise suggests turning right and left as opposed to spinning, but other responses could be added, such as blinking lights, playing a sound, or operating some additional servo or motor. 18

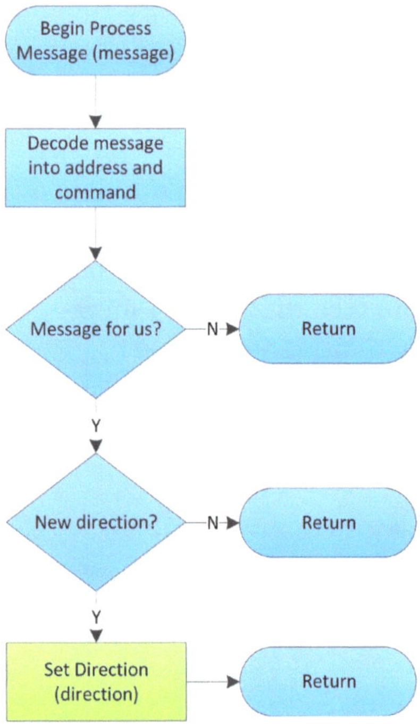

Called by the `loop()` method if a valid message has been detected and decoded, the `processMessage()` method first determines whether the message is meant for some other recipient. If it is not, the method then tests that the command is a change from what the robot is currently doing. If the message is to go forward, for example, and if the robot is currently going forward, then no action is taken. But if the command is a change, then `processMessage()` calls yet another method, `setDirection()`, to effect the change.

Figure 18-4. Flow chart of the `processMessage()` *method*

The `setDirection()` *method*

This method is a sort of switch. It sends the appropriate commands to the servos that reflect the command. Notice the set of options is easily expanded to include other buttons on the remote control.

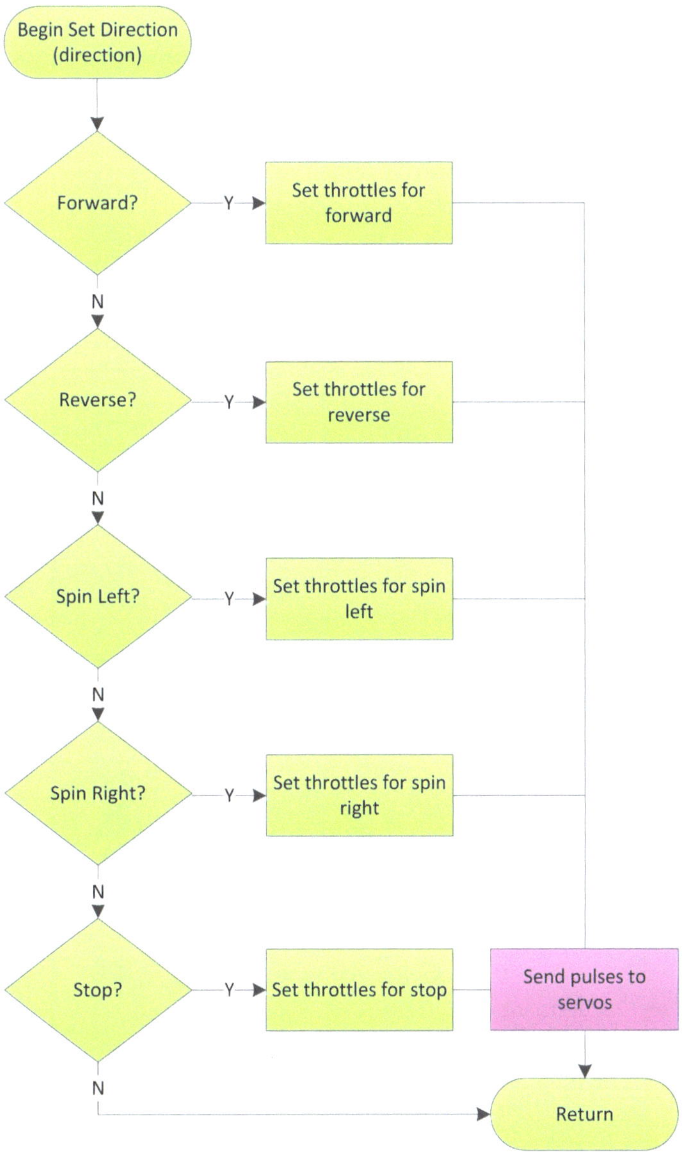

Figure 18-5. Flow chart of the `setDirection()` method

Called by `processMessage()` from within `loop()` the `setDirection()` method translates the infrared message's command into specific actions for the motors. Notice that the five commands recognized here are for the servos. Other commands are easily added to extend the types of commands the servos receive as well as to perform just about any other task, such as playing a sound effect or blinking some lights. This method is intended to be expanded.

18

Materials:

Quantity	Part	Image	Notes	Catalog Number
1	Arduino™ Uno		Single-board computer. This board is delicate and should be handled with care. When you are not using it, keep it in a box or plastic bag.	3102
1	USB Cable		This is a standard USB adapter cable with a flat connector on one end and a square connector on the other.	2301
1	Computer with at least one USB port and access to the Arduino™ website, http://www.arduino.cc.	---	The operating system of this computer must be Windows, Macintosh OS/X, or Linux.	---
1	Rolling Robot		This is the robot constructed in Lesson 15. It must include at least one infrared receiver.	Robot 101
1	Remote Control		Any remote control compatible with Sony devices will serve.	3120
1	IR Sensor		Lesson 16 used two such sensors. One of these will suffice.	1302

Goals:

By the end of this lesson readers will:

1. Understand how an Arduino™ sketch can be constructed to perform two complementary tasks, in this case to control the DC motors and to watch for and respond to infrared messages from a remote control.
2. Be able to expand the Arduino™ sketch to respond to other control buttons and to perform tasks in addition to the control of DC motors.

Procedure:

1. Begin with the rolling robot as created for Lesson 15. Remove the infrared sensors, headlights, and associated wiring. The only remaining wiring should be the motors themselves. Viewed from the top, the motor controller and H-bridge will look like Figure 18-6.

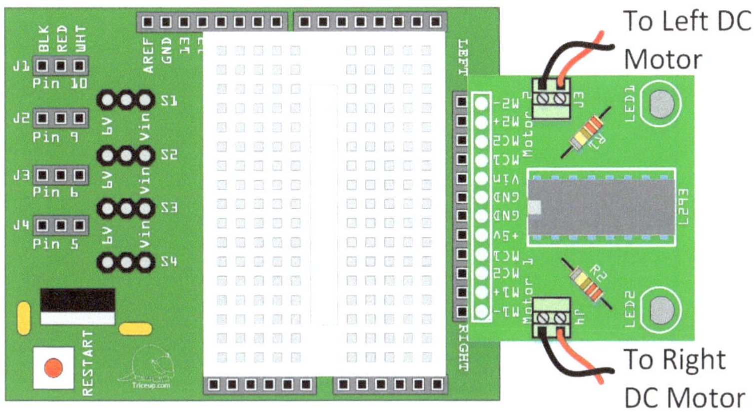

Figure 18-6. Position of the motor controller and H-bridge

2. Insert the infrared sensor and connect it to +5v, GND, and the Arduino™ pin 7 as shown in Figure 18-7.

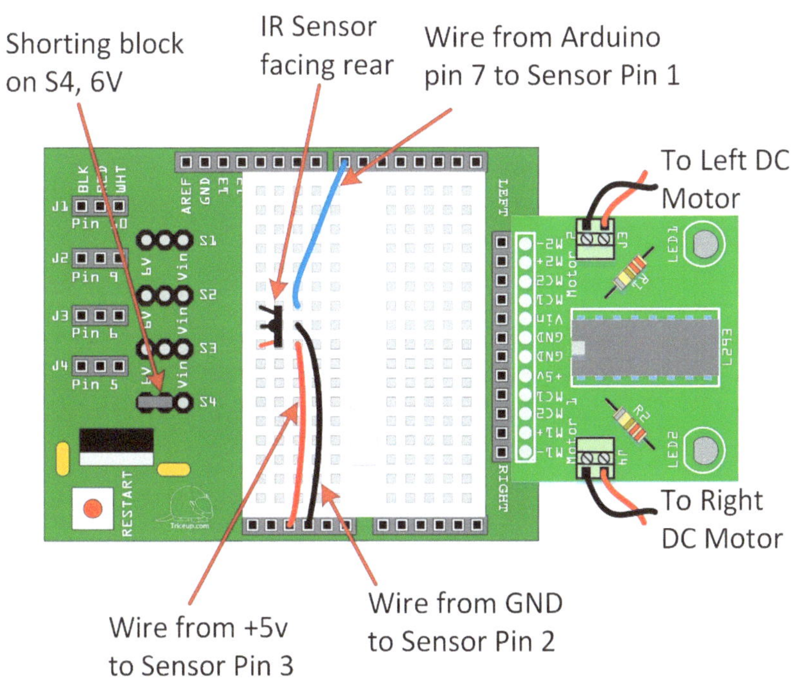

Figure 18-7. Wiring the DC motors

3. Download the starter sketch for remote control of a rolling robot, `Lesson18HBridgeMotorIRControl.ino` sketch, and save it to a folder of the same name in the Arduino™ folder.

4. Open the Arduino™ IDE and then open the `Lesson18HBridgeMotorIRControl.ino` sketch.

5. Modify line 118 to reflect which device code the robot is to respond to. In the case of the VCR, for example, this line would be:

   ```
   uint_8 addressUS = ADDRESS_VCR;
   ```

6. Connect the robot's Arduino™ to the PC. Upload the `Lesson18HBridgeMotorIRControl.ino` sketch to the Arduino.™

7. Connect the robot's battery pack to the Arduino.™

8. Remove the USB cable connecting the robot to the computer.

9. Set the remote control command to the type of device selected in step 5. In this example the remote would be set to control a VCR.

10. Test the control by pressing the 2 button. The robot should roll forward. Verify the other directions by pressing 4, 5, 6, and 8. The robot should spin left when the 4 is pressed and right when the 6 is pressed. The robot should roll backward when 8 is pressed. Pressing 5 should cause the robot to stop.

Exercises:

Exercise 18-1. Add direction buttons to arrows

This exercise may not work with your Sony-compatible remote control. The goal is to make control of your robot more intuitive by having it respond to up, down, left, and right arrows common on controls. These are usually grouped around a center button that might say something like stop or select or maybe have a simple symbol.

Take a look at your remote control. If it has such arrows, and these arrows are not marked as changing volume or channel, refer to the table of addresses and commands you made in Lesson 16. Notice here that each arrow button, including the center one, transmits an address and a command. But unlike the 0 through 9 number buttons, the command values may not be the same for different addresses. Up Arrow for TV may be different than Up Arrow for DVD.

Make a copy of the `Lesson18HBridgeMotorIRControl.ino` sketch and save it as `Lesson18Exercise1.ino`. Modify `Lesson18Exercise1.ino` as follows:

1. Set the address to be sent to ADDRESS_TV.

2. Locate where the command values for different buttons are defined. This section is about line 100 and has some comments titled

    ```
    // DEFINE WHICH BUTTON ON THE REMOTE DOES WHAT.
    ```

3. Add definitions for each of the four arrow buttons and for the center button. Following are two examples. Do not trust the values to be correct.

    ```
    #define MOTORS_FORWARD_ARROWUP   65
    #define MOTORS_REVERSE_ARROWDOWN 76
    ```
    and so on. Again, these particular values are probably wrong. Use the ones on your table.

4. Modify any other parts of the sketch to make your robot respond to the arrow keys as well as the number keys.

HINT: Motors forward might look something like this:

```
case MOTORS_FORWARD:
case MOTORS_FORWARD_ARROWUP:
forward();
break;
```

18

Exercise 18-2. Add the ability to pivot

The sketch `Lesson18HBridgeMotorIRControl.ino` provides for changing direction only by spinning, which can be difficult to manage.

If you completed Exercise 18-1 and created `Lesson18Exercise1.ino`, make a copy of that sketch and save it as `Lesson18Exercise2.ino.` Otherwise, make a copy of `Lesson118HBridgeMotorIRControl.ino` and save it as `Lesson 18Exercise2`.

Extend the capabilities of `Lesson18Exercise2.ino` by adding the ability to pivot four different ways:

1. pivot right going forward when the number 3 is pressed. This means the right wheel is stopped and the left is turning counterclockwise. Put the code for this in a method named `pivotRightForward()`.
2. pivot left going forward when the number 1 is pressed. This means the left wheel is stopped and the right is turning clockwise. Put the code for this in a method named `pivotLeftForward()`.
3. pivot right going backwards when the number 9 is pressed. This means the left wheel is stopped and the right is turning counterclockwise. Put the code for this in a method named `pivotLeftReverse()`.
4. pivot left going backwards when the number 7 is pressed. This means the right wheel is stopped and the left is turning clockwise. Put the code for this in a method named `pivotRightReverse()`.

To make this work, you will need to define four new commands at the top of the sketch. Add these commands to the switch in the `setDirection()` method.

Exercise 18-3. Add sound to the robot

Make a copy of `Lesson18HBridgeIRControl.ino`, `Lesson18Exercise1.ino`, or `Lesson18Exercise2.ino` and save it as `Lesson18Exercise3.ino`. Then, add a speaker and the field effect transistor of Lesson 10. Modify `Lesson18Exercise3.ino` such that your robot makes a warning "beep, beep" sound when backing up.

Exercise 18-4. Add an LED to robot and turn LED on and off

One of the problems with remote control of robots is that when the wheels are not turning the robot can be thought of as off. But it's not really off; it's just waiting for a command from your remote control. Meanwhile, the robot is consuming power from the batteries. (In addition, it's possible for your robot to respond to commands issued by remote controls other than your own.) In this exercise, you add a current-limiting resistor and LED to your robot such that it lights whenever the robot is on but stopped. You can then tell at a glance whether the robot is on or off. The LED turns off when the robot is in motion.

Make a copy of your choice of a working Lesson18 sketch and save it as `Lesson18Exercise14.`

How-To #1: Assemble DC-Motor Robot Chassis

Background:

A chassis is the frame of a device. The components are attached to this frame. The chassis described in this How-To is for two geared DC motors with wheels, an Arduino™ with a motor controller shield, a battery pack, an H-bridge circuit board, and a rear wheel.

This chassis is made from wood, although other materials will certainly serve. The wood is pre-cut into five pieces: the front panel, the rear panel, two side panels, and a deck. Modeling glue for wood is the recommended adhesive. For precisely rectangular construction a corner clamp is highly recommended, although it is not absolutely required.

Materials:

Included in Robot Body kit (part RB103)

All the parts necessary to assemble the chassis and attach it to the Arduino,™ its navigation shield, the battery pack, and the DC motors are included in the kit.

Quantity	Part	Image	Notes	Catalog Number
1	Deck	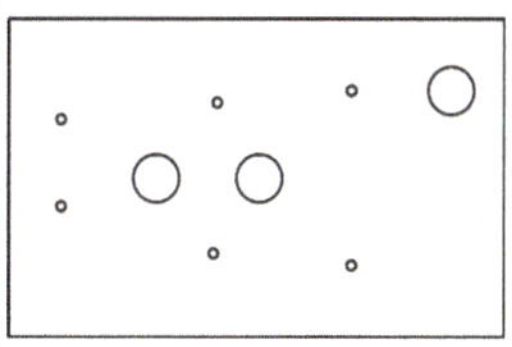	The top flat surface of the robot. The armadillo logo should be visible when the chassis is complete.	RB103
1	Front Panel	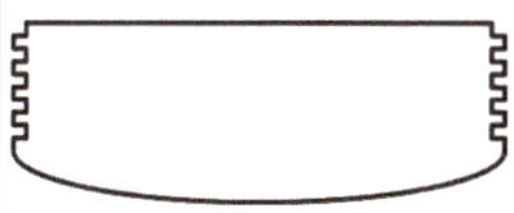	Curved along the bottom. Attaches on each side to the end of the side panel with the large rectangular cutout.	
2	Side Panels	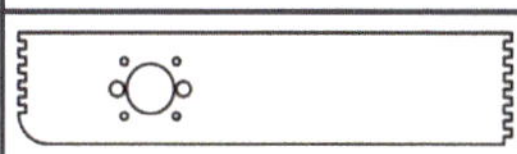	End with large rectangular cutout should be near the front panel.	
1	Rear Panel	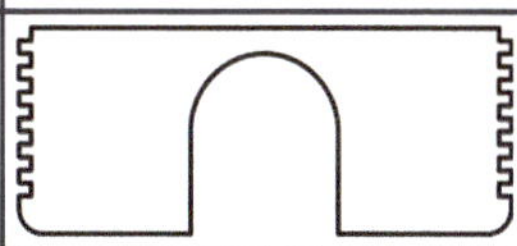	U-shaped opening, should be attached with the U opening downward.	
1	Rear Wheel		One-inch diameter wood ball with a hole through the center.	
1	Rear Wheel Axel		3-inch dowel.	

Quantity	Part	Image	Notes	Catalog Number
4	Nylon Spacers		4-40 threaded for mounting Arduino™ Uno.	RB103
8	Nylon Pan Head Screws		For attaching the Arduino™ Uno to the nylon spacers, and the spacers to the robot deck.	
8	Stainless 4-40 Pan Head Screws		For attaching DC motors to the side panels.	
8	Stainless 4-40 Hex Nuts		For attaching DC motors to the side panels.	

Not included in kit:

Quantity	Part	Image	Notes	Catalog Number
1	Arduino™ Uno		Single-board computer. This board is delicate and should be handled with care. When you are not using it, keep it in a box or plastic bag.	3102
1	Motor Controller Shield		May be assembled from parts or purchased as a kit. Find How-To instructions can be found on http://www.LearnCSE.com.	MC101
2	DC Motors		Geared DC motors, 6 volts.	3132
1	Battery Holder with 2.1mm connector. Holds 6 AA cells.		May be assembled from kit or by following instructions on LearnCSE.com.	3131
4	AA cells		Alkaline or rechargeable.	3118

Quan-tity	Part	Image	Notes	Catalog Number
2	Wheels to match the geared DC motors		Rubber-tired wheel to fit DC motors.	3133
1	H-bridge	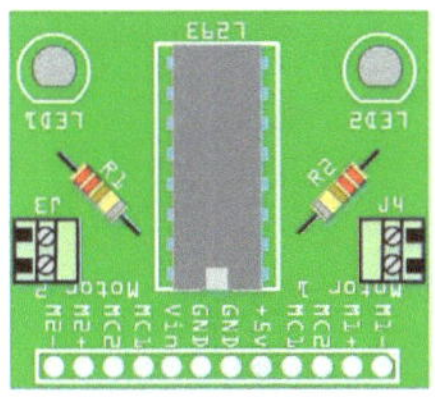	May be assembled from parts or purchased as a kit. Instructions are in How-To #7 on LearnCSE.com.	1307

Tools:

In addition to the parts, the following tools aid in the assembly of the robot chassis:

Quan-tity	Tool	Image	Notes
Small tube	Modeling glue for wood		Most wood glues will work, but Testors Cement for Wood Models sets quickly and is sufficiently strong. It is available from most hobby stores.
1	Corner clamp (optional)	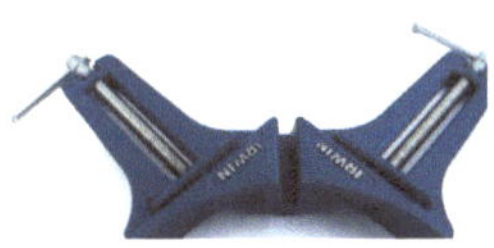	This device is an easy way to ensure 90- degree corners for the chassis. It is inexpensive and available from Home Depot and most other tools suppliers. The one shown here, purchased from Home Depot, sells for approximately $9.
1	Screw driver		Phillips-head, suitable for the pan head screws.

Procedure:

Follow the instructions for the type of glue. Drying and curing times are different. "Dry" often means the glued object does not need continued support. But the glue hasn't reached its full strength until it is "cured," that is, when the chemical reactions are complete. Curing usually requires several hours.

1. Glue the front and rear panels to the side panels as shown in Figure HT1-1.

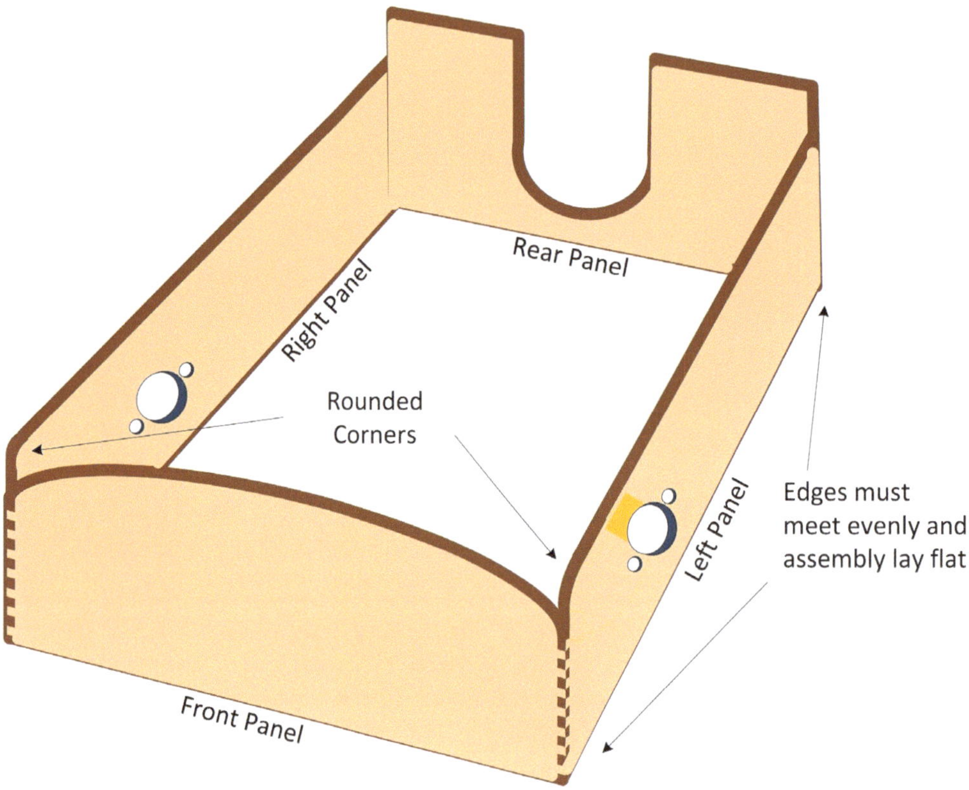

Figure HT1-1. Front, rear, and side panels of robot chassis

Important	In Figure HT1-1 the panels are all upside down. It's important to ensure that: • the assembly lies perfectly flat when put together as shown. • the rectangle cutouts on the side panels are toward the front panel. • each of the corners is as close to a perfect 90-degree angle as possible. • the rounded corners of the side panels meet the rounded side of the front panel.

2. After the glue has dried and cured, turn the assembly over.

3. Glue the deck to the top.

Important	The location of the Armadillo image is critical. It must be on top and at the opposite end of the curved front panel. See Figure HT1-2.

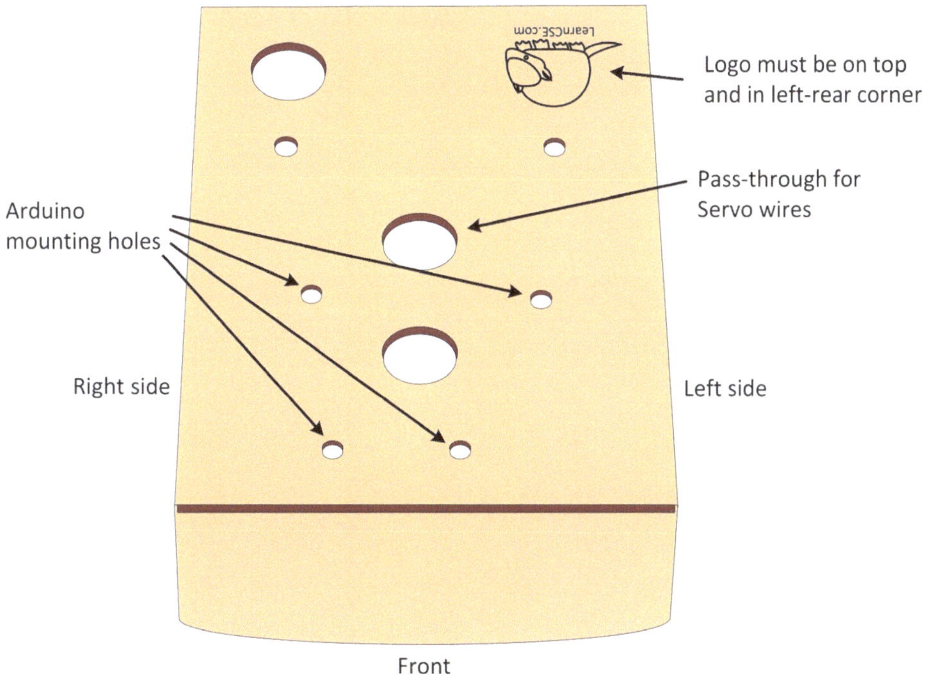

Figure HT1-2. Placement of chassis deck to front panel

4. Attach the rear wheel. This is accomplished by gluing the dowel, passed through the center of the wood bead, to the rear panel.

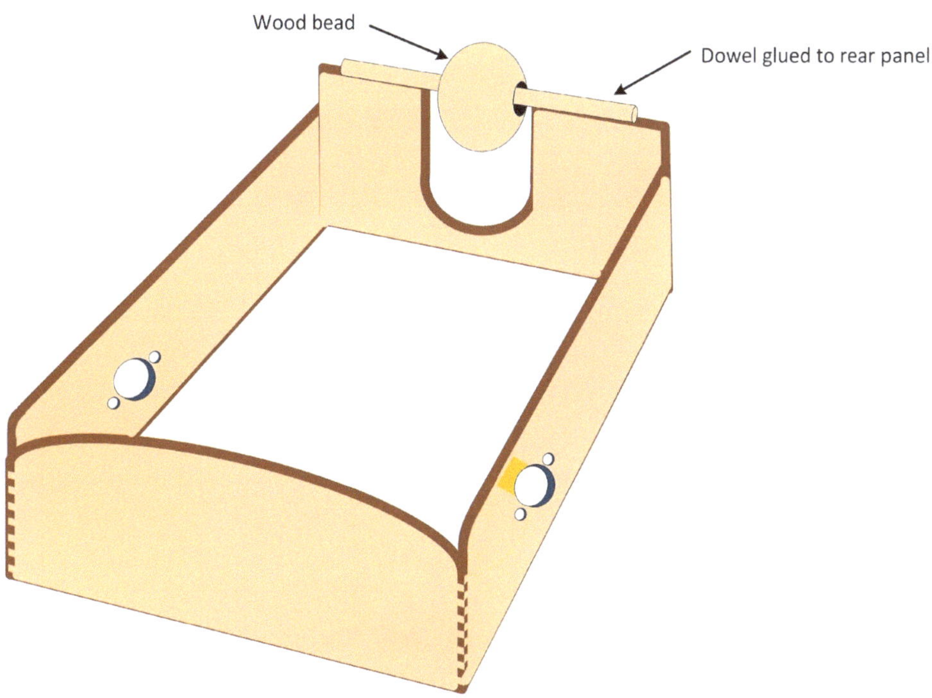

Figure HT1-3. Adding the rear wheel and axel to chassis

5. Turn the robot body over after the glue used to attach the rear wheel is dry and cured. Use the nylon screws to attach the four nylon standoffs to the top of the robot deck.

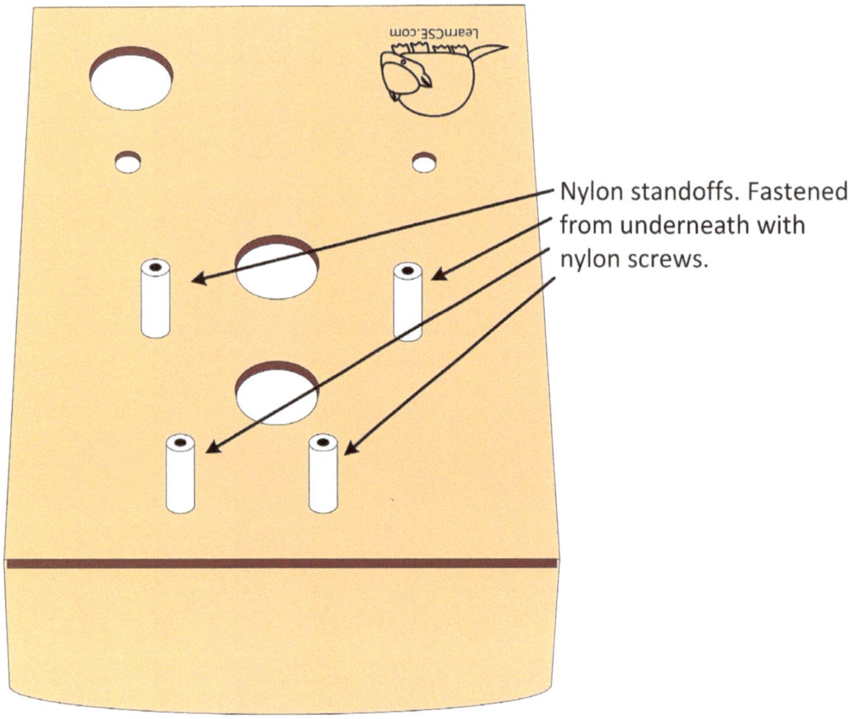

Figure HT1-4. Chassis with nylon standoffs

Caution	Use only nylon screws to mount the Arduino.™ Metal screws can damage the nylon standoffs and—on some versions of the Arduino™—can cause an electrical short.

6. Attach the Arduino™ Uno to the standoffs, again using the nylon screws.

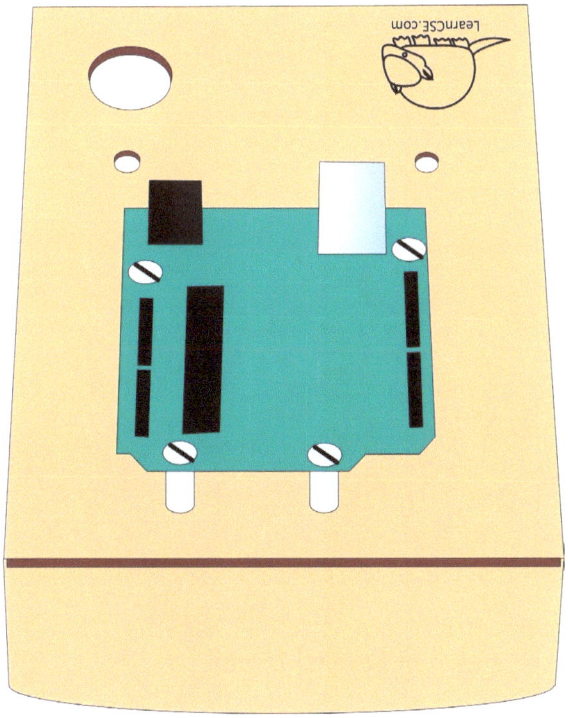

Figure HT1-5. Arduino™ Uno attached to chassis body with nylon screws

7. Use the metal screws and hex nuts to mount the DC motors to the side panels of the robot body:

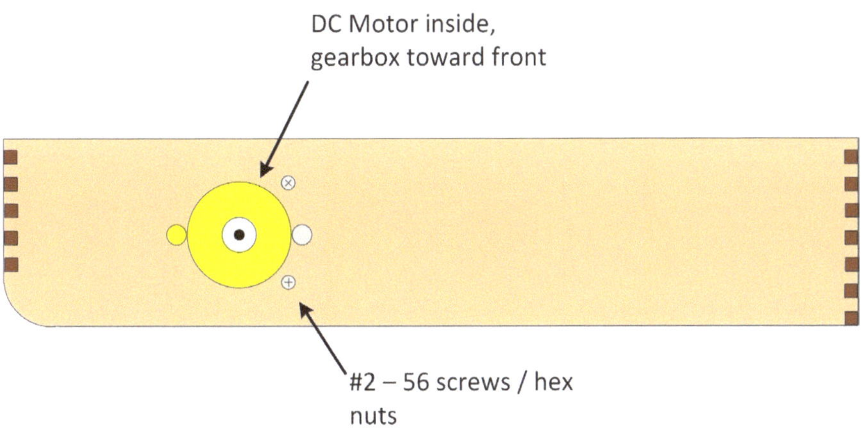

Figure HT1-6. DC motor mounted to side panel of robot chassis

8. Mount the wheels to the motors by first aligning them with the flat sides of the motor shaft and then pressing the wheels on gently.

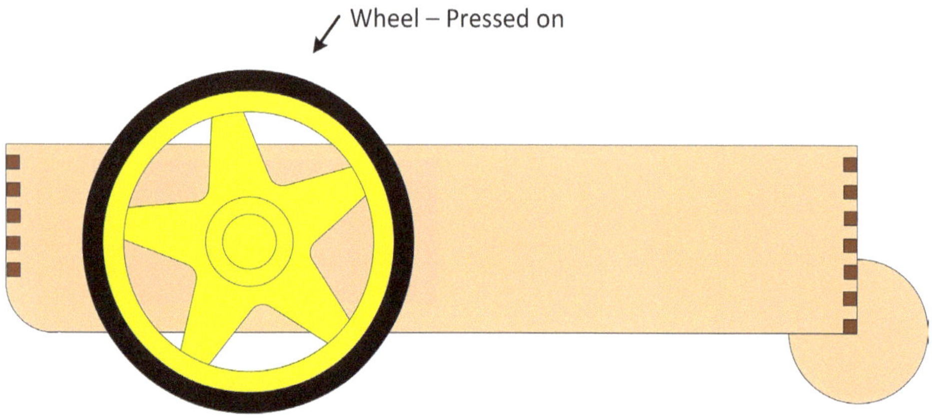

HT1-7. Wheels mounted to DC motors

The rolling robot body is now ready to be used. This robot is used in Lessons 15 and 18.

How-To #2: Create a PCB using Fritzing and OSH Park

Background:

This How-To provides instructions on how to create a printed circuit board (PCB) using the Fritzing (http://www.fritzing.org/) open-source design tool and then prepare that design for fabrication by OSH Park (http://www.oshpark.com/), which provides an economical fabrication service well suited for small volumes.

Because the production files Fritzing produces are not a perfect match to the requirements of OSH Park, this document provides step-by-step instructions for modifying the Fritzing files and then uploading the results to OSH Park for production. The instructions assume the circuit-board designer has an account with OSH Park; accounts are free and easy to set up on the website.

Important	This How-To does not include information about using the Fritzing software to design a circuit board. The Fritzing website provides excellent tutorials for this purpose. Keep in mind that circuit-board design is both an art and a science. Fritzing will help with the science, but the art is mastered only with practice.

Fritzing is unusual in that it allows a designer to begin with an interactive pictorial of a bread-board, jumper wires, components, and an Arduino™ single-board computer. The user can enter her bread-board experiment, then edit the schematic diagram generated by Fritzing, and finish by laying out the resulting circuit board. Some users prefer to go directly to the circuit-board layout and bypass the bread-board and schematic views.

The Infrared Navigation circuit board used by the Rolling Robot project is the example used here. Figure HT2-1 shows the three views of this circuit as seen inside the Fritzing software.

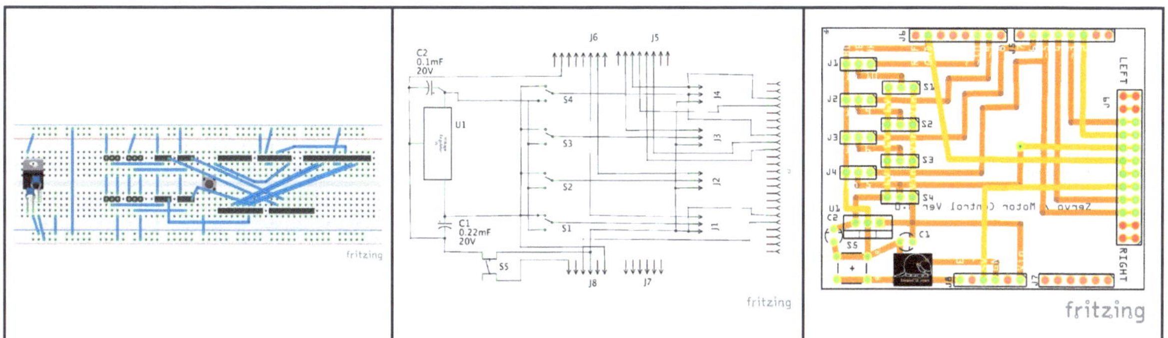

Bread-board (pictorial) view	Schematic view	Circuit-board view

Figure HT2-1. Three views of IR navigation circuit-board

The bread-board view in HT2-1, is a pictorial view — a picture or drawing of how the parts are physically connected.

The schematic view is an economical representation of the way the electricity flows.

The actual Fritzing design file for this circuit board can be found on LearnCSE.com.

Procedure:

1. Design the circuit board using Fritzing. (Instructions and tutorials for Fritzing are found on the organization's website, http://www.fritzing.org.)

2. Create a set of Gerber files by exporting for production. The menu path is:

   File -> Export -> for Production -> Extended Gerber (RS-274X…)

A set of nine files will be created. For the IR Navigation board, the files are:

```
IRNavigationVerPt6DoubleSidedGroundFill_contour.gm1
IRNavigationVerPt6DoubleSidedGroundFill_copperBottom.gbl
IRNavigationVerPt6DoubleSidedGroundFill_copperTop.gtl
IRNavigationVerPt6DoubleSidedGroundFill_maskBottom.gbs
IRNavigationVerPt6DoubleSidedGroundFill_maskTop.gts
IRNavigationVerPt6DoubleSidedGroundFill_silkBottom.gbo
IRNavigationVerPt6DoubleSidedGroundFill_silkTop.gto
IRNavigationVerPt6DoubleSidedGroundFill_drill.txt
IRNavigationVerPt6DoubleSidedGroundFill_pnp.txt
```

This listing was taken from a Macintosh computer. The listing on a Windows computer will be similar, but the `.txt` file suffix will be missing from the `_drill` file.

3. Look for the file that ends with `_drill`. On a Macintosh it will also have the suffix `.txt`, indicating it is a text file. Change this suffix to `.xln`. Thus, in this example,

```
IRNavigationVerPt6DoubleSidedGroundFill_drill.txt
```

becomes

```
IRNavigationVerPt6DoubleSidedGroundFill_drill.xln
```

For a Macintosh computer, simply editing the file name is sufficient.

On Windows computers, the `.txt` suffix exists but is hidden from the user. (The file would be named `IRNavigationVerPt6DoubleSidedGroundFill_drill`.) Windows computer users then will open the file with a good text editor, such as Notepad++. Then save the file as a `*.*` type and add the file extension `.xln` to the name. This will result in two files ending in `_drill`. Delete the one without the `.xln` suffix.

4. Locate the file that specifies the top silk screen. It will end with `_silkTop`, followed by the suffix `.gto`. Make a copy of this file but change the suffix to `.gko`. This will result in two files for the top silk screen, one with the suffix `.gto` and the other with the suffix `.gko`.

HT

5. OSH Park will not use all the files created by the Fritzing software. Zip the following Fritzing files into a single file:

```
boardname.GTL
boardname.GBL
boardname.GTS
boardname.GBS
boardname.GTO
boardname.GBO
boardname.GKO
boardname.G2L - only if a four-layer board
boardname.G3L - only if a four-layer board
boardname.XLN
```

   In this example the files to be zipped are:

```
IRNavigationVerPt6DoubleSidedGroundFill_copperTop.gtl
IRNavigationVerPt6DoubleSidedGroundFill_copperBottom.gbl
IRNavigationVerPt6DoubleSidedGroundFill_maskTop.gts
IRNavigationVerPt6DoubleSidedGroundFill_maskBottom.gbs
IRNavigationVerPt6DoubleSidedGroundFill_silkTop.gto
IRNavigationVerPt6DoubleSidedGroundFill_silkBottom.gbo
IRNavigationVerPt6DoubleSidedGroundFill_silkTop.gko
IRNavigationVerPt6DoubleSidedGroundFill_drill.xln
```

The zip file can be given any valid name. In the example, the name is:

```
IRNavigationVerPt6DoubleSidedGroundFill.zip
```

6. Go to http://www.oshpark.com/, click the [Get Started Now] button, and follow the instructions.

How-To #3: Make and Use a Motor Controller Shield

The Arduino™ single-board computer can be used to control servos and motors. But sometimes more current is required than the Arduino™ can provide, either because the motors chosen demand high current or because the applications requires multiple motors to operate at the same time.

The motor controller shield constructed in this How-To is an inexpensive way to deliver adequate current to and simultaneous control of several motors and servos. Each motor can have this current delivered at a regulated six volts or the voltage provided by a power source plugged into the power connector of the Arduino.™

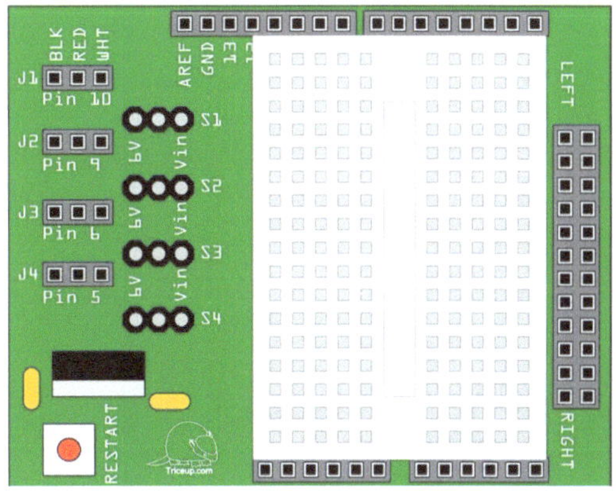

Figure HT3-1. Motor controller shield

The shield also provides a small prototyping board for adding related components such as infrared navigation, remote control, indicator lights, and sounds.

A special two-row header permits the addition of the H-bridge breakout board desribed in How-To #7, enabling control of two additional DC motors or a stepper motors or a single stepper motor.

Background:

Many of the devices made with the Arduino™ involve motion. Wheels turn, propellers spin, arms reach out, pincers grip, and flags wave. The devices that cause these motions are called motors. The shield built in these instructions is designed to control the types of motors commonly found in robotics.

These motors can be divided into three groups:

Group 1: Motors that move back and forth. These are called servos. Typical uses are to raise and lower elevators on an aircraft and to open and close arms on a robot. The direction and amount of motion is specified by the width of a pulse sent by the Arduino.™

Servos used with an Arduino™ are usually designed for six volts.

Group 2: Motors that spin but are controlled by the Arduino™ as if they are servos. These, in turn, fall into two subgroups: continuous rotation sersvos and motors controlled with electronic speed controllers (ESCs).

Continuous rotation servos: these are servos similar in appearance to those that move back and forth but have been modified to move a certain amount in one direction without returning. They are often used as propulsion for small robots, such as the Boe-bot from the Parallax Corporation. As with other servos, the continuous rotation servo usually requires six volts.

ESC-controlled motors: these are motors that are connected to the Arduino™ via an electronic speed controller, a special device that uses pulses from the Arduino™ to set the direction and speed of the motor. The controlled motor, in turn, connects to the ESC and not to the Arduino™ itself.

Because the ESC controls the delivered current, ESC-controlled motors can be high power and high speed. Such motors are used to turn the propellers of model airplanes and the wheels of larger, powerful model cars.

Group 3: Motors that spin clockwise or counterclockwise, depending on the polarity of their connection to their power source, and whose speed is determined by the average voltage. Proper operation of these motors requires a special control circuit called an H-bridge. The yellow motors used in the rolling robot of Lessons 15 and 18 are examples of such motors.

What is important to notice is that all the types of motors in groups 1 and 2 are controlled in the same way. Regardless of their task, whether moving the rudder of an airplane or spinning the propeller that powers it, these motors appear to the Arduino™ as servos and are programmed as shown in Lesson 11.

This shield can control up to four of these motors. Group 3 motors, by contrast, are programmed as shown in Lesson 14.

Table HT3-1. Motors that can be controlled with this motor controller shield

Type	**Description**	**Image**
VEX model 393 with Motor Controller 29 (brushed motor)	A flexible and powerful motor commonly used in competitive robotics. The VEX Motor Controller 29 is the ESC that allows the motor to be controlled by the Arduino.™	
Brushless Outrunner	Commonly used for powering model airplanes and helicopters. These motors are connected via an ESC to the Arduino.™ ESCs are matched to motors by current and voltage and are purchased separately.	

Type	Description	Image
Parallax Servo	A motor that rotates a specific distance when it's sent a pulse. Some are modified to turn continuously and are used for rolling robots. A servo also makes back and forth motions possible. A servo is specifically designed to translate pulses into motion and, therefore, does not require an external ESC.	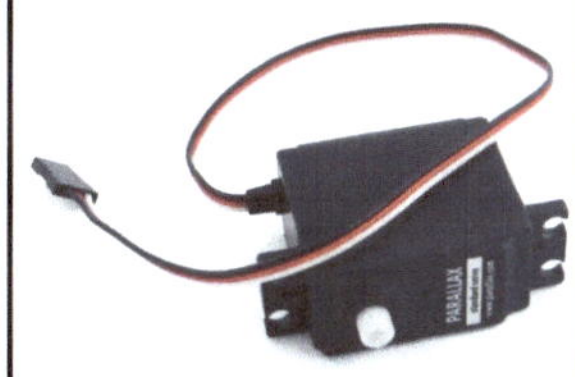
Geared, brushed DC Motor	An inexpensive and responsive DC motor with gears that reduce the rotation speed to one appropriate for driving wheels. This motor requires the H-bridge.	

HT

Description:

This controller shield can be extremely useful in the exploration of robotic devices controlled by the Arduino.™ For this reason, its design optimizes the following:

1. Flexibility. Any combination of up to four motors and servos can be controlled.
2. Extendibility. Stacking headers are used to allow for additional shields and breakout boards.
3. Broad application. In addition to controlling motors, the stacking headers and the bread-board prototyping areas provide for experimentation with complementary technologies such as infrared communication, radio transceivers, Bluetooth communication, and sensors.
4. DIY compatibility. The shield can be constructed entirely from scratch, including fabrication of the underlying circuit board.

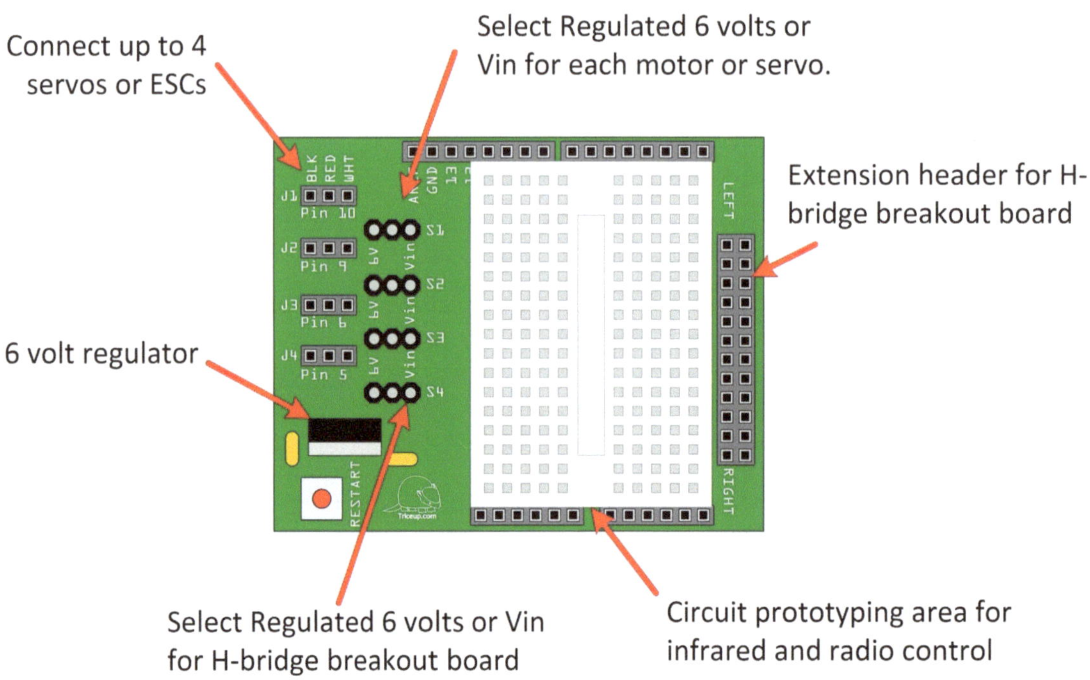

Figure HT3-2. Top view of a completed motor controller shield with feature callouts

The features of the motor controller shield are:

1. Servo and Motor Connection Headers. These are a set of four three-pin female headers into which servos are plugged. Most servos, including those from Parallax Inc., the most commonly used servos, also have female connectors. For the female connectors, a double-sided male three-pin header is used as an adapter (part number 2303 in Parts Catalog). ESCs for brushed motors usually have three-pin male headers and, thus, do not require adapters.

   The right-hand side of each header connects to a digital pin. From top to bottom in the figure, these pins are 10, 9, 6, and 5.

2. Power Source Selection Pins. Using a single shorting block, these pins connect the power (center) pin of its corresponding Connection Header to six volts coming from the voltage regulator, to Vin from the Arduino,™ or to nothing. Table HT3-2 illustrates the three possible configurations.

3. Prototyping board. This is a workspace for experimenting with components that complement the servos and motors. It is used in the IR Navigation Lesson (Lesson 14) and the IR Robot Remote Control Lesson (Lesson 17).

4. Stacking headers. These are special connectors that allow this shield to be plugged into an Arduino™ Uno, Mega, and any other board with similar printout. And they have female sockets on the top allowing other shields to be plugged into this one.

5. Restart push button. This button restarts the Arduino™ sketch.

6. Voltage regulator. It provides a stable +6 volts to the servos.

Table HT3-2. Motor power option jumper settings

Connection	Purpose	Jumper placement
Shorting block connects motor power to regulated +6 volts.	A wide variety of rotation applications, from high speed through high torque, are made possible by attaching a brushed motor to gears.	
Shorting block connects motor to raw, incoming voltage.	A brushless motor is commonly used for spinning propellers for model aircraft and drive shafts for model cars and boats.	
Shorting block not used.	A servo makes back and forth motions and, in the case of continuous rotation servos, low-speed turning motion possible.	

Important	Brushless and other motors with batteries connected directly to ESCs can be used to power the Arduino.™ This is both helpful and necessary if the Arduino™ has no other source of power, as is the case on an airplane. In this case, the jumper of one, and only one, of the used motor headers can be used to connect to Vin.

Building or Buying the Circuit Board

The circuit board for this shield has been designed for ease of assembly by using large traces for easy soldering and providing wide spacing between parts. It can be obtained in the following ways:

1. Buy it directly from LearnCSE.com. The board can be purchased by itself or as part of a kit containing all the other necessary components.

2. Have the board commercially made by a board fabricator such as OSH Park. Instructions for submitting a Fritzing-designed board to OSH Park can be found on LearnCSE.com.

3. Do-It-Yourself fabrication. The Fritzing (www.fritzing.org) project file is available for download from LearnCSE.com. The board is double-sided, but the top layer has only a few traces, which can be replaced with jumpers. Instructions for making your own circuit boards can be found in the How-To instruction "How To Make a Printed Circuit Board," also from LearnCSE.com.

Procedure:

Begin by assembling the materials. Among the options for finding these parts are:

1. Buy a kit of parts directly from the LearnCSE.com store. If you are also purchasing the prefabricated circuit board, both the board and the parts can be purchased as a kit.
2. Purchase each part from various suppliers. Look up each item in the LearnCSE.com Parts Catalog via the catalog number in the Materials table. The catalog provides a source and, usually, the source's part number.

Materials:

Quantity	Part	Image	Notes	Part Number	Catalog Number
4	Headers, 3-pin, female		J1 -> J4. Cut from 20-pin header	J1, J2, J3, J4	2201
4	Headers, 3-pin, male. Notice how each part has a corresponding location identified by its part number on the top of the board. J5 and J6, for example, are the part numbers for two 8-pin stacking headers. They are placed into the areas marked J5 and J6 on the circuit board.		S1 -> S4. Cut from 20-pin header.	S1, S2, S3, S4	2204
4	Shorting Blocks		To be used with S1 - S4.	SB1, SB2, SB3, SB4	2205
2	8-pin Stacking Headers		Can be purchased together as one item.	J5, J6	2203
2	6-pin Stacking Headers		Matches 6-pin female header on Arduino™ Uno.	J7, J8	2202
1	Voltage Regulator		1.5 amp, model 7806	U1	1104

Quan-tity	Part	Image	Notes	Part Number	Catalog Number
1	0.33 capacitor		Ceramic capacitor. May be marked 334.	C1	0202
1	0.10 capacitor		Ceramic capacitor. May be marked 104.	C2	0203
1	Circuit board	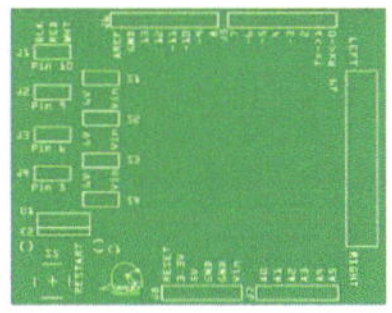	Gerber files and finished board both available from LearnCSE.com.	---	PCB502
1	Small Bread-board	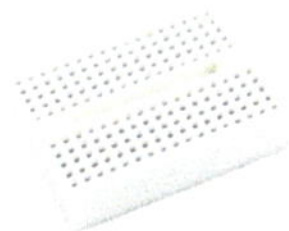	170 contact.	---	2305
1	Push button		Bread-board and PCB friendly.	S5	3106

Steps

1. Familiarize yourself with the parts. Be sure you recognize each part and know where it goes on the circuit board. Remember, all parts go on the top of the board, that side with all the white outlines and labels. In the image on the materials list the circuit board is green, but the actual color will depend on where the board itself was made. Boards fabricated by OSH Park, for example, are purple. Still, the white outlines and lettering are always the same.

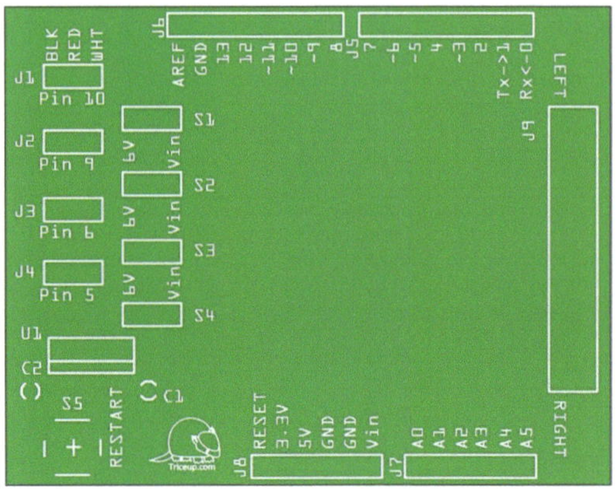

Figure HT3-3. Top of circuit board

Notice how each part has a corresponding location identified by its part number on the top of the board. J5 and J6, for example, are the part numbers for two 8-pin stacking headers. They are placed into the areas marked J5 and J6 on the circuit board.

2. Insert the two 8-pin stacking headers into the positions marked J5 and J6, as shown in Figure HT3-4. Solder on bottom of the board.

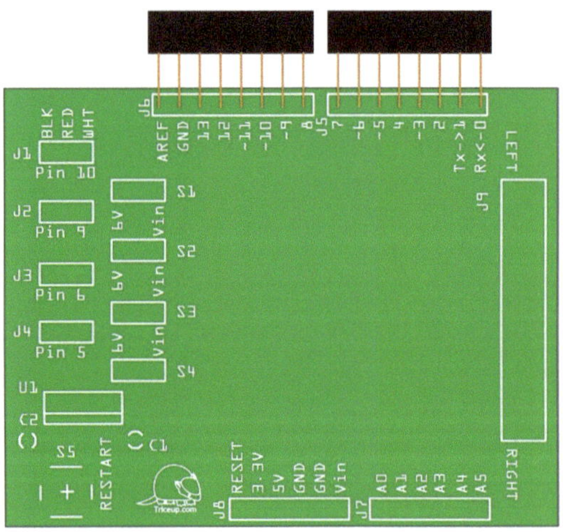

Figure HT3-4. Location to insert 8-pin stacking headers

3. In a similar manner, insert and solder the two 6-pin stacking headers into the positions marked J7 and J8, as shown in Figure HT3-5.

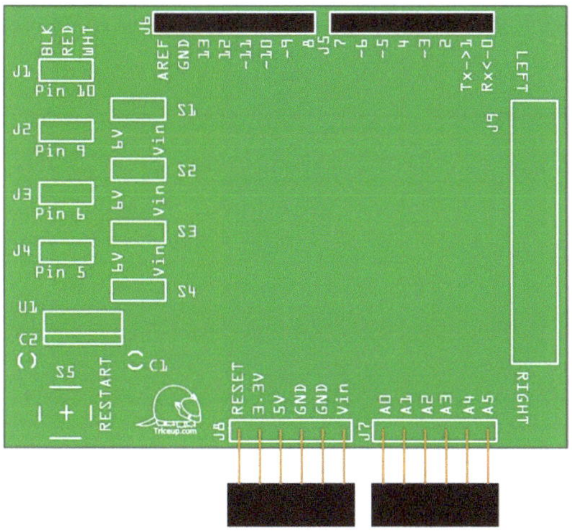

Figure HT3-5. Location to insert 6-pin stacking headers

HT

4. Locate a strip of female headers used for parts J1, J2, J3, and J4. Use a pair of strong wire cutters to cut four 3-pin headers from this strip, as shown in Figure HT3-6. These become parts J1, J2, J3, and J4.

Important	To yield a 3-pin header, the strip must be cut directly on top of the fourth pin, as shown in Figure HT3-6.

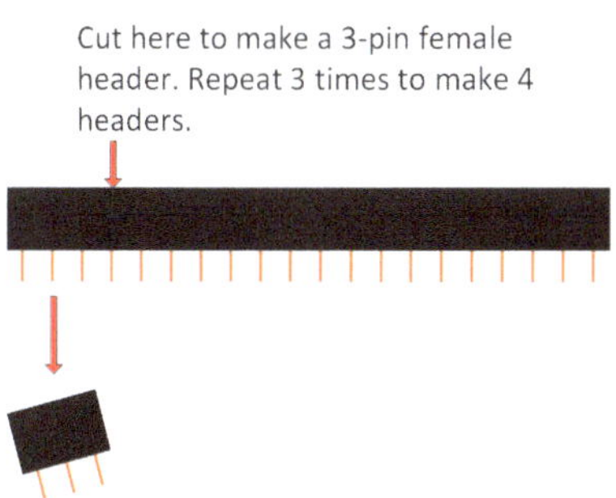

Figure HT3-6. Location to cut female header strip

Light sandpaper can be used to smooth the rough edges of the cut end.

5. Insert the four female headers into the top of the circuit through the locations marked J1, J2, J3, and J4, as shown in Figure HT3-7. Solder from the bottom.

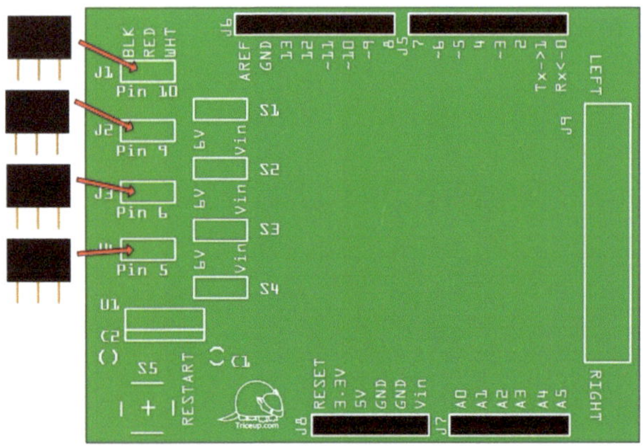

Figure HT3-7. Location to insert female headers

6. Locate a strip of male headers used for making parts S1, S2, S3, and S4. As with step 4, use wire cutters to cut three times, creating four male headers of 3 pins each.

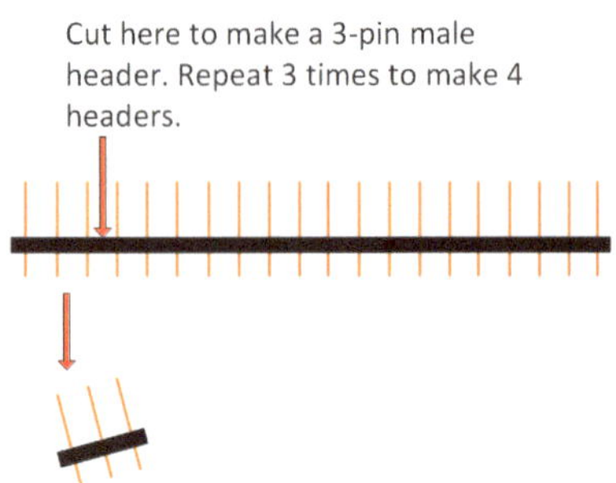

Figure HT3-8. Location to cut male header strip

Important	Notice that for male headers, the cut is made between pins, not on top of a pin.

7. Insert and solder the four male headers into the top of the circuit board through locations marked S1, S2, S3, and S4. See Figure HT3-9.

Important	The short pins go through the circuit board. The long pins stick up.

HT

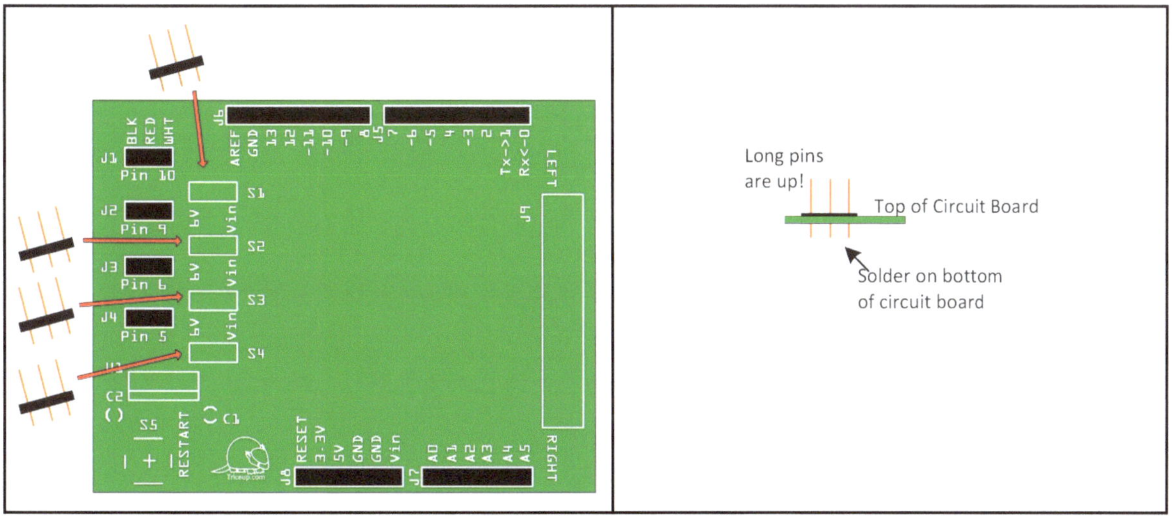

Figure HT3-9. Location to insert and solder male headers

8. Insert and solder the two capacitors, C1 and C2.

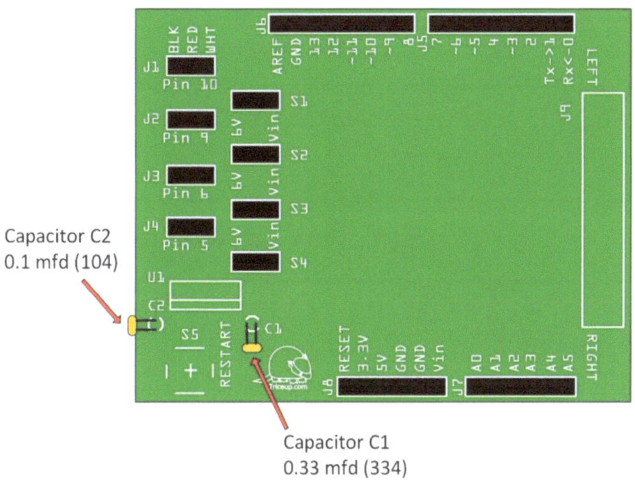

Figure HT3-10. Location to solder capacitors

9. Insert and solder the push button, S5, as shown in Figure HT3-11.

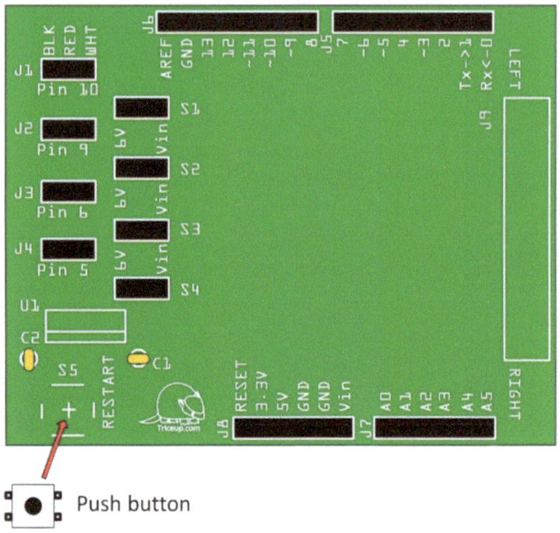

Figure HT3-11. Location to solder push button

10. Insert and solder the voltage regulator, U1 as shown in HT3-12. Insert the regulator as far as it will comfortably go, which is up to the point where the pins widen. The regulator will sit somewhat above the board. This is useful, should it need to be bent down out of the way so another Arduino™ shield can be plugged into the top of this one.

Caution	Take care not to install the voltage regulator backwards. The metal plate of the regulator must face the push button, S5.	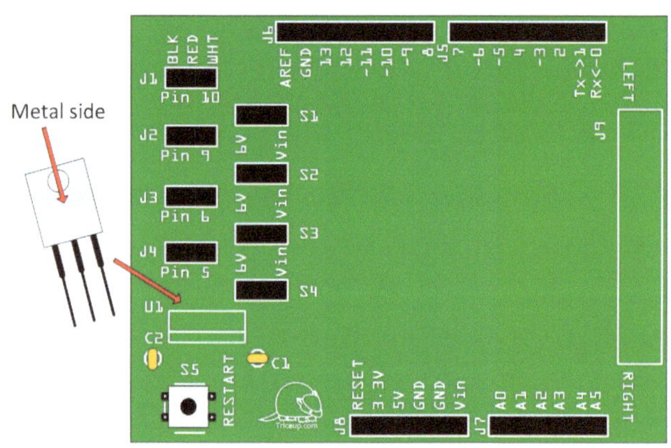

Figure HT3-12. Location to solder voltage regulator

11. Insert and solder the double-row female header (12 pins in each row) into the location marked J9.

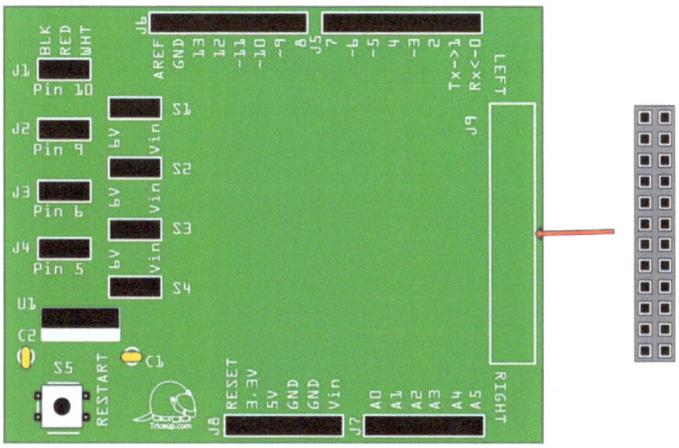

Figure HT3-13. Location to insert double-row female header

12. Finally, pull the protective cover off the tape on the bottom of the small bread-board and set the bread-board directly onto the surface of the circuit board between the six- and eight-pin headers.

The completed board should look like Figure HT3-14.

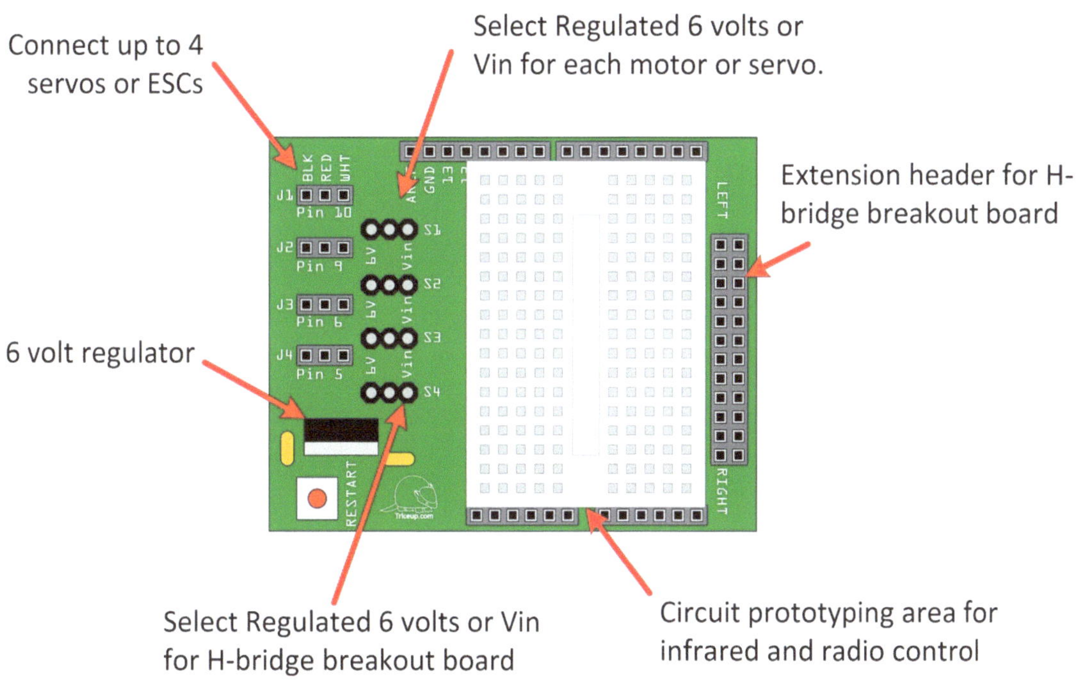

Figure HT3-14. Completed motor controller shield with feature callouts

How-To #4: Read Resistor Values

Many of the experiments and projects in these lessons use resistors. Resistors come in different values, representing the amount of resistance offered the flow of electrons. The unit of measure is the ohm, named after the German physicist and mathematician Georg Simon Ohm.

The value of any particular resistor is usually indicated by a set of colored stripes on the body. This How-To illustrates how to determine a resistor's value by reading these colors.

Figure HT4-1. Georg Ohm
(Wikipedia*)

HT

Background:

Electricity is the flow of electrons through some conductive medium. For the circuits made in the lessons in this book and on the website LearnCSE.com, the medium is usually copper wire or copper foil on a printed circuit board. Electrons flow through copper very easily, so easily we can think of them as meeting no resistance.

But there are times when we want electrons to meet with resistance. This might be to protect an electronic device. Too many electrons through a light-emitting diode, for example, can cause its internal components to overheat and melt or burn.

Other times we want a voltage that is somewhere between zero and some value. This is called a voltage divider; and Lesson 9: Analog IO uses a voltage divider to determine the position of a knob that can be turned.

The important point is that a resistor is a device that presents "resistance" to the flow of electrons. This resistance results in a measurable voltage across the resistor. The relationship between resistance of a resistor, the quantity of electrons that flow through that resistor, and the voltage measurable across that resistor was determined by Herr Ohm and is expressed in the law that bears his name, Ohm's Law.

Figure HT4-2 shows a resistor of value 220 ohms connected across a 9-volt battery. Notice current (I) flows through the resistor and encounters resistance (R). This results in the voltage (V) that can be measured across the resistor.

*Ⓟ Image of Georg Simon Ohm: Public domain, Wikimedia Commons via German Wikipedia. {{PD-1923}}

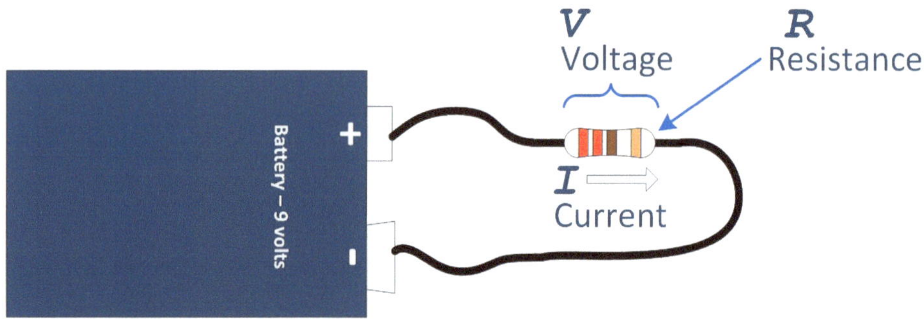

Figure HT4-2. Resistor connected across a 9-volt battery

The relation of voltage to resistance and current is expressed by Ohm's Law: ***V=IR***

Description:

Reading the colors

Consider the resistor shown in Figure HT4-3. Remember, an actual resistor is less than ½-inch in length. To make reading instructions easier to understand, resistor images are magnified greatly in this How-To.

Figure HT4-3: Resistor (expanded greatly from actual size)

Notice that this resistor, like a typical resistor, has four stripes. Three are close together, as seen in Figure HT4-3. The fourth is by itself and is a metallic color, usually silver or gold. The colored stripes indicate the value, whereas the metallic color indicates the tolerance, an estimate of how close the actual value of the resistor comes to the indicated value.

The colors are read from left to right, with the metallic color on the right-hand side. A gold band indicates that the actual value of the resistor is within 5 percent of what the stripes indicate. A silver band indicates that the actual value is within 10 percent.

The value of a resistor is expressed in ohms and encoded in the colors. Each color is associated with a number, as shown in Table HT4-1.

Table HT4-1. Resistor color codes

Color	Value
Black	0
Brown	1
Red	2
Orange	3
Yellow	4
Green	5
Blue	6
Violet	7
Gray	8
White	9

HT

The first two colors on the resistor shown in Figure HT4-3 are actual numbers, read directly from the color table, as shown in Table HT4-1. In this case the colors are brown (with a value of 1) followed by black (value of 0). Together, they produce the number 10.

The third color is red. But instead of being read as the number 2, it is interpreted as the number of zeros to be added to the number produced by the first two colors. In this case, red is 2, meaning two zeroes are added. The final resistance is 1000 ohms.

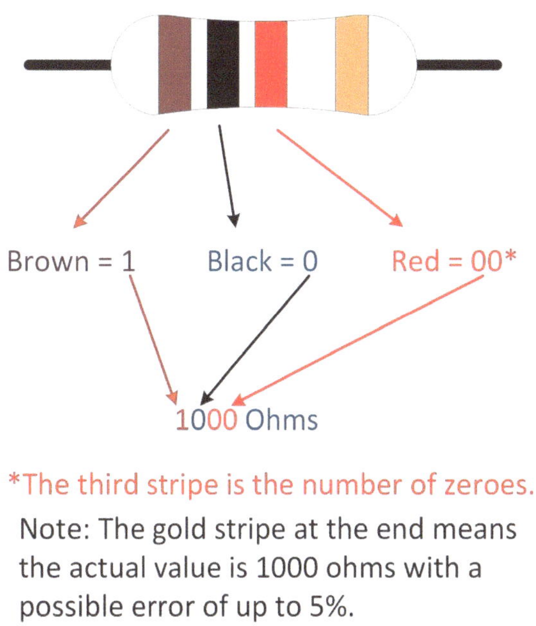

Figure HT4-4. Diagram for reading 1000 ohm resistor

Figure HT4-5 is another example of a resistor, this time a resistor with colors yellow-violet- yellow. The resulting value, 470,000 ohms, can also be written 470k ohms, where the letter k is representing three zeros.

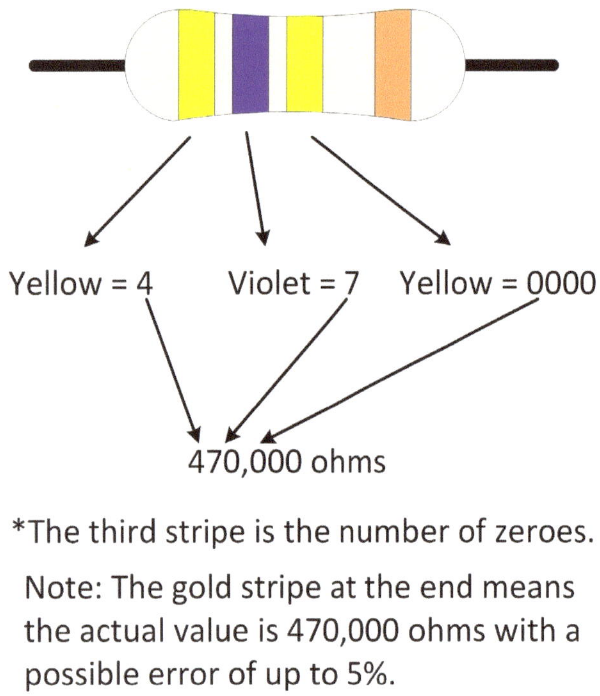

Figure HT4-5. Diagram for reading 470,000 ohm resistor

How-To #5: Make Arduino™ Tones Louder

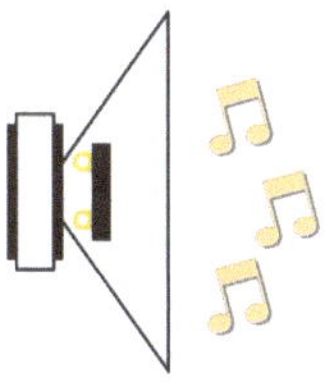

The Arduino™ can generate what can be called a passable tone using the function `tone()`. This How-To shows how a few inexpensive parts can be used to make these tones dramatically louder than those heard when a speaker is connected directly to an Arduino™ output pin.

HT

Background:

The Arduino™ can make sounds, but they aren/t loud.

Many Arduino™ tutorials, including those on our home site LearnCSE.com, have a lesson that uses the Arduino™ function `tone()` to generate a sound. Typically a speaker is connected to an Arduino™ pin, either by a coupling capacitor or a resistor.

While this connection works well for teaching the use of the function, it has the disadvantage of producing a low-volume tone. Many of us, particularly when we want to add sound effects to something we've made that is powered by an Arduino,™ want a much louder sound.

A linear audio amplifier can make them louder, but at the expense of several parts.

An audio amplifier, such as the ubiquitous LM386, can be added but at the cost of the integrated circuit and all its supporting components, including up to four capacitors, a resistor, and some sort of potentiometer if volume control is desired.

Arduino™ tones are square waves, providing a simple alternative.

But an Arduino™ tone is a square wave with a 50% duty cycle repeated at the desired frequency. It's not very musical, but it is simple. It doesn't need to be "amplified." To sound louder all that's needed is a way to increase current through the speaker. And this can be done by reducing the overall resistance of the speaker circuit.

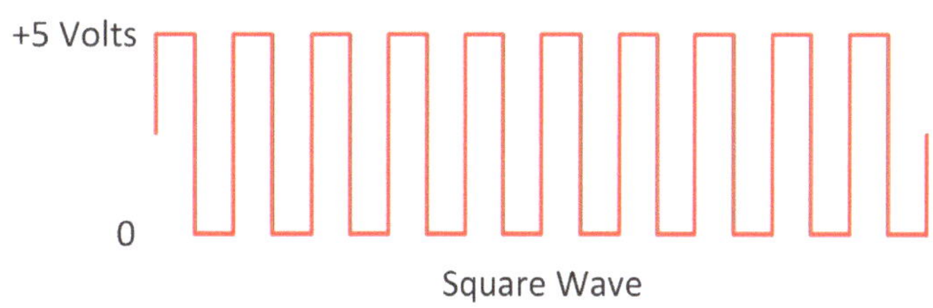

Figure HT5-1. Square wave

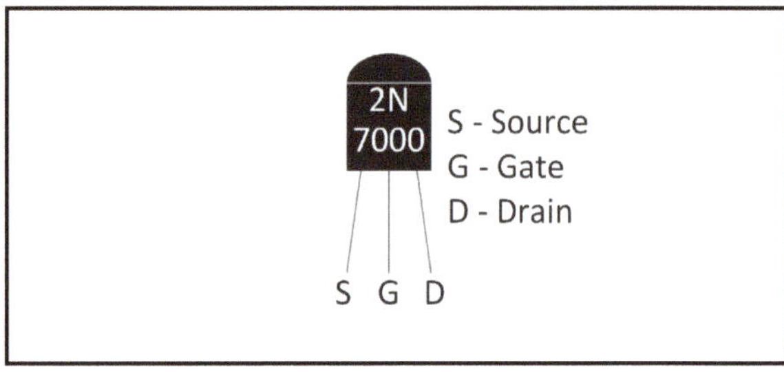

Figure HT5-2. Pictorial for FET

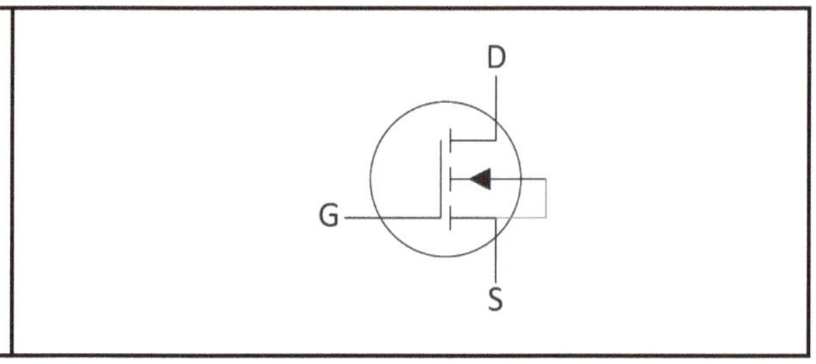

Figure HT5-3. Schematic for FET

To do this all we need is to connect the speaker directly to a source of electrical current, then switch this current on and off as the square wave goes to +5 volts and zero. The device that can do this is a *Field Effect Transistor (FET)*. There are many types of FETs; we will use a 2N7000, which is an *N-channel, Metal Oxide Semiconductor, Field Effect Transistor (MOSFET)*. As Figure HT5-2 shows, this device has three pins labeled Source (S), Gate (G), and Drain (D). The schematic symbol for this FET is shown in Figure HT5-3.

The feature of the FET that will be taken advantage of is that when the gate is positive relative to the source the resistance between the drain and source drops to nearly zero. This is the "switch." As the schematic Figure HT5-4 shows, the drain is connected to the Vin of the Arduino™ via the speaker. The source is connected to ground. And, finally, the gate, as the switch, is connected to the pin of the Arduino™ that is generating the square wave.

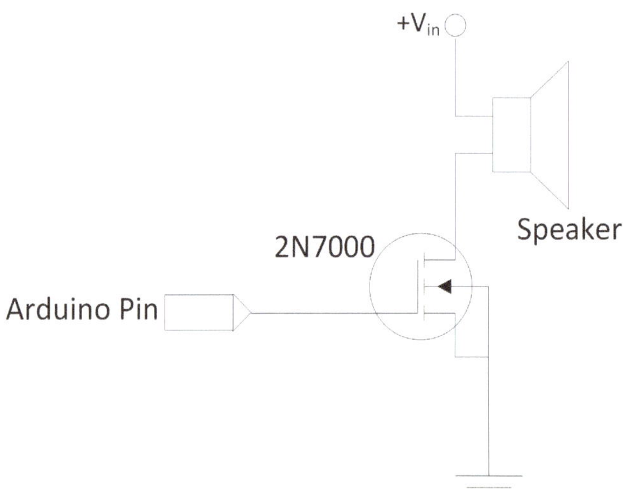

Notice the connection to Vin rather than +5 volts. This allows greater current than can be delivered via the Arduino™ itself.

Figure HT5-4. Schematic for using FET to amplify square wave generated by Arduino™

Procedure:

These instructions show how to prototype a MOSFET switch to drive audio-frequency square waves through a speaker. The resulting sound should be significantly louder than those heard when a speaker is connected directly to an Arduino™ pin.

Among the advantages of this approach is that just a few new, inexpensive parts are needed.

Materials:

Quantity	Part	Image	Notes	Catalog Number
1	Arduino™ Uno		Single-board computer.	3102
1	USB Cable		This is a standard USB adapter cable with a flat connector on one end and a square connector on the other.	2301
1	Computer with at least one USB port and access to the Arduino™ website, http://www.arduino.cc.	---	The operating system of this computer must be Windows, Macintosh OS/X, or Linux.	---
1	Field effect transistor (FET) 2N7000		N-channel, MOSFET.	1305
1	Magnetic speaker		4, 8, or 16 ohm.	3119

Steps

1. Assemble the parts shown in the Materials list.
2. Wire the parts as shown in the Figure HT5-5.

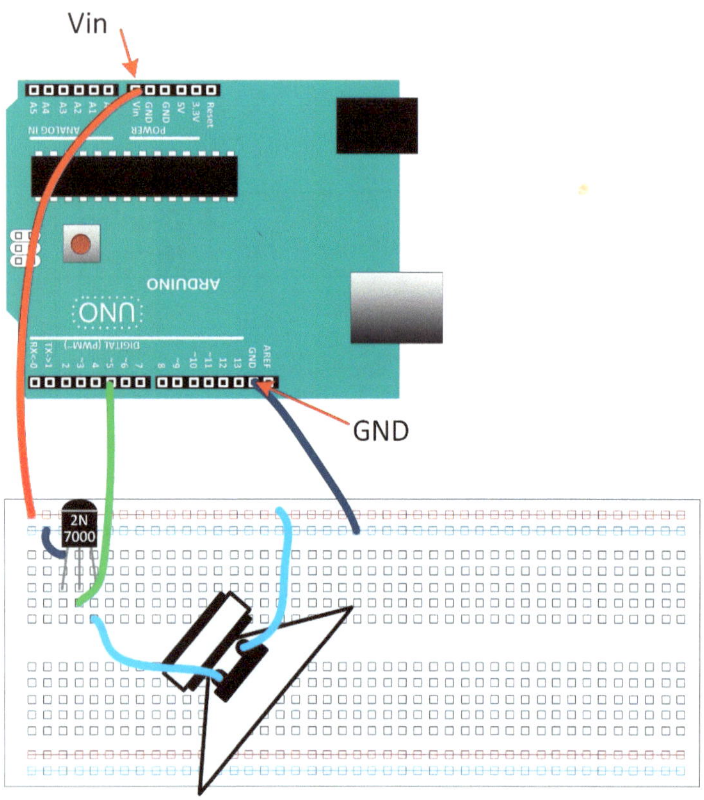

Figure HT5-5. Pictorial diagram for connecting Arduino™ to speaker

3. Connect the Arduino™ to the programming computer via a USB cable.
4. Enter then upload the test sketch from Lesson 10, `Lesson10SimpleTones.ino`.

The louder sounds should now be obvious.

How-To #6: Make an Infrared Headlight

Background:

An infrared (IR) headlight is a small device that shines infrared light in only one direction, much as a hand-held flashlight shines light in only one direction. IR headlights are commonly used on small rolling robots to detect obstacles or illuminate some path to be followed.

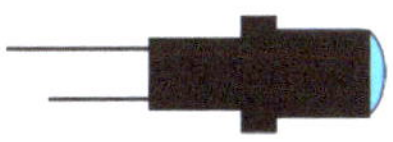

An infrared-emitting diode (IRED) cannot be used for this purpose all by itself because, while it focuses infrared in the forward direction, it also allows emissions from the sides and the back.

IR headlights are very simple, consisting of an IRED and some sort of cover that prevents these spurious emissions by surrounding the diode with an infrared-opaque material. A rough analogy is putting a light bulb in a soup can that is open at one end.

This method of making infrared diodes is simple and inexpensive. The materials are available almost everywhere.

Materials:

Quantity	Part	Image	Notes	Catalog Number
1	Infrared-emitting diode	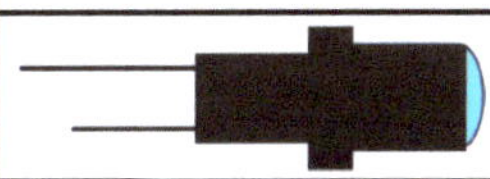	---	1303
1 inch	3/8-inch diameter shrink tubing	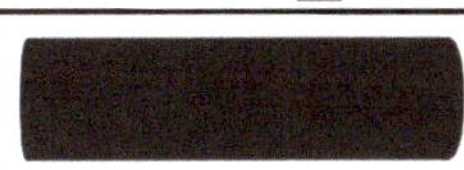	The tubing must be opaque to infrared light.	4105

Heat shrink tubing comes in many colors, but black seems to work best because other colors are often transparent to infrared.

You will also need a pair of scissors and a butane lighter. Other heat sources will work, including matches. But matches and candles tend to darken the tubing.

Procedure:

1. Using the scissors, cut the 1-inch tubing into two pieces of length ½-inch each.

Figure HT6-1. Heat-shrink tubing

2. Place one of the pieces of tubing over the IRED, allowing the end of the diode to project just beyond the tubing.
3. Shrink the tubing by applying heat from the butane lighter. Move the flame while rotating the diode with the tubing. The tubing will shrink tightly around the diode.
4. Repeat step 3 with the second piece of tubing. Pay special attention to the tubing around the wires. It needs to be as flat as possible.

The final diode should look something like Figure HT6-2.

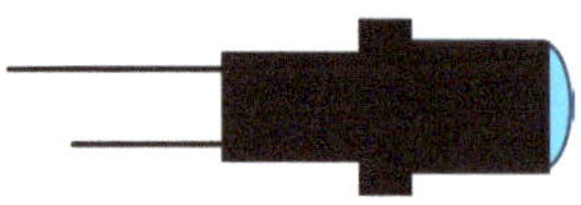

Figure HT6-2. IR Headlight

How-To #7: Assemble an H-bridge Circuit Board

Making a DC motor turn is relatively easy: simply connect the motor's terminals to a power supply. But what if the motor is to be controlled by an Arduino,™ and what if that motor requires more current at a higher voltage than the Arduino™ can deliver?

For this we use the H-bridge, a device under the control of two digital pins that can turn a motor on and off and set its direction. Further, if one of these pins is capable of pulse-width modulation, the H-bridge can also control the speed of that motor.

In this How-To we assemble an H-bridge that brings the ability to control two DC motors to the Motor Controller Shield of How-To #3, simply by plugging it in.

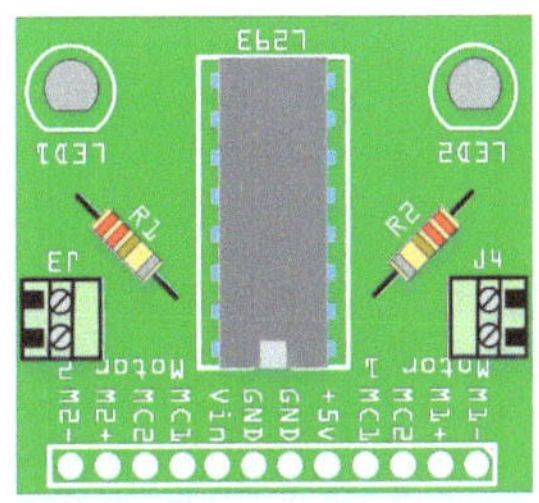

Figure HT7-1. H-bridge circuit board

Background:

The DC motors this H-bridge can control are common, inexpensive, and extremely useful. They are "brushed" motors, meaning each is composed of a coil of wire inside a magnet. When electrical current is run through the wire a magnetic field is created that opposes the field of the permanent magnet, causing the coil to move. How such a motor works is described and illustrated on Wikipedia at https://en.wikipedia.org/wiki/Brushed_DC_electric_motor#Simple_two-pole_DC_motor.

An Arduino™ can directly control such a motor, provided the motor requires about 5 volts and very little current. Most useful motors, however, are designed for higher voltages and currents. The motors used in the lessons in this book and the companion website (LearnCSE.com), for example, run best at six volts and draw between 0.15 and 0.4 amps, depending on how much work they are attempting.

An H-bridge connects a DC motor to an appropriate power supply but does it in such a way that a pair of Arduino™ digital pins can turn that power on and off, and set the polarity, thus setting the spin direction.

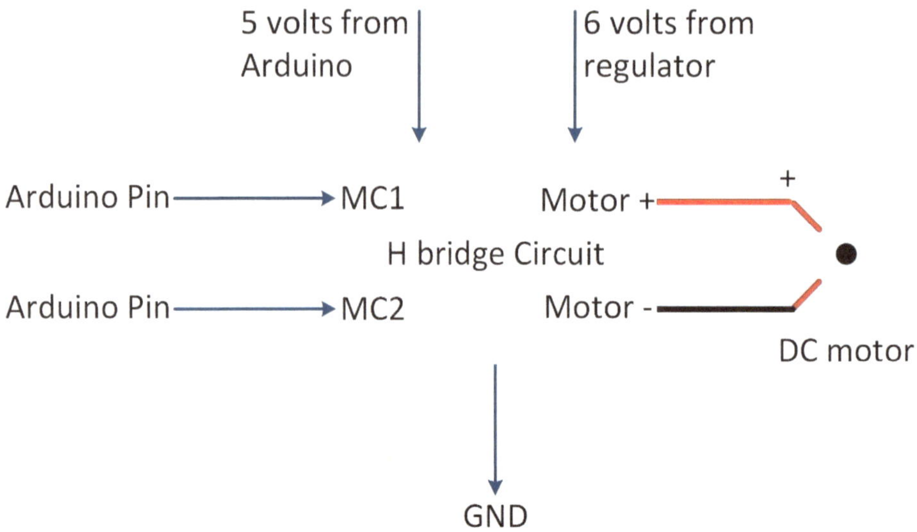

Figure HT7-2. H-bridge control of a DC motor

The values of the Arduino™ pins turn the DC motor on or off and set the directions, as shown in Table HT7-1.

Table HT7-1. Motor direction as a function of inputs to MC pins

MC1	**MC2**	**Motor**
HIGH	HIGH	Stopped
HIGH	LOW	Spins one direction
LOW	HIGH	Spins reverse direction
LOW	LOW	Stopped

Description:

The heart of the H-bridge circuit board built here is the L293 integrated circuit. The pinout for these is in Figure HT7-3.

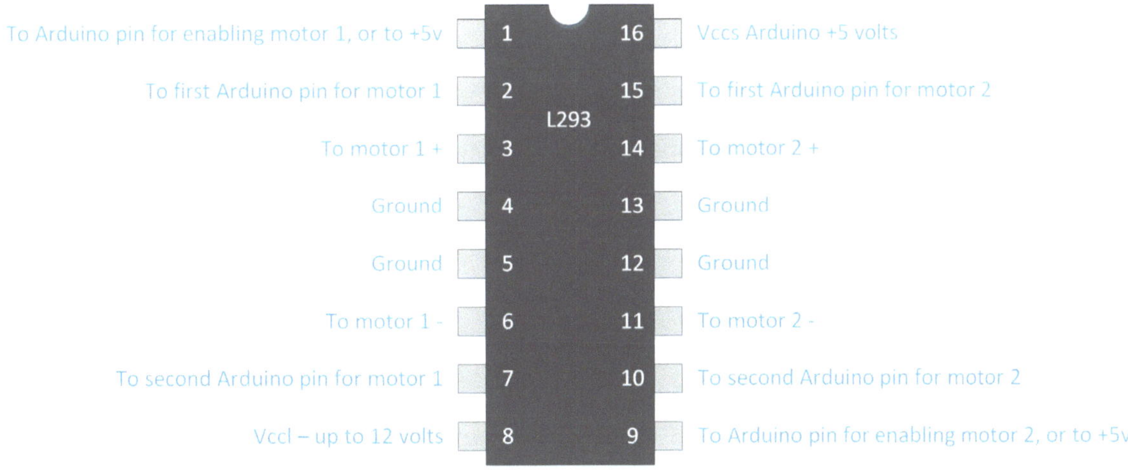

Figure HT7-3. Pinout of L293 integrated circuit

Notice how each side of this integrated circuit controls one motor from a pair of Arduino™ pins.

Pins 1 and 9 can be used to enable and disable their respective motors. For this circuit board we permanently enable both motors by connecting these pins to +5 volts.

Important	The notch at the top indicates the end of the integrated circuit close to pin 1. Use this notch to orient the circuit with the circuit board. Reversing it will result in an H-bridge circuit board that cannot function.

Building or Buying the Circuit Board

The raw circuit board used here is double-sided. It has been designed for ease of assembly by using large traces for easy soldering. It can be obtained in the following ways:

1. Buy it directly from LearnCSE.com. The board can be purchased by itself or as part of a kit containing all the other necessary components.
2. Do-It-Yourself fabrication. The Fritzing (www.fritzing.org) project file is available for download from LearnCSE.com. The Fritzing application can print accurately scaled masks for each side of the board.
3. Have the board commercially made by a board fabricator such as OSH Park. Instructions for submitting a Fritzing-designed board to OSH Park can be found on LearnCSE.com.

Procedure:

Where to get the parts

Begin by assembling the materials. Among the options for finding these parts are:

1. Buy a kit of parts directly from the LearnCSE.com store. If you are also purchasing the prefabricated circuit board, both the board and the parts can be purchased as a kit.
2. Purchase each part from various suppliers. Look up each item in the LearnCSE.com Parts Catalog via the catalog number in the Materials table. The catalog provides a source and, usually, the source's part number.

Materials:

Quantity	Part	Image	Notes	Catalog Number
1	Arduino™ Uno		Single-board computer. This board is delicate and should be handled with care. When you are not using it, keep it in a box or plastic bag.	3102
1	USB Cable	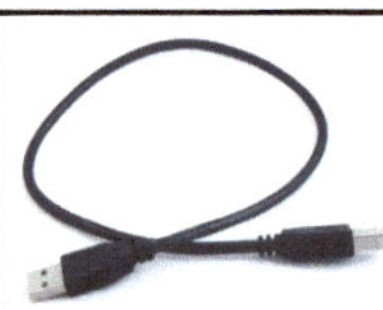	This is a standard USB adapter cable with a flat connector on one end and a square connector on the other.	2301
1	Circuit board	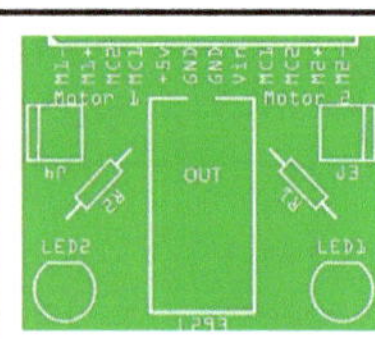	Purchase from LearnCSE.com or DIY.	PCB505
1	H-bridge integrated circuit, L293		Dual-inline pin. UI	1307
2	Resistor, 220 ohm (red-red-brown)		R1, R2	0102
2	Screw Terminal		2 position, J2, J3	4108

Quan-tity	Part	Image	Notes	Catalog Number
2	Red / Green bi-color LED		2 lead, LED1, LED2	1310
1	Male header, 12 pin		J1.	2204

Steps

1. Familiarize yourself with the parts. Be sure you recognize each part and know where it goes on the circuit board. In the image on the materials list, the circuit board is green, but the actual color will depend on where the board itself was made. Still, the white outlines and lettering are always the same.

Important	All parts are inserted on the top of the raw board and soldered on the bottom except the male header. It is inserted from the bottom of the board and soldered on the top.

2. Begin by placing the integrated circuit on the top of the circuit board, taking care to align the notch on the top of the board to the gap in the white rectangle drawn on the board, as shown in Figure HT7-4.

   Solder the integrated circuit in place from the bottom.

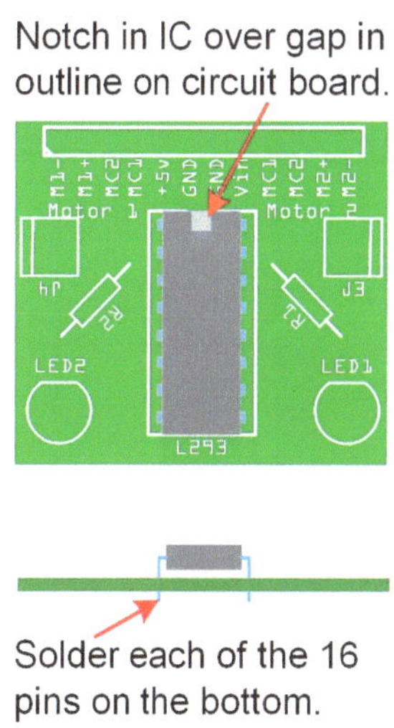

Figure HT7-4. Pin soldered to integrated circuit

3. Insert and solder the two 220 ohm resistors. Trim excees leads from the bottom.

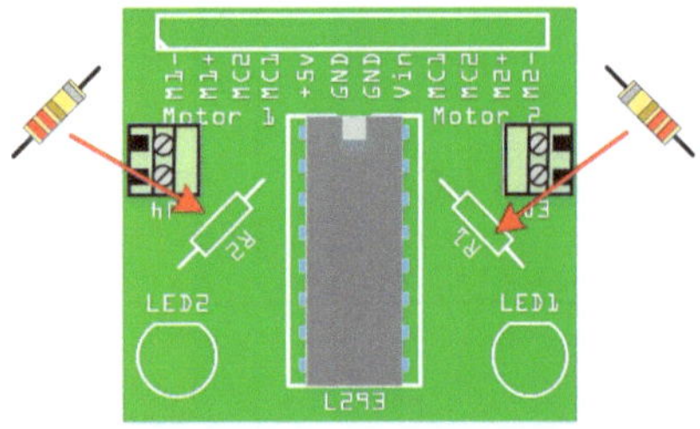

Figure HT7-5. Resistors soldered

4. Insert and solder the two screw terminals.

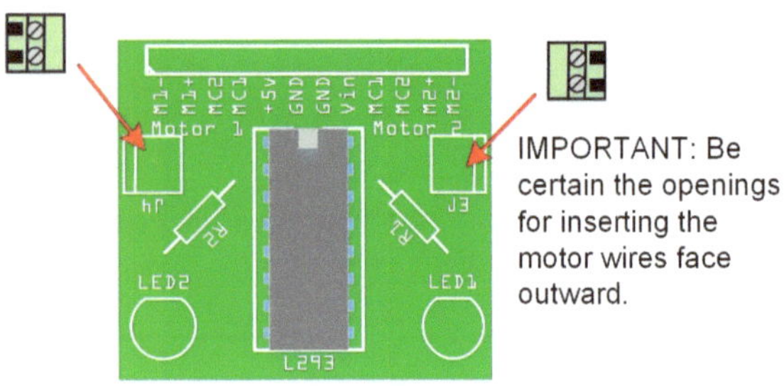

Figure HT7-6. Screw terminals soldered

5. Prepare a 12-pin male header as shown in HT7-7.

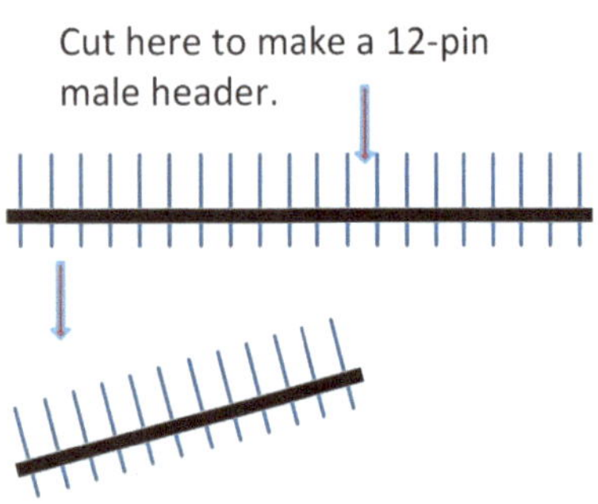

Figure HT7-7. 12-pin male header

6. Insert the male header through the bottom of the circuit board and solder on the top.

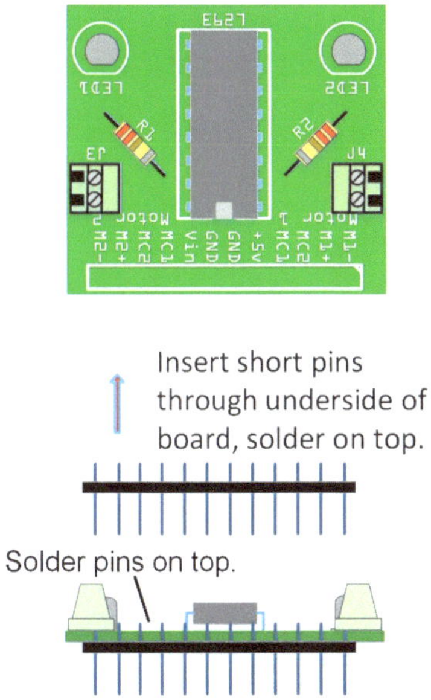

Figure HT7-8. Header inserted into circuit board, then soldered

The H-bridge, as shown in HT7-9, is now complete. Check for good solder connections and remove any solder that bridges connections.

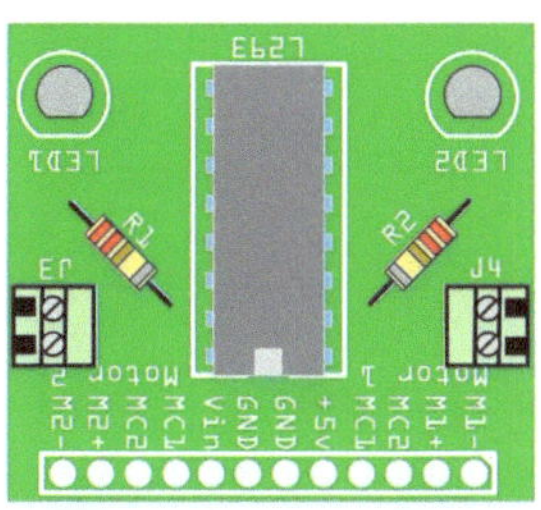

Figure HT7-9. Complete H-bridge

How-To #8: Work with Smart LEDs

This How-To shows how to connect and control a number of special light-emitting diodes, each of which can be set to any color and brightness. We will use NeoPixels from AdaFruit and control them with the Arduino™ library AdaFruit provides.

Background

We love LEDs. But most of them light in only one color. True, so-called bicolor LEDs light one color when connected one way and a second color when the connection is reversed. But what we really want is an LED that can light up in any color and can be generated by mixing red, green, and blue light.

Tricolor LEDs that will do this are available. But to drive one of these LEDs requires three separate digital Arduino™ pins, one for each color. And that's for each LED. Want five in a row? Get ready to find 15 digital pins. This is just not practical.

Adafruit offers LEDs it refers to as NeoPixels that meet our requirements perfectly. These LEDs come in several forms, from small discs that can be sewn into clothing to strips and even individual NeoPixels that look a lot like ordinary LEDs with a few too many wires. These devices are perfect for us because each NeoPixel mixes the light from three LEDs—one green, one blue, and one red. Even better, each NeoPixel comes with its own tiny built-in microprocessor that lets it be controlled with just one wire.

Even better still, data that comes in through that wire can be sent out another wire to another NeoPixel, meaning that multiple NeoPixels can be connected all in a row. We can set the brightness and color of as many LEDs as we might want from only one Arduino™ digital pin. Figure HT8-1 shows a pinout of the NeoPixel used in this How-To.

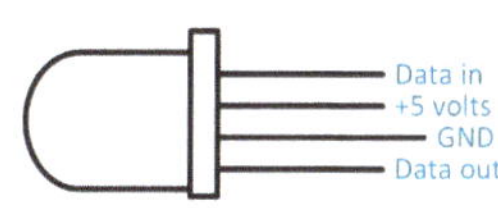

Figure HT8-1. NeoPixel with pins identified

Important	An individual NeoPixel can require up to 60 milliamperes. This may not sound like a lot, but the upper limit of the Arduino™ is about 400 milliamperes and can be quickly exhausted. So, while we show the NeoPixels connected to the +5 volts pin of the Arduino,™ sizeable projects will require a separate five-volt power supply.

Procedure:

This How-To shows how to connect five NeoPixels together and, using the Adafruit library, drive them. It also reviews the methods the library makes available for the programmer and concludes with a modest sample sketch.

Materials:

Quantity	Part	Image	Notes	Catalog Number
1	Arduino™ Uno		Single-board computer. This board is delicate and should be handled with care. When you are not using it, keep it in a box or plastic bag.	3102
1	USB Cable		This is a standard USB adapter cable with a flat connector on one end and a square connector on the other.	2301
1	Solderless bread-board	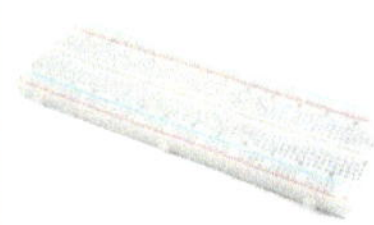	Solderless bread-boards are reusable.	3108
5	Adafruit NeoPixel diffused 5mm through-hole LEDs	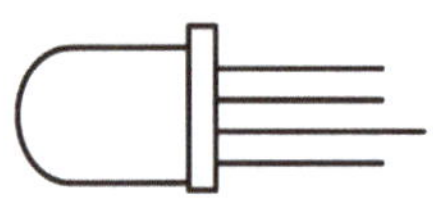	Adafruit product ID 1938	N/A
1	Capacitor, 1000 mfd, at least 10 volt		Electrolytic	0205
1	Resistor		470 ohm, 1/4 watt	0105

Steps

1. Assemble the parts shown in the Materials table.
2. Wire the parts as shown in Figure HT8-2.

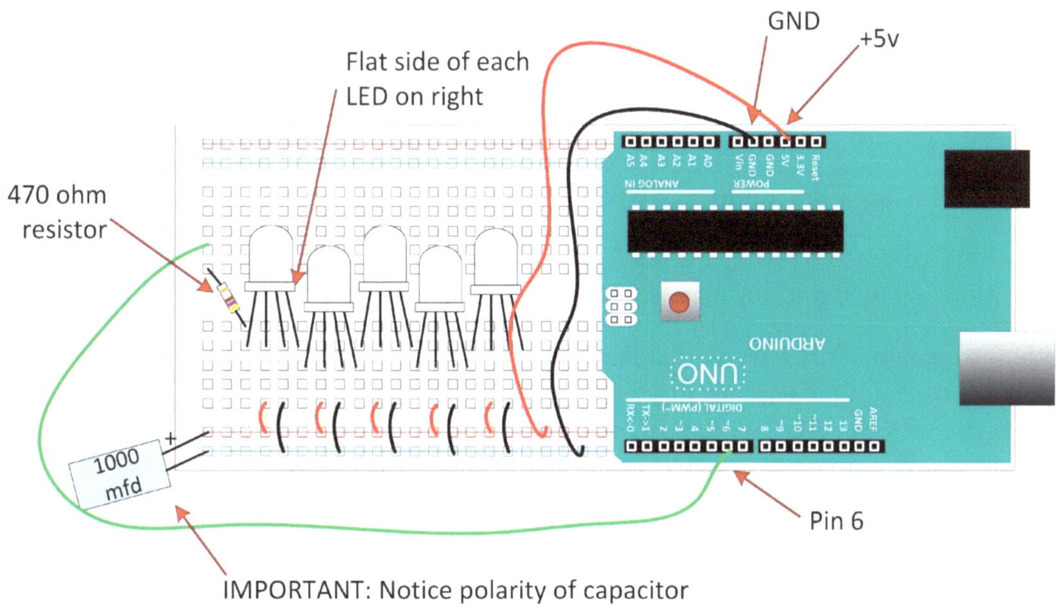

Figure HT8-2. Schematic and pictorial of wiring for NeoPixel and Arduino™

3. Connect the Arduino™ to the programming computer via a USB cable.

Important	Be certain the flat side of each NeoPixel is oriented the same as in Figure HT8-2, and make sure that the positive and negative leads of the capacitor are not reversed.

Also notice the data-in pin of each LED is in the same row as the data-out pin of the preceding LED, except for the first, which is connected via a 470 ohm resistor to pin 6 of the Arduino.™

4. Download and install the Adafruit NeoPixel library, which can be found at https://github.com/adafruit/Adafruit_NeoPixel. Install the library by:
   a. Placing the zip file in your Arduino™\libraries folder.
   b. Unzipping the file in place. A new folder will be created.
   c. Renaming the new folder `Adafruit_NeoPixel`.
   d. Closing any open Arduino™ windows then restarting Arduino.™

5. Open the `strandtest` sketch that comes with the library. It may be found under the File menu:

   File -> Examples -> Adafruit_NeoPixel -> strandtest

6. Look closely at the sketch that appears in the Arduino™ IDE.

   a. Line 3 specifies the Arduino™ pin that sends data to the LEDs. Make certain it is set to 6.

   b. Line 12 is where the object to communicate with the LEDs is created. Make sure the following parameters are correct. If they are not, change them.

      i. The first parameter is the number of NeoPixels in your strand. In this case there are 5.

      ii. The second parameter is the Arduino™ data pin defined in line 3. To change the pin number, modify line 3, not this parameter.

      iii. The third parameter is a set of two flags that together specify what type of NeoPixels are being controlled. One flag specifies the order in which values for colors are to be sent. The other specifies the rate at which that data is to be sent. These NeoPixels expect the colors to be in red, then green, and then blue order. This is specified by the flag `NEO_RGB`. The data rate is 800 kilohertz. That flag is `NEO_KHZ800`. So, this parameter should be `NEO_RGB + NEO_KHZ800`.

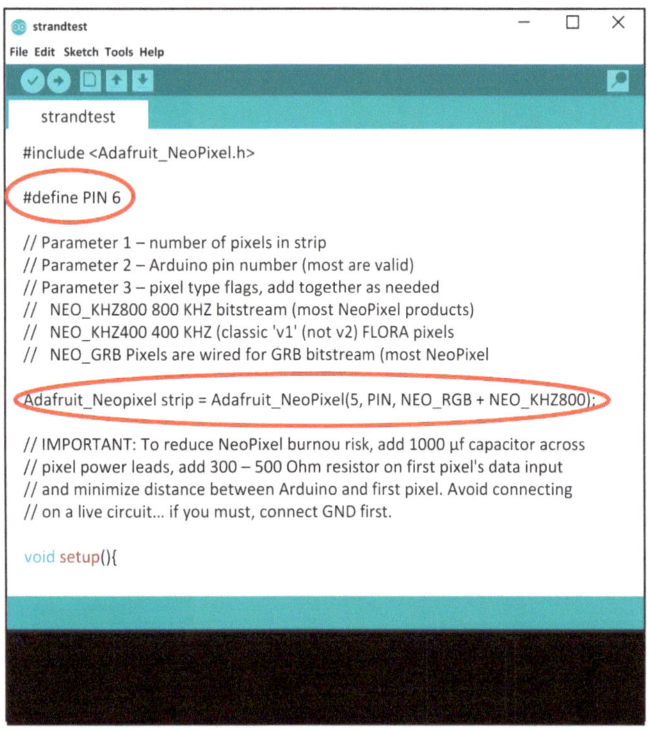

Figure HT8-3. Defining pin 6

7. Upload `strandtest` to your Arduino.™ The NeoPixels should provide a rather entertaining display. All five LEDs should light, flash, and change color.

Writing your own sketches

The strandtest is fun, but the real reason for the NeoPixel library is to provide programming tools for making your own color patterns. To this end, the AdaFruit library provides the following methods:

Constructor

Use this method to create an object to communicate with your string of NeoPixels:

```
Adafruit_NeoPixel(unsigned int numberOfNeoPixels,
                  byte pinNumber,
                  byte flags)
```

where

`numberOfNeoPixels` is the number of NeoPixels to be controlled

`pinNumber` is the Arduino™ pin connected to the first NeoPixel in the string

flags specifies the color order and communication data rate. These are dependent on the type of NeoPixel being used. These are defined as:

`NEO_GRB` = green then blue then red

`NEO_RGB` = red then green then blue

`NEO_KHZ400` = 400 kilohertz

`NEO_KHZ800` = 800 kilohertz

Example HT8-1.

```
Adafruit_NeoPixel myPixels = Adafruit_NeoPixel( 5, 6,
                                 NEO_RGB + NEO_KHZ800);
```

Other methods

Update the entire string of NeoPixels to the values set in the sketch. No color or brightness settings appear on any NeoPixels until this method is called.

```
void show()
```

Example HT8-2.

```
myPixels.show();
```

Initialize communication with the NeoPixels. This method typically is called from the Arduino™ `setup()` method.

```
void begin()
```

HT

Example HT8-3.
```
myPixels.begin();
```

Set the Arduino™ output pin. This step is not typically needed unless a pin different from that specified in the constructor is desired.

```
setPin(byte pin)
```

where

`pin` is the Arduino™ pin to be used to communicate with the NeoPixels

Example HT8-4.
```
myPixels.setPin(4); // set output pin to 4
```

Set the color of a specific NeoPixel by specifying the amounts of red, green, and blue.

```
void setPixelColor(unsigned int pixelNumber, byte red,
              byte green, byte blue)
```
where

`pixelNumber` is which NeoPixel is to be set. Keep in mind that the number of the first pixel is zero, the second is one, the third is two, and so on until the last, which is the number of NeoPixels in the string minus 1.

`red` is a number from 0 through 255 that specifies the amount of red in the final color.

`green` is a number from 0 through 255 that specifies the amount of green in the final color.

`blue` is a number from 0 through 255 that specifies the amount of blue in the final color.

Example HT8-5.
```
// set 3rd NeoPixel to yellow
   myPixels.setPixelColor( 2, 255, 255, 0);
   myPixels.show();
```

Set the color of a specific NeoPixel with a "packed" 32-bit unsigned integer

```
setPixelColor(unsigned int pixelNumber, unsigned long
color)
```

where

`pixelNumber` is which NeoPixel is to be set. Keep in mind that the number of the first pixel is zero, the second is one, the third is two, and so on until the last, which is the number of NeoPixels in the string minus 1.

`color` is an integer of 4 bytes. Three of the bytes contain the amounts of red, green, and blue of the color to appear on the NeoPixel.

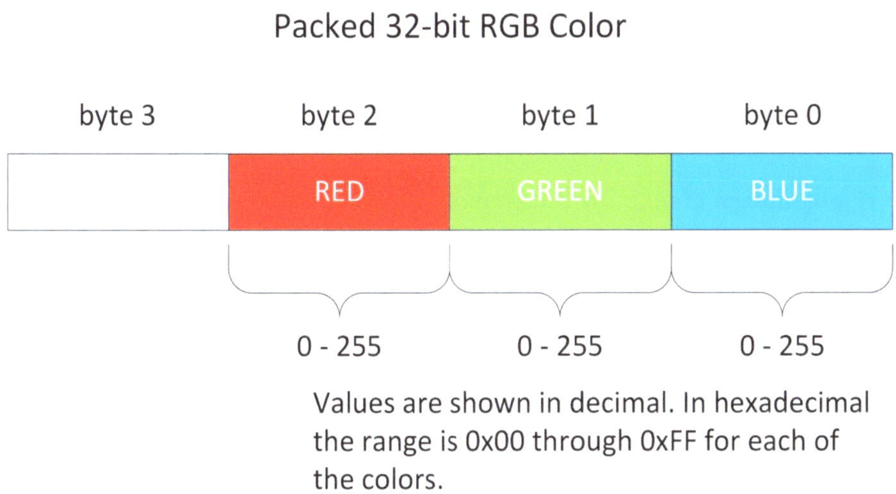

Figure HT8-4. Packed 32-bit RGB color

Although you can create and decode packed 32-bit colors for the purposes of controlling NeoPixels with the Adafruit library, you needn't. Methods for these tasks are provided.

Example HT8-6.

```
unsigned long myColor;
myColor =  0x00FFFF;

// Set 5th NeoPixel to cyan
myPixels.setPixelColor( 4, myColor);
myPixels.show();
```

HT

Convert separate red, green, and blue colors into a packed 32-bit RGB color.

```
unsigned long Color( byte red, byte green, byte blue);
```

where

`packedColor` is an integer of 4 bytes. Three of the bytes contain the amounts of red, green, and blue of the color to appear on the NeoPixel.

`red` a number from 0 through 255 that specifies the amount of red in the final color.

`green` a number from 0 through 255 that specifies the amount of green in the final color.

`blue` a number from 0 through 255 that specifies the amount of blue in the final color.

returns an unsigned long integer containing the amounts of red, green, and blue encoded in the packed 32-bit color format.

Example HT8-7.

```
unsigned long myPackedColor;

// color values for magenta
byte red = 255;
byte green = 0;
byte blue = 255;

myPackedColor = myPixels.Color(red, green, blue);
```

Get the color of a particular NeoPixel

```
unsigned getPixelColor(byte whichNeoPixel)
```

where

`whichNeoPixel` is which NeoPixel is to be read. Keep in mind that the number of the first pixel is zero, the second is one, the third is two, and so on until the last, which is the number of NeoPixels in the string minus 1.

returns an unsigned integer containing the amounts of red, green, and blue in the color of `whichNeoPixel`.

Example HT8-8.

```
unsigned long myPackedColor;

// get color of 4th NeoPixel
myPackedColor = myPixels.getPixelColor(3);
```

Get an array of all the NeoPixel color values in NeoPixel order

```
byte* myPixels.getPixels();
```

where

`myPixelArray` holds the address in memory of an array of data for each NeoPixel. The use of this method is not discussed in this note.

HT

Get the number of NeoPixels being controlled.

```
unsigned int numPixels();
```

Example HT8-9.

```
unsigned int number = myPixels.numPixels();
```

Set overall brightness

```
void setBrightness( byte level)
```

where

`level` is a positive integer from 0 through 255 that specifies overall brightness for the string of NeoPixels. 0 is off; 255 is maximum brightness.

Example HT8-10.

```
myPixels.setBrightness(127);  // Half brightness
myPixels.show();
```

Putting it all together

To use the library for your own sketch, follow these steps:

1. In the Arduino™ IDE create a new sketch.
2. At the top of the sketch file include the library sketch header file with the statement:

```
#include <Adafruit_NeoPixel.h>
```

3. Before writing any methods, create a NeoPixel object. This example assumes five NeoPixels with data coming from pin 6.

```
Adafruit_NeoPixel myStrip = Adafruit_NeoPixel(5,
6, NEO_RGB + NEO_KHZ800);
```

4. Initialize the string of NeoPixels inside the `setup()` method.

```
myStrip.begin();
```

5. Use the NeoPixel methods as needed in the rest of the sketch. Remember, in this example each begins with `myStrip`.

How-To #9: Make a Printed Circuit Board

Background:

Fabricating a circuit board is a four-step process.

1. Expose: Use light and a mask to set the image of the desired traces on the circuit board.
2. Develop: Chemically remove the light-sensitive coating of the circuit board, except for the image of the traces.
3. Etch: Chemically remove copper from the board everywhere except in the image of the traces.
4. Drill: Use a drill press to make holes for mounting and soldering components.

Many methods exist to create a circuit board from a trace pattern. The methods shown in this How-To were developed at a large public high school, where they have been used for several years. Other methods may be faster or more precise, but the methods have proven to be reliable and reasonably safe.

Materials:

Tool	Image	Notes
Photo exposure lamp	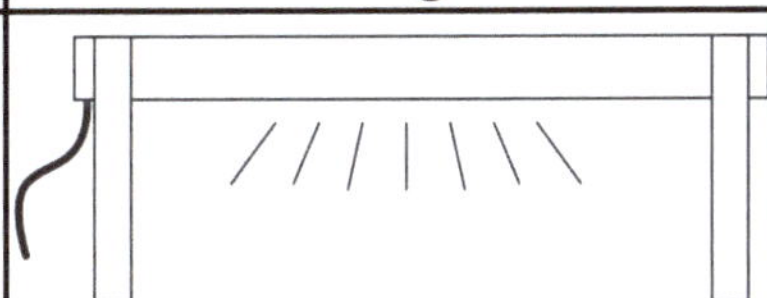	Light is from an appliance flourescent bulb, very bright.
Developer		Used to develop image after exposure.  Caution: The developer contains sodium hydroxide. Dilute 10:1 (10 parts water to 1 part developer) before using.
Ferric chloride	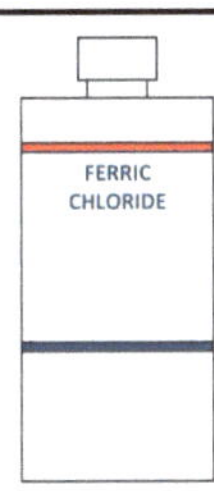	Used to etch all exposed copper from the developed circuit board.

Tool	Image	Notes
2 Trays	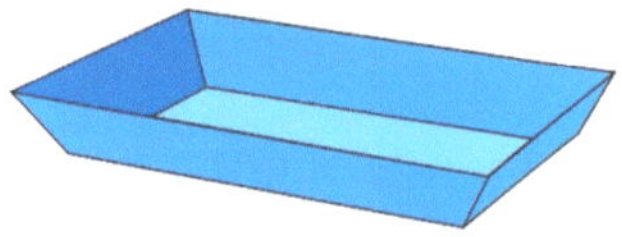	Need two small plastic photographic trays, one for developing and the other for etching.
Electric tea kettle		Used to heat water for a hot water bath to speed etching.
Glass or plastic pan		Holds hot water for bathing the tray when etching the circuit board.
Flat board and matching glass		Used to hold raw circuit board and mask during exposure.
Sponge		Used to gently wipe the raw circuit board during development.
Paper towels		Used to dry board after developing and again after etching.

Procedure:

Expose

Important	Exposure is a photographic process. The copper foil on your raw circuit board is coated with a light-sensitive material. Do not peel the protective tape from the board until just before making the exposure. After the exposure, protect the board from light until after it is developed.

Make the photo exposure as follows:

1. Make an "exposure carrier" using the flat 8" by 10" board along with a matching sheet of glass. Make certain the glass is clean and dry.

2. Make a "sandwich" of the carrier as follows and as shown in Figure HT10-1:
    a. The bottom layer is the carrier board.
    b. The next layer up is the raw circuit board with the white tape removed, photosensitive side facing up. This is the side from which the tape was removed.
    c. The next layer up is the mask. Make certain the mask is placed in the center of the raw board and that the text is clearly readable, left to right.
    d. The top layer is the sheet of glass. It presses the mask close to the raw board, assuring a sharp image.

Assembled "sandwich" as seen from top. Glass, mask, and raw board must be clean and dry. Any dust or scratch will appear on the finished board.

Sandwich as seen from end.

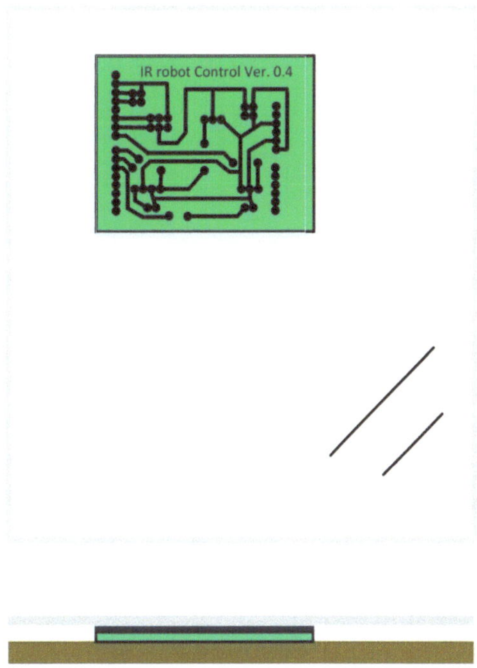

Figure HT10-1. Assembled "sandwich" as seen from top and from end

Important	The mask must be positioned near the center of the raw board with the words clearly readable—not mirror imaged. The glass must be clean; it must also press the mask flat against the raw board.

3. Place the sandwich under the exposure light. Leave it undisturbed for twelve minutes.

Caution	Do not touch the sandwich or the light during exposure. Even careful movement of the board can result in a blurred image on the raw circuit board.

4. After exposure, disassemble the sandwich and protect the raw board from exposure to light until you are ready to develop the image.

Develop corrected image

This step uses a chemical labeled "Developer" on the bottle. The active solution is sodium hydroxide. The sodium hydroxide dissolves the coating on the raw circuit board, but only where that coating was exposed to the light. The result will be a green pattern on the board that looks exactly like the black pattern on the mask. Where the mask was clear, the board will now be bare copper.

CAUTION	**During developing, ALWAYS wear lab safety goggles and gloves!**

1. In one of the trays, mix 20 ml of developer with 200 ml of water. This is more dilute than the instructions on the bottle produce, but it also slows the development process enough to make it easily managed.

2. Submerge the exposed board in the developer in the tray. Use the sponge to gently brush the board until the trace pattern is clearly visible.

3. Remove the board the moment no trace of green is seen in the bare copper portions of the board.

Important	An underdeveloped board will appear light green in the non-trace areas and will not etch properly. However, developing too long will result in the traces as well as the non-trace areas being erased. Developing must be stopped the moment the light areas are clear of all trace of green.

A properly developed board has crisp, green traces and text. Copper in open areas is clear and shiny.

4. Wrap the developed board in a paper towel to prevent scratching the green pattern before etching.

5. The developer is good for several more boards. It may be kept in a tightly closed plastic bottle. Either store the developer or pour it down the drain with plenty of water.

6. Rinse and dry the developer tray and anything else that came in contact with the developer.

7. Rinse your gloves to remove all traces of the developer. Remove them and throw them away.

Etch

This step uses an aqueous solution of ferric chloride, sometimes known as iron chloride. The ferric chloride will dissolve the exposed copper on the circuit board. The copper under the green trace pattern will remain on the board.

CAUTION!	**During developing, ALWAYS wear lab safety goggles and gloves!** **Work in a well-ventilated space.**

Caution	Ferric chloride stains almost anything, permanently!

1. Fill the electric tea kettle with water and heat it to a boil.
2. While the water is heating place the circuit board pattern side up in the second plastic tray.
3. Pour enough ferric chloride in the plastic tray to cover the circuit board by about 1/8 inch.
4. Pour the hot water from the tea kettle into the plastic tub.
5. Float the tray containing the circuit board and ferric chloride on the hot water. The idea is to raise the temperature of the ferric chloride and, thus, reduce the time required to etch the board.
6. Gently rock the tray to "slosh" the ferric chloride over the circuit board. The entire etching process should take between 10 and 15 minutes.
7. Occasionally pull the board out of the ferric chloride to assess progress. Stop when light can be seen through the circuit board everywhere except where the traces are.
8. Wash the board and your gloves thoroughly in running water.
9. Place the ferric chloride in a closable plastic bottle for later use.

CAUTION!	**NEVER POUR FERRIC CHLORIDE DOWN A DRAIN!** Damage to the plumbing is possible. Spent ferric chloride can be disposed of at a hazardous waste site. The solution now contains copper chloride, which is not healthy for the environment.

10. Pour the water out of the tub. Rinse it and the tray thoroughly.
11. Rinse your gloves one more time, then remove them and throw them away.

You are now ready to drill.

Drill

This How-To is not a tutorial on the use of a drill press. Do not attempt to adjust or use a drill press if you've not been shown how to do so safely.

The recommended drill size is 3/64th inch. Holes are in what are called solder pads, round circles of copper.

How-To #10: Add Bluetooth LE Control to Rolling Robot

The robot built in Lesson 15 and operated with an infrared remote control in Lesson 18 can be upgraded for control with a smartphone running either Apple's IOS or Google's Android operating systems. This upgrade takes advantage of Bluetooth Low Energy (Bluetooth LE), a 2010 addition to the Bluetooth standard. More can be learned about Bluetooth, including technical specifications, at https://www.bluetooth.com/.

Adding Bluetooth LE to the robot comes with several advantages over infrared control. Among these are:

- Much crisper responsiveness of robots because of reduced signal interference, even when dozens of robots are being operated simultaneously.
- Ability to take advantage of smartphone sensors, including the accelerometer. For example, a robot or devices on it may be controlled by simply tilting the phone.
- Robots respond to button "pushes" in a more natural way. The robot moves while the button is being touched and stops instantly when the button is released.
- A path is opened for student-written IOS and Android applications.

HT

About Bluetooth LE Devices

This How-To describes how to use either of the two Bluetooth LE devices made by the Adafruit company and available for purchase from them and from our own LearnCSE.com store. The devices are:

Bluefruit LE SPI Friend communicates with the robot's Arduino™ via hardware Serial Peripheral Interface.

Bluefruit LE UART Friend communicates with the robot's Arduino™ via a software serial port.

The devices sell for the same price and, for our purposes, provide the same service—receipt of text data from the smartphone that is then used to control the robot. There are, however, two important differences:

1. The two devices are wired differently.
2. A few lines of program code need to be added to manage communications. These lines are different for each of the devices.

Once wired and configured for the proper communication protocol, the devices are identical in how they are accessed and how their data is used.

Materials

Quantity	Part	Image	Notes	Catalog Number
1	Complete Rolling Robot	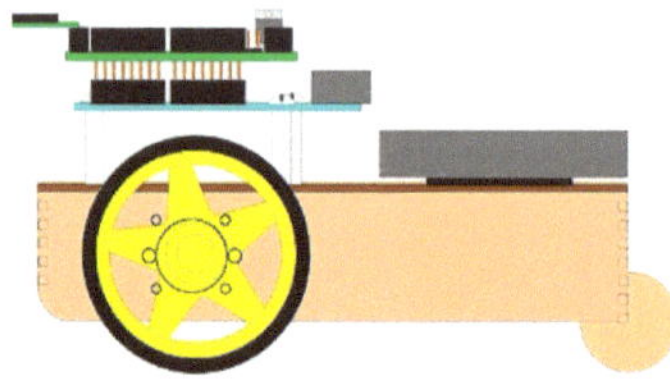	From Lesson 15 or Lesson 18	5101
1	Bluetooth LE Receiver	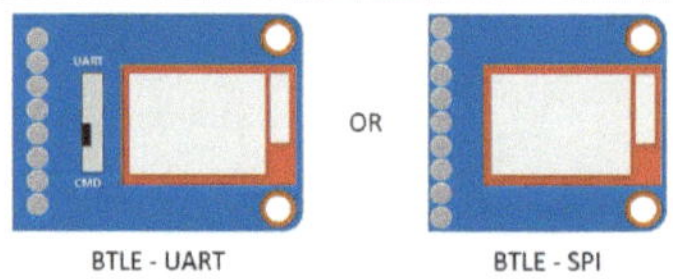	Either UART or SPI Bluefruit LE Friend	3140 or 3141
1	Smartphone		Android or Apple IOS	User supplied
7	Jumper wires		Male – Male	3105

Procedure:

The following steps will result in an Adafruit Bluetooth LE (low-energy) device being used to control the rolling robot of Lesson 15 from a smartphone. The smartphone application itself is from Adafruit (Adafruit.com) and may be found in the IOS and Android app stores.

Wiring

1. Determine which Bluefruit LE Friend you are working with. The images in Figure HT10-1 are taken from the Adafruit website:

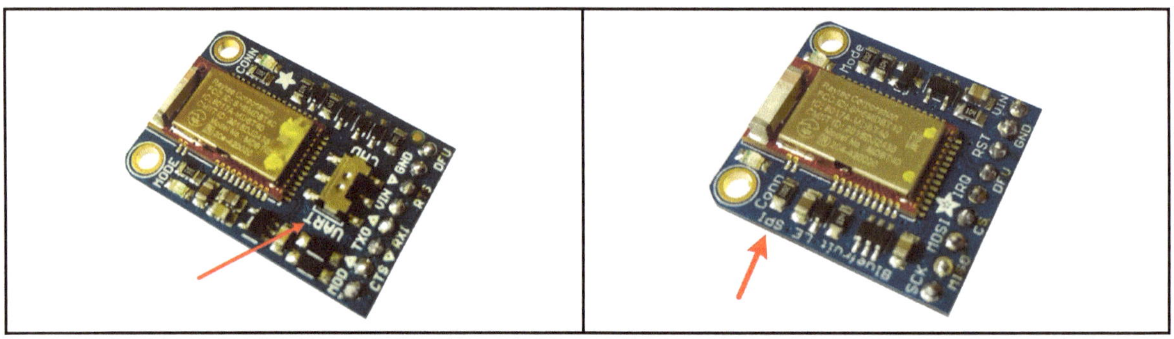

Figure HT10-1. Bluefruit LE UART Friend and Bluefruit LE SPI Friend

These two boards perform similar functions but communicate with the Arduino™ via different protocols.

UART: Universal Asynchronous Receiver / Transmitter is an integrated circuit for serial communication of data between a computer and a device. In our case the computer is an Arduino,™ and the device is the Adafruit Bluefruit LE UART Friend. While the definition assumes an integrated circuit is managing this communication, the process can also be emulated in software running on the Arduino.™ The former is called hardware UART; the latter software UART.

SPI: Serial Peripheral Interface, a protocol for exchange of data between two electronic devices one bit at a time. One device is declared the master, the other the slave. In our case the master device is the Arduino,™ with the Bluefruit LE SPI Friend the slave. The Arduino™ includes electronics specifically for managing this interface, but it can also be emulated in software running on the Arduino.™ The former is called hardware SPI, the latter software SPI.

2. Solder the male headers to the underside of the BT device as shown in Figure HT10-2. This is a three-step process:

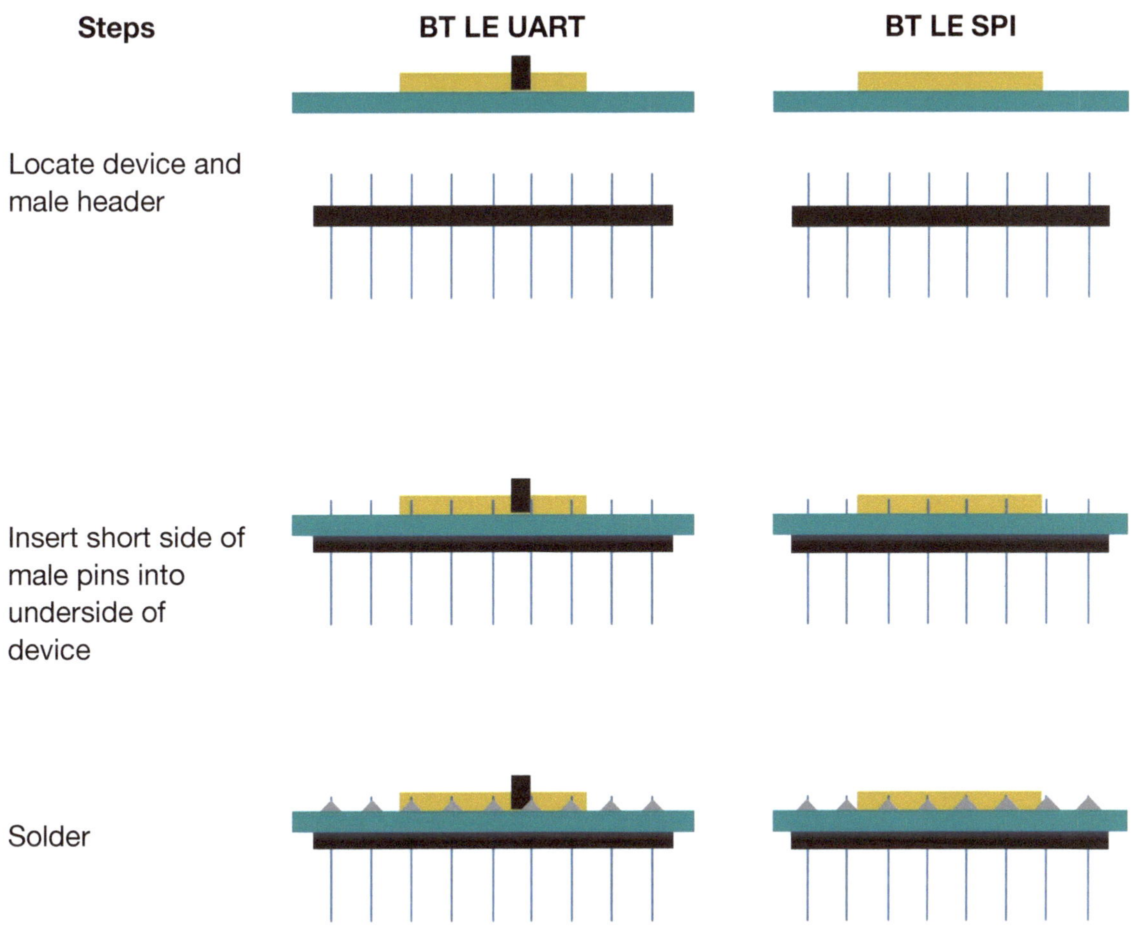

Figure HT10-2. Soldering male headers to BT device

HT

3. Using jumper wires, connect your BT device to your Arduino.™ A standard-sized solderless breadboard works well.

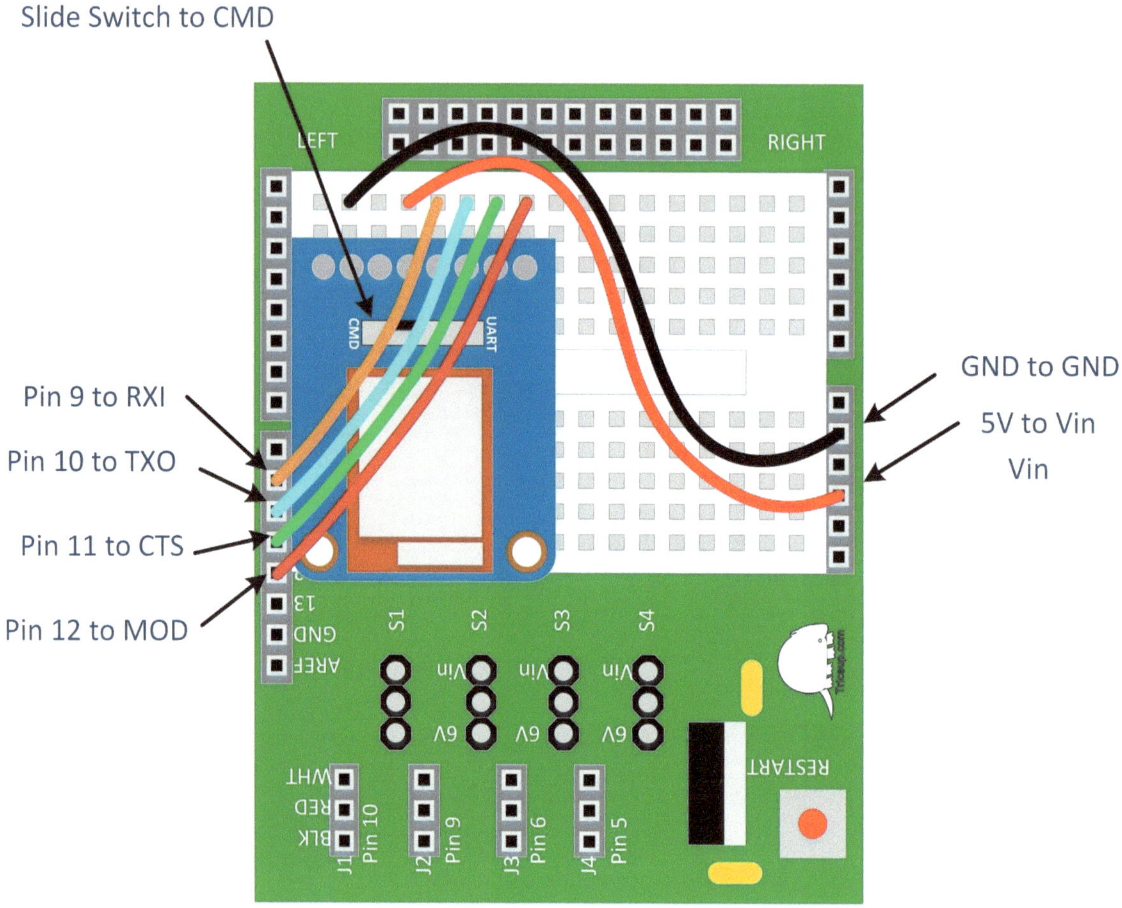

Figure HT10-3. Robot Wiring for Bluefruit LE UART Friend

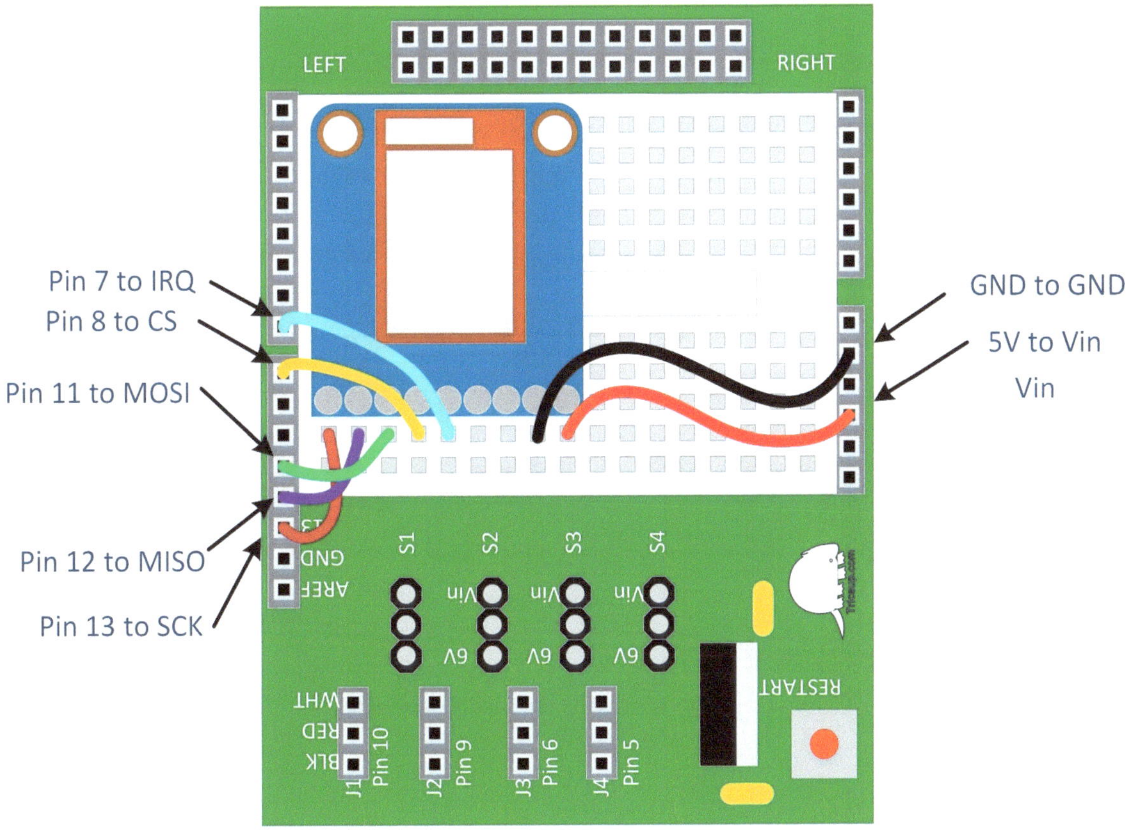

Figure HT10-4. Robot Wiring for Bluefruit LE SPI Friend

HT

Library

4. Download and install the Adafruit library Adafruit_BluefruitLE_nRF51.

   a. Download the zip file by visiting *https://learn.adafruit.com/introducing-the-adafruit-bluefruit-le-uart-friend/software* and clicking the green download button.

   Download Adafruit_BluefruitLE_nRF51

   b. Unzip the file. When you do, it will create a folder named Adafruit_BluefruitLE_nRF51_master.

   c. Rename the folder Adafruit_BluefruitLE_nRF51.

   d. Move this folder to the libraries folder of your Arduino™ folder.

5. If you have the Arduino™ IDE running, close all open instances.

6. Connect the Arduino™ to the computer with the USB cable.

7. Start the Arduino™ IDE.

Install Adafruit Bluefruit Connect on smartphone or tablet

8. This is a free application that is used to connect to the Bluetooth device. It may be found and downloaded from the app stores for Apple's IOS and Google's Android operating systems.

Update Bluefruit LE device firmware

Important	This is an absolutely essential step. Many features of the Adafruit Bluefruit LE library will not function without doing this. Fortunately, the process is simple.

9. Apply power to the Arduino™ to which the Bluefruit device is connected. The red indicator LED will begin to flash.
10. Open the Adafruit Bluefruit application on the smartphone or tablet. A list of detected devices will appear. A new Bluefruit LE device will appear in a box labeled Bluefruit LE.
11. Select the device by touching the rectangle. If a firmware update is required, a notice will appear. If this happens, follow the steps to install the update.

Caution	This firmware update comes from a GitHub project. Sometimes Internet-filtered systems, often including those found in public schools, will block access to GitHub. If this happens, the update will appear to happen quickly when, in fact, no update has occured at all. If you have any reason to suspect the update was not installed, connect to the phone service's Internet access instead of WiFi and try again.

Test connectivity with BTLETerminal

12. Download the BTLETerminal.zip file from LearnCSE.com. This file may be found in the Sketches menu on the right side of the Learn to Program page and the How-To page.
13. Unzip this file into the Arduino™ folder so that BTLETerminal appears as an Arduino™ sketch.

Figure HT10-5. File structure of BTLETerminal sketch after being unzipped

14. Using File -> Sketchbook open BTLETerminal. The Arduino™ IDE should look something like Figure HT10-6.

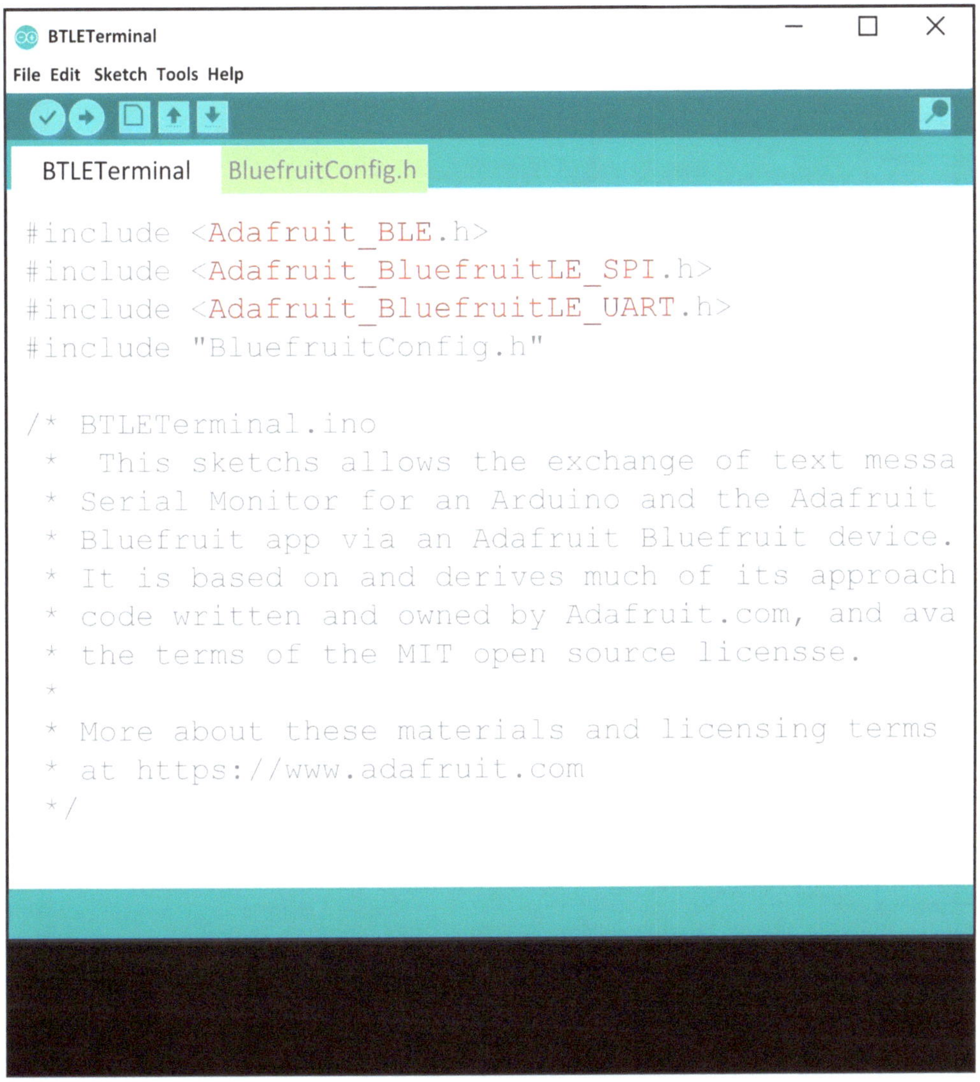

Figure HT10-6. BTLETerminal sketch opened in Arduino™

Notice the sketch has two tabs—BTLETerminal and BluefruitConfig.h. BTLETerminal sets up communication with the Bluefruit device and the Arduino.™ The latter, meanwhile, identifies options and pin assignments for the Bluefruit devices.

15. Verify the pin assignments and constants in BluefruitConfig.h. An error here can prevent successful communication between the Bluefruit LE device and the Arduino.™ The definitions should be:

```
// COMMON SETTINGS
// ----------------------------------------------------------------------
// These settings are used in both SW UART, HW UART and SPI mode
// ----------------------------------------------------------------------
#define BUFSIZE                        128   // Size of the read buffer for incoming data
#define VERBOSE_MODE                   true  // If set to 'true' enables debug output
#define BLE_READPACKET_TIMEOUT         500   // Timeout in ms waiting to read a response


// SOFTWARE UART SETTINGS
// ----------------------------------------------------------------------
// The following macros declare the pins that will be used for 'SW' serial.
// You should use this option if you are connecting the UART Friend to an UNO
// ----------------------------------------------------------------------
#define BLUEFRUIT_SWUART_RXD_PIN       9    // Required for software serial!
#define BLUEFRUIT_SWUART_TXD_PIN       10   // Required for software serial!
#define BLUEFRUIT_UART_CTS_PIN         11   // Required for software serial!
#define BLUEFRUIT_UART_RTS_PIN         -1   // Optional, set to -1 if unused


// HARDWARE UART SETTINGS
// ----------------------------------------------------------------------
// The following macros declare the HW serial port you are using. Uncomment
// this line if you are connecting the BLE to Leonardo/Micro or Flora
// ----------------------------------------------------------------------
#ifdef Serial1    // this makes it not complain on compilation if there's no Serial1
  #define BLUEFRUIT_HWSERIAL_NAME      Serial1
#endif


// SHARED UART SETTINGS
// ----------------------------------------------------------------------
// The following sets the optional Mode pin, its recommended but not required
// ----------------------------------------------------------------------
#define BLUEFRUIT_UART_MODE_PIN        12    // Set to -1 if unused


// SHARED SPI SETTINGS
// ----------------------------------------------------------------------
// The following macros declare the pins to use for HW and SW SPI communication.
// SCK, MISO and MOSI should be connected to the HW SPI pins on the Uno when
// using HW SPI.  This should be used with nRF51822 based Bluefruit LE modules
// that use SPI (Bluefruit LE SPI Friend).
// ----------------------------------------------------------------------
#define BLUEFRUIT_SPI_CS               8
#define BLUEFRUIT_SPI_IRQ              7
#define BLUEFRUIT_SPI_RST              -1    // Optional but recommended, set to -1 if unused

// SOFTWARE SPI SETTINGS
// ----------------------------------------------------------------------
// The following macros declare the pins to use for SW SPI communication.
// This should be used with nRF51822 based Bluefruit LE modules that use SPI
// (Bluefruit LE SPI Friend).
// ----------------------------------------------------------------------
#define BLUEFRUIT_SPI_SCK              13
#define BLUEFRUIT_SPI_MISO             12
#define BLUEFRUIT_SPI_MOSI             11
```

16. Upload the sketch to the Arduino.™

17. After uploading, open the Serial Monitor. Change the data rate to 115200 baud. Something like the screen shown in Figure HT10-7 should appear.

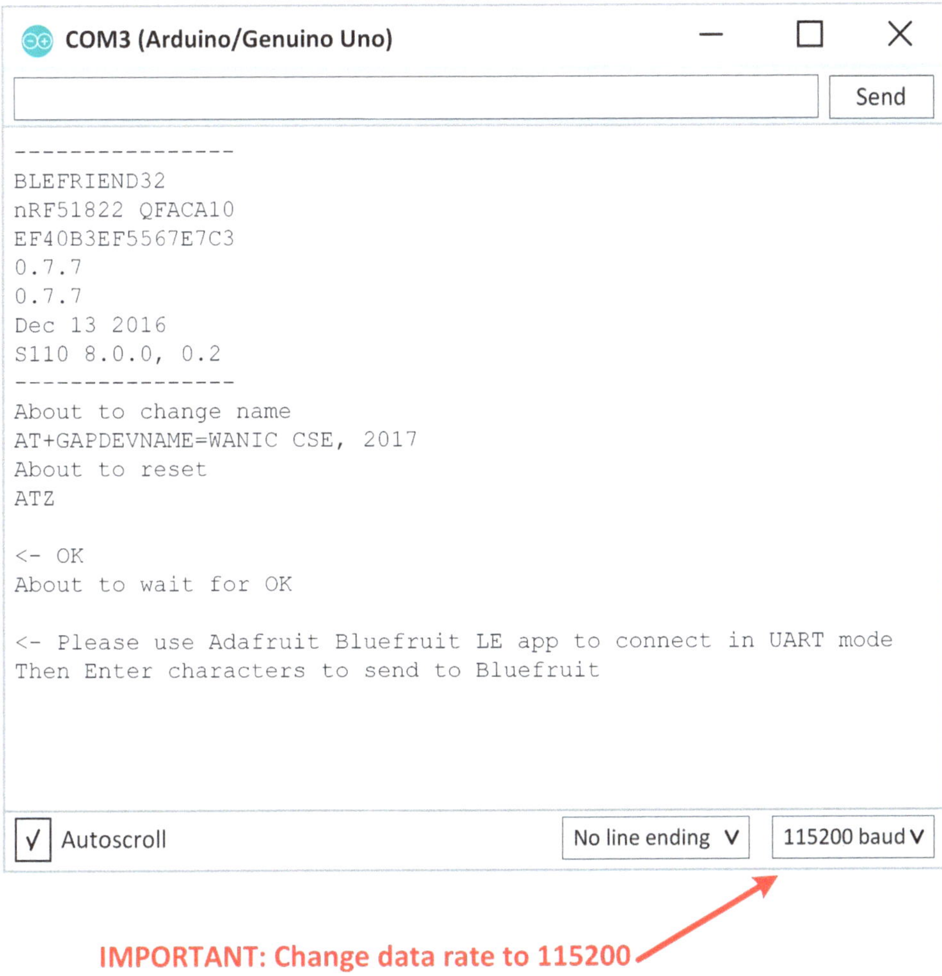

Figure HT10-7. Output of sketch on Serial Monitor

18. Select the type of Bluefruit LE device you're connecting to by commenting and uncommenting some programming statements near the beginning of the sketch.

Adafruit Bluefruit LE devices are capable of four different communications protocols. Of these we can use two with the Arduino™ Uno.

Table HT10-1. Bluefruit LE communications protocols

Type	Bluetooth LE device connected to Arduino™ Uno
SPI Hardware	Bluefruit LE SPI Friend
SPI Software	Not used in these instructions
UART Hardware	Not used in these instructions
UART Software	Bluefruit LE UART Friend

For Bluefruit LE SPI Friend comment out these lines.

```
/*
SoftwareSerial bluefruitSS = SoftwareSerial(BLUEFRUIT_SWUART_TXD_PIN, BLUEFRUIT_SWUART_RXD_PIN);

Adafruit_BluefruitLE_UART ble(bluefruitSS, BLUEFRUIT_UART_MODE_PIN,
                      BLUEFRUIT_UART_CTS_PIN, BLUEFRUIT_UART_RTS_PIN);
*/

// If Bluefruit LE SPI Friend uncomment the following line:
Adafruit_BluefruitLE_SPI ble(BLUEFRUIT_SPI_CS, BLUEFRUIT_SPI_IRQ, BLUEFRUIT_SPI_RST);
```

Uncomment this line.

Figure HT10-8. Programming configuration statements for Bluefruit LE SPI Friend

For Bluefruit LE UART Friend uncomment these lines.

```
SoftwareSerial bluefruitSS = SoftwareSerial(BLUEFRUIT_SWUART_TXD_PIN, BLUEFRUIT_SWUART_RXD_PIN);

Adafruit_BluefruitLE_UART ble(bluefruitSS, BLUEFRUIT_UART_MODE_PIN,
                      BLUEFRUIT_UART_CTS_PIN, BLUEFRUIT_UART_RTS_PIN);

// If Bluefruit LE SPI Friend uncomment the following line:
// Adafruit_BluefruitLE_SPI ble(BLUEFRUIT_SPI_CS, BLUEFRUIT_SPI_IRQ, BLUEFRUIT_SPI_RST);
```

Comment out this line.

Figure HT10-9. Programming configuration statements for Bluefruit LE UART

19. Open the Adafruit Bluefruit app on your cell phone or tablet. Look for a rounded rectangle that indicates that your device has been detected.

Important	The BTLETerminal sketch changes the name that is broadcast for the device to WANIC CSE 2017. But the Adafruit application will not update this name until it has been connected to at least once. So, look for a device with a more generic name such as Bluefruit LE.

20. Connect to your device. It may appear as one of the three options shown in Figure HT10-10 or even something else:

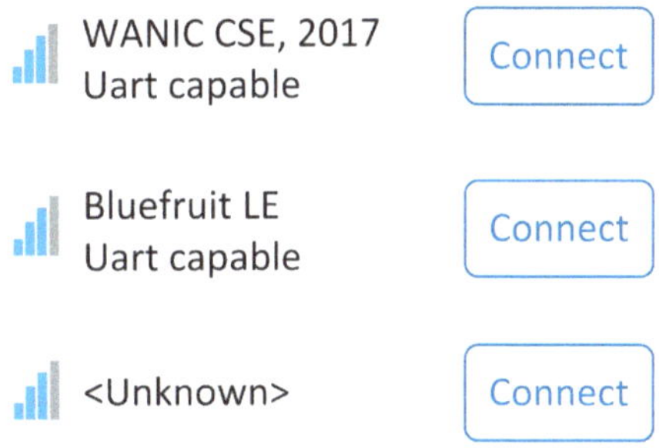

Figure HT10-10. Bluetooth devices as they appear on Adafruit cell phone app

Once connected, the Serial Monitor updates, as shown in Figure HT10-11.

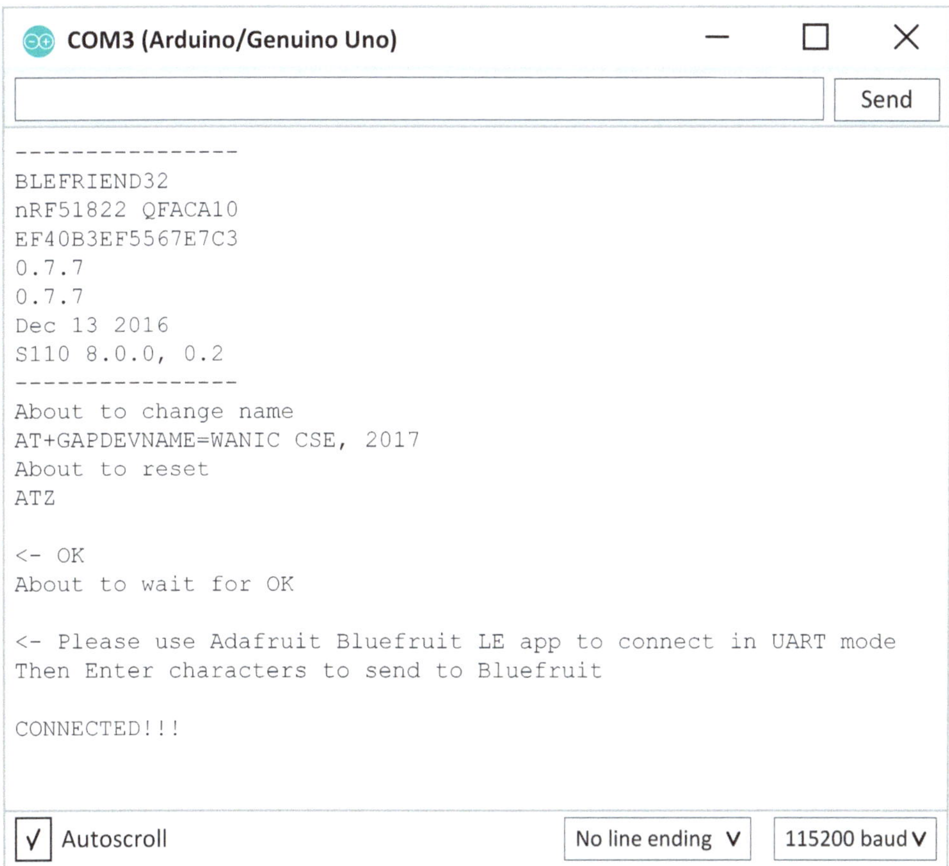

Figure HT10-11. Confirmation of connection as appears on Serial Monitor

HT

21. From the list of modules that appear in the Adafruit Bluefruit app after a connection is made, select UART. Verify the connection by sending text to the device. The text should appear in the Serial Monitor.

22. Enter text in the top field of the Serial Monitor, then click Send. That text should appear in the UART application.

Congratulations! You have established text communication between the robot and a smart phone / tablet.

Configure for Robot

BTLERobotNameAndPINSetup is a sketch that allows you to personalize the Bluefruit LE device to make it easier to identify in a list of Bluetooth LE devices and for you to require entry of a four-digit PIN before turning over control of the robot.

23. In the same manner as used for the BTLETerminal sketch, download and install the BTLERobotNameAndPINSetup sketch.

24. Open the sketch via File -> Sketchbook. Verify that two file tabs are visible: BTLERobotNameAndPINSetup and BluefruitConfig.h.

25. Verify the constants in BluefruitConfig.h. These should be the same as in BluefruitConfig.h in the BFLETerminal sketch.

26. Make certain the Bluefruit LE device is properly connected to the Arduino™ and the Arduino™ to the computer.

27. Select the communications protocol in BTLERobotNameAndPINSetup for software UART for a Bluefruit LE UART Friend or hardware SPI for Bluefruit LE SPI Friend.

28. Upload the sketch, open the Serial Monitor, and follow the instructions that appear.

Control Robot

29. In the same manner as used for the BTLETerminal sketch, download and install the BTLERobotControl sketch.

30. Open the sketch via File -> Sketchbook. Verify that three file tabs are visible: BTLERobotControl, BluefruitConfig.h, and RobotControl.

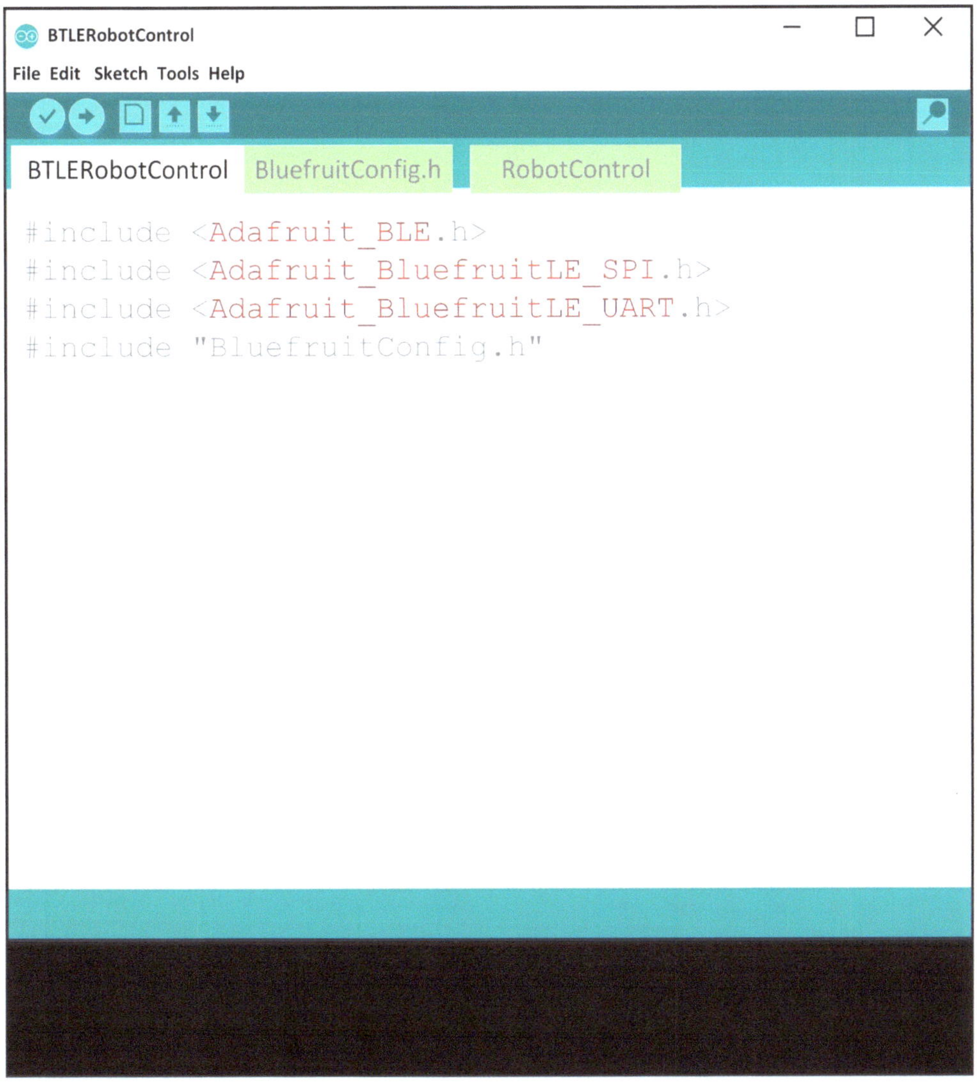

Figure HT10-12. BTLERobotControl sketch

HT

31. Select the communications protocol appropriate for the type of board.
32. Upload to the Arduino.™
33. Open the Adafruit Bluefruit LE app and connect to the Bluefruit device.
34. If a PIN has been set, go to the UART module and enter it.

Important	The UART module will neither prompt for nor confirm the PIN entry. But if the Arduino™ is connected to a computer with the Serial Monitor open, both a prompt and confirmation will appear there.

35. Return to the modules and select Controller.
36. From the Controller module, select the Control Pad. The robot should respond to touching the arrows on the controller.

Index

J

K

L

M

N

O

P

R

S

T

U

V

www.ingramcontent.com/pod-product-compliance
Lightning Source LLC
LaVergne TN
LVHW070933210926
848482LV00003B/235